Letters to Simon

ON THE CONDUCT OF PSYCHOTHERAPY

Letters to Simon

ON THE CONDUCT OF PSYCHOTHERAPY

I. H. PAUL

INTERNATIONAL UNIVERSITIES PRESS, INC.
NEW YORK

Library of Congress Cataloging in Publication Data

Paul, Irving H
    Letters to Simon: on the conduct of psychotherapy.

    1. Psychotherapy. I. Title. [DNLM:
1. Psychotherapy. WM 420 P324L 1973]
RC480.P39   616.8'914   72-8792
ISBN 0-8236-3010-2

Second Printing, 1973

Contents

v

I. H. Paul

Foreword

Reading about psychotherapy in advance of actually doing it has proven of such limited value that anyone who attempts a didactic treatise on the subject must experience the impulse to apologize. His only justification may lie in the fact that there remains a certain value and a necessary function to acquiring a reading knowledge of psychotherapy's concepts, formulations, and techniques. It is that certain value and necessary function which motivated me to write this book. My intention was to supplement, not to replace, what has proven to be the method of choice—the supervision of students during their conduct of psychotherapy.

I am convinced, moreover, that reading about psychotherapy maintains its value not only before and during the beginning stages of actually doing it, but also after the student has become an experienced practitioner. It is a truism, if something of a cliche, that we are learning it all the time. Therefore, though my intended audience—my Simon—is a student in the usual sense of the term, I have written also with a second audience in mind—the student in the strict sense of the term—and I believe that what I've written can also be of value and interest to my professional colleagues.

A treatise on psychotherapy—even one that promulgates, as this one does, a particular form and method of it—may require little more apology than that. But when it is cast into letters, then some further explanation is called for. One explanation is that the subject matter is quite personal and even literary; it lends itself therefore to a corresponding format. Another is that Merton Gill gave me the idea, and I took it gladly because I found that my intention—which was to present things concretely and practically—could best be served by the flexible and informal letter format (the debt I also owe to C. S. Lewis will be apparent to readers familiar with his *Screwtape Letters*).

The first two letters tell everything else you might expect to learn from this foreword with the big exception of to whom thanks must be given and with whom credit shared. Merton Gill is the main one—for his wisdom, his expertise, and his encouragement have counted for a great deal. I want also to single out four colleagues who gave me good counsel: Arthur Arkin, Francis Baudry, Donald Gerard, and Harold Wilensky. I don't mean to imply that they concurred with my point of view either in general or in specifics. Neither did my wife Edith. In fact, she has taken sharp exception to many of the lessons I've given Simon; but her support and inspiration were great, nonetheless. To her do I lovingly dedicate this book.

I. H. Paul

City College of New York
April, 1972

One

Dear Simon,

You're surrounded out there, are you?—on the one side by the Modifiers and on the other by the Encounterers. (Quite a contrast, isn't it?) They are now the radicals, the firebrands; theirs are the new methods, the pioneer spirit, the exhilaration of being liberated from tradition. We who still cling to the "talking cure"—we traditional psychotherapists—are the conservatives of an entrenched authority. The way we once had Science and Culture on our side, they have it on theirs (the Modifiers have the Science and the Encounterers have the Culture); the way we once proclaimed triumphantly that our treatment works, they now boast that theirs works better; and like fathers before their adolescent offspring, our inconsistencies and shortcomings are brandished before us. That analogy, Simon, coming from your father's brother, is defensive I admit. I guess that ours, like any orthodoxy, looks for all the world like a rearguard holding action against the wave of the future.

But you say you're not yet committed—buffeted and tempted, but still undecided. And so, Simon, you want a close look at the older psychotherapy. Since I'm one of its practitioners, you turn to me with a question that has long intrigued you: What actually goes on when I'm with a patient? The standard answer I used to give you won't do any more. Now you want me to show you the actual methods and techniques by which I practice the traditional psychotherapy.

1

Alright, I will. How can I pass up an opportunity to influence my favorite nephew at such a juncture in his professional development? Moreover, it's another kind of opportunity as well: it's bound to be useful for me to articulate my thoughts about psychotherapy and commit them to writing where I can take a fresh look at them. (A therapist gets complacent and rigid if he doesn't periodically re-examine his principles and methods.) That's one of the important side benefits of teaching. And I expect to discover things about my work that I didn't fully realize were there—principles that I didn't know were so articulated and definite, opinions and prejudices that I never fully acknowledged and therefore never thought through. So I may want to digress from time to time in order to argue and defend (i.e., think through) some aspect of my position. If, therefore, I seem occasionally to be writing you as if you were an experienced colleague, you will understand, Simon, that the subject at hand is difficult, ambiguous, and controversial.

At first I thought what you wanted from me was advice on how to become a traditional therapist, for you did write, "Tell me how a good psychotherapist of the so-called dynamic persuasion treats his patients with interpretations and technique." And my impulse was to give you the same advice I would have offered if you had asked me to tell you how to play the piano or tennis: "Get the right teacher—and practice!" But that would seem to minimize the value of reading about it; and I don't mean to do that. After all, unlike tennis and piano, the traditional psychotherapy is substantially verbal; and so at the verbal-intellectual level there's much to be learned about it—albeit only so much. Anyway, I can try to tell you that much.

I'll also try my best to stick to the conditions of your request—in your words, "I would like a treatise, please, not a polemic; elucidation, explication, and demonstration, and not an argument." I do appreciate that you go on to apologize for asking for so much—though you don't apologize for the implications of these conditions for my personality. It's not going to be easy for me to avoid polemics on psychotherapy-in-the-large and disquisitions on Big Questions. Though I can abstain from telling you what the nature of Human Nature is, some "editorializing" is bound to be unavoidable, and a certain kind of theorizing is essential up to a certain point. And occasionally I may find myself engaging in polemics more for my own sake than yours. Otherwise, however, I promise to stick to the terms of your request: a description, explication, and articulation of the form of psychotherapy that I regard as optimal and ideal—the one that I practice with those of my patients for whom I deem it to be appropriate, and which is for the others the form that I deviate from.

But first I must write you some rather general Introductions. If I didn't then I would later on worry about your misunderstanding or misconstruing me. That's perhaps a rationalization; maybe I'm merely indulging my pedantic streak. Still, I need some Introductions to warm up with. The pitcher does it by flexing his muscles, rubbing the baseball, and lobbing it in the general direction of his catcher a few times. The teacher does it by flexing his rhetoric, defining some terms, and talking generally about what it is he's going to talk about particularly. So please bear with me, my dear nephew—I'll try to be brief. If I'm to leave no stone unturned I must warm up.

* * * * * *

There are two points to begin with that I wish I could make simultaneously instead of laying end-to-end (which is going to be a steady problem). The one that will go second is that the form of psychotherapy I practice may merit the label *traditional,* but certain of my methods and principles are far from old, and some are quite radical. The first point is that none of them is unique to me—I make no claims to originality. Now, insofar as the methods and principles have been developed and refined over the past several decades by a variety of psychotherapists, it should be possible to fulfil your request by giving you a selected reading list. It isn't. For while various of the principles and techniques have been written about (by orthodox Psychoanalysts, by neo-Freudians, by Ego Psychologists, by Existentialists, Humanists, and Nondirectivists, and by some who defy classification), and written about very well, no one has set them all down in a coherent and integrated and systematic way. In fact, there are remarkably few books available that attempt to give a complete and detailed account of how any form of the traditional psychotherapy works.

The scarcity of good-and-complete treatises on psychotherapy is something of an embarrassment, and I sometimes wonder why my colleagues have such a great preference for writing about their theories and their patients rather than their session-to-session work. True, most of us regard the apprenticeship mode to be the most appropriate one for learning the work—like playing tennis and the piano, the learning has to be tailored to the individual pupil, and there is only so much that can be gained from reading about it. But I suspect that there are other and less laudatory reasons as well.

Too many of us, I suspect, have grown lax and even careless. Our work is so private, so shielded from outside scrutiny, that it invites undiscipline. In the extended contacts with our patients we tend to permit a wide variety of interactions that cannot be justified by our formal system of principles and methods. Perhaps we are smarting under the repeated attacks that have been leveled against Technique—no one likes to be accused of being "mechanical" and "cold" and "inhuman." As you know, the technique of the traditional psychotherapist has been the subject of enormous criticism and ridicule from all sides. And when the complaints are made by our patients in the privacy of our office then it is difficult to withstand the temptation to bend to them—to be "flexible" and "human." In any case, I suspect that the paucity of didactic treatises reflects the workings of a defense that we share with our clients and friends: a form of disavowal best expressed as sweeping-under-the-rug-in-order-to-keep-up-appearances.

Still, as I mentioned, aspects of the method have been well written about by psychotherapists of varying persuasion; and later on I may take time out to give you a list of these readings. Now to the second point.

My methods and principles aren't all that old and traditional—some are, some aren't. While the structure and spirit of the thing is Psychoanalytic, many of the principles derive from Existentialist thought, from the Humanistic tradition, and from Nondirective methodology; and some can only be called Eclectic. Moreover, they have developed quite gradually—evolved, really—both in the field and in my application; and they are still doing it. Perhaps I should take the time here to trace the heritage, to tell you which teachers and writers have influenced me. If this were a formal treatise I would want to do that; but it isn't, so I'll resist the temptation. Giving credit where it is due is a clear virtue, but I don't see much value to you in having the historical and intellectual context of the method spelled out in advance. For one thing, I believe you will recognize them well enough; for another, I believe you'd rather examine and critically evaluate the methods and principles on their own grounds with a minimum of Appeal to Authority.

Since I'm going to be concentrating on actual methods and on actualized principles, and since I'll want to write you about them as comprehensively and completely as I can, I'm going to have to leave some important things out and assume that you know them. I'll rely on your letters to tell me when I am presuming too much or too little. I know that you've already gained a substantial familiarity with psychotherapy, with its history and its major phenomena; and I assume that your course-work has already acquainted you with the major theories of psychopathology and of psychological change. So when I write about such things as Defense and Transference, for instance, I won't take time out to explicate them except insofar as my conception of them may bear directly on some technical point. Similarly, I'll give little if any consideration to such vital questions as the formation and functions of symptoms, the diagnosis of disorders, and the like. From time to time I will want to write about the origins of this or that aspect of the method, where it fits into the babel of methods, and some of the connections with psychological theory and philosophical thought. But I'll try at all times to keep in mind the terms of your request and to fulfill them as directly as I am able.

Your aunt sends her love and admonishes you to write often to your parents.

Your affectionate uncle

Two

Dear Simon,

Yes, I remember how Ezra used to explain what it was I did with my patients when I was closeted with them in my office. He'd say smugly (because it intrigued him too), "Daddy knows people who have lots of problems; he just talks to them a long time in his office, and then all the problems go away." And now because soon you will be closeted with people who have lots of problems—you want a more precise answer from me.

You characterize your method of psychotherapy as traditional and yet not all that traditional. What I'm eager to know is how it is and isn't. And I'm eager to know what the therapist who follows this particular approach to therapy actually does—not just what he says he does." In time, in time. First I must temporize and write you further Introductions. For one thing, I can see that I'm going to have a prose problem. "This particular approach to therapy"— "Your (my) method of psychotherapy"—these are awkward phrases, and they're going to be unavoidable unless I use a name to label the thing. Moreover, insofar as my method is quite distinctive—as you will see—it may even deserve a name.

But a name is bound to be a mixed blessing. For one thing, it can imply too much—for instance, that the methods and principles so named comprise a unified and formal system. But more serious than that, names have connotations, and therefore can be misleading in one way or another. I

7

would consider using such names as Autonomy Therapy, Ego Analysis, Effective Dynamic Psychotherapy, Paul's Method, and the like, were it not for the fact that they all strike me as misleading, presumptuous, or both. I like the neutral and confident ring of Effective Psychotherapy; but that, unfortunately, has been preempted (by Hellmuth Kaiser). I would call it Analytic Psychotherapy if not for the fact that that is too close to Analytically oriented Psychotherapy on the one hand, and to the Jungians' occasional use of it on the other.

So here's what I'll do to avoid the handicaps of a formal name and at the same time gain the advantage of simple exposition. I'll do it with capital letters. You'll notice, Simon, that the way I like to solve the problem of the term with special meaning is to begin it with a capital (e.g., *T*echnique, *D*efense, *T*act, *U*nderstanding, and the like—something I learned from *Winnie-The-Pooh*). I'll simply do the same with "psychotherapy" when I mean it to have the special meaning of "my method of psychotherapy." Thus, when I write Psychotherapy with a capital *P*, I mean "this particular set of methods and principles for psychotherapy." And to futher support that connotation I will also underscore the word: *Psychotherapy*.

(If you forget, after a while, that by *Psychotherapy* I do not mean simply psychotherapy, then I'll be far from dismayed. For I won't deny that *deep down* I believe that my methods and principles apply to all forms of psychotherapy that are good and effective.)

Psychotherapy is traditional and yet not all that traditional. So how shall I characterize it? First let me claim that no system of psychotherapy can be simply and generally characterized. The literature (particularly the textbook literature) gives the impression that each of the five or six "schools" has a coherent and unified set of principles and methods. That's a quite misleading impression; for only at the highest—and most impractical—level of abstraction do we find much unity within any of the school systems. When it comes down to actual techniques, methods, and usages there are substantial differences among those who subscribe to the same larger system.

With that in mind, I would locate *Psychotherapy* within the family of methods that make up the Psychoanalytic school. You undoubtedly know how proud and quarrelsome a family it is; how much argument has gone on about which of the offspring have abided by the true Freudian traditions; how there are by now several distinct generations, a good many intermarriages, and members of the family have been officially disowned. Still, appearances sometimes to the contrary notwithstanding, the spirit of individuality has remained strong in it. And because analysts have generally preferred to write about their theory and their patients than about their therapeutic methods, it has gone largely unnoticed that not only have their methods undergone a gradual but significant change, but they have diverged into a heterodoxy. Students have long known, from their contact with supervisors and teachers at the institutes, that there are wide differences in the way that orthodox analysts conduct their psychoanalysis. For example, some have abandoned the standard silent posture in favor of an active involvement in the free association process, making freer use of interrogation and confrontation; others haven't. Some pursue each and every manifestation of Transference and Resistance; others do it only when it constitutes an impasse. And there are further divergences that make substantial differences in how the therapy will proceed.

There remains, nevertheless, an underlying spirit and attitude that cuts across all forms of psychoanalysis; and *Psychotherapy* shares in it. As you will see, the process of Understanding that I rely upon so heavily is closely related to the Analytic mode of articulation and explanation. Further-more, when I conduct *Psychotherapy* I pay special attention to those phenomena that the analysts have taught us to pay attention to—to Conflicts, to Defenses, to forms of Resistance and Transference, to fantasies. And like the orthodox analyst, I encourage my patient to freely examine his Mind—to express his thoughts, to articulate his feelings, to reminisce and fantasy. Finally, and most importantly, I take as my central theoretical concept the psychoanalytic concept of Ego Autonomy; and that concept provides the basis for *Psychotherapy's* major Technical principles.

But *Psychotherapy* also differs from orthodox psychoanalysis in several important ways. For one thing, it eschews the so-called procedural rules (the use of the couch, the requirement of daily sessions, and the reliance on free association). For another, it does not select for emphasis any particular aspects of the patient's experience (for example, I don't place such a high premium on the recollection of early childhood experiences). Moreover, it conceptualizes the role of the therapist in a somewhat different way

At the same time, *Psychotherapy* is not what is commonly referred to as Analytically oriented Psychotherapy, which usually entails a diluted form of psychoanalysis with significant ingredients of support, reassurance, and focusing upon the present tense. In fact, far from being diluted psychoanalysis, I regard *Psychotherapy* as an even stricter and more purified form of it. You will shortly see why I make that claim. Let me add here that, while it maintains the formal structure and the clinical attitudes of psychoanalysis, *Psychotherapy* borrows from Nondirective Counselling and from Existential Psychotherapy their concepts of Freedom and Caring and their therapeutic goals of self-determination and authentic Selfness.

Like most forms of traditional psychotherapy whose heritage is psychoanalysis, *Psychotherapy* is Mental. It deals with a patient's private experience—his phenomenological realm—and gives it ontological primacy. This in no way means that one of its chief goals is not to influence his actions. But it doesn't pursue that goal directly. Instead, it deals with a patient's experiences—his Mind—and leaves the rest to Human Nature

The relationship between thought and action is a problem not only for theoretically minded psychologists, but also for philosophers and politicians. It's our old Mind-Body Problem in all its exquisite complexity and fascination; and it's one of the Big Questions that I promised to sidestep. So I'll simply proclaim that *Psychotherapy* makes commerce with the Mind and trusts that the Body will follow suit in some appropriate way—be it in Interaction, in Transcendental Harmony, in Double-Aspect, or whatever. "I will not be telling you what to do; I will not suggest what decisions you should make, or how I think you should behave"—that is a fundamental limitation that I impose on myself and make clear to my patients. This hardly means that I remain aloof from their actions: "I will try to help you understand your actions; and I may sometimes help to clarify the reasons for your decisions. But what you do and how you decide will be up to you."

This limitation, I'm afraid, is only one of many. In fact, that it places stringent restrictions on the therapist's behavior and his participation in the treatment is probably one of *Psychotherapy's* most distinctive features. The list of restrictions may strike you as prohibitive and puzzling, Simon, because it includes the following. The therapist does not counsel, direct, or interview the patient; he provides little if any guidance, advice, and evaluation; he gives no rewards or punishments; he doesn't relate as a mentor, or teacher, or friend; he maintains a neutrality, an impersonality, and an impassivity that is quite severe; he observes without much participation, he comments without judging, and he shows only a narrow and selective range of feelings.

I am deliberately exaggerating the strictures, Simon, in order to emphasize that the therapist's behavior is unique (when he is conducting *Psychotherapy*, that is). For what reasons is it unique in these ways? Because his principal goal is to promote in his patient an altogether unique kind of experience. *Psychotherapy*, you see, places a high priority on uniqueness; and it does it in order to provide the patient with an extended and profound experience in a unique kind of process. Since I'll be writing about that process repeatedly, and since I welcome your suspended anticipation, I'll postpone the subject for now and make one additional point in this letter.

I regard the methods and principles of *Psychotherapy* to be in direct antithesis to those of Behavior Modification as well as those of Interpersonal Encounter. Instead of the systematic and deliberate manipulation of a patient's behavior (by means of conditioning and learning methods, or by means of exercises and games), there is in my "system" a deliberate avoidance of any and all manipulation. When you conduct *Psychotherapy*, Simon, you eschew reliance on External or Extrinsic Reinforcement. To repeat: you try your best to give no advice of any kind—you don't instruct, interview, counsel, or guide your patient, nor do you play any direct role in influencing his actions. Your overriding goal is to provide for him a special kind of experience in examining and expressing his Mind. What that actually means and entails will be the chief subject of my correspondence with you.

Your affectionate uncle

Three

Dear Simon,

In this letter I'll give you an overview of *Psychotherapy* by writing about its most basic concepts and principles. I'm as eager as you to get down to concrete details, so I'll keep the purely theoretical matters down to a minimum—for now, at least. When I write you about the different aspects of the method, I expect I'll digress into relevant theory in order to amplify and complete the account I give you in this letter.

The core principles of *Psychotherapy* (and I remind you, Simon, that it means "a particular set of methods and principles of psychotherapy") are embodied in the instruction that I give my patient at the outset. I will refer to it as The Basic Instruction (I'll have to amplify on it in later letters); and it is this:

The Basic Instruction

> You can tell me the things you want to tell me. It's up to you. I will listen and try to understand. When I have something useful to say, I will say it.

This means, first and foremost, that my patient is free to express his feelings and to speak his mind in whatever way he will. During the sessions he is to behave as freely and as self-directedly as he can. Please notice that, even in this "instruction," my patient is being notified instead of instructed. I don't ask him to say what's on his mind; I don't request him to speak his thoughts to me or to express his feelings; I don't direct him, "Tell me about yourself." He can if he

13

chooses to—it's up to him. It is clear, then—and if it isn't sufficiently clear then I take pains to make it so—that he is to decide for himself.

Now, to support and promote that freedom of self-expression and of self-experience, I behave in ways that hold to a minimum all forms of direction, guidance, and control. My principal role is that of an interested but neutral observer and commentator. I listen actively, I supervise the Therapeutic Process, and I help my patient to understand his experiences by articulating and analyzing them. But throughout I take special pains to keep from unduly influencing those experiences or shaping his behavior.

I structure the therapy and relate to my patient in ways that are designed to achieve a fundamental goal for him. That goal is Ego Autonomy. Or call it Freedom—freedom from "neurosis" in the broad sense of the term. Phenomenologically it is freedom from ego-alien experiences and compulsions, from inner as well as outer compulsions and conflicts. That fundamental goal, however conceived of, shapes most of my behavior, for virtually all of the principles that guide me have some bearing on the patient's acquiring greater Autonomy. My central assumption is that he will benefit from the therapy to the extent that he attains greater Autonomy from—and therefore greater control over—the forces that operate upon his Ego from within as well as from without.

My central theoretical concept, as you can see, is Ego. It denotes the core of one's personality, consisting of the self-image and the so-called executive functions of behavior—and it also denotes the phenomenological Self that the reflective person comes to recognize as his autonomous sense of Me-ness. My central assumption (strictly speaking it is probably a theorem) is that Ego is embedded in a matrix of processes and forces that originate both from within the personality and from without. The former may be thoughts, action tendencies, even fantasies; they can include feelings and needs; they may be experienced as conflicts and ambivalences. In any case, they represent Inner processes and pressures that are never in perfect harmony with the core Me-ness; and when that harmony reaches a certain degree of dissonance we refer to them as Ego-Alien. From without, Ego is subject to the pressures and demands of reality that are also never in perfect harmony; and when that dissonance becomes excessive we speak of Maladaptiveness.

The task of mediating and harmonizing these relatively independent configurations of processes and forces (which can, but need not, be conceptualized as Id, Superego, and Reality) is one of Ego's chief functions. Add to this the hypothesis that Ego too has substantial interests and claims upon behavior, and we have a picture of a complicated and dynamic interplay and counterpoint. This interplay and counterpoint are what the concept of Ego Autonomy—and its essential relativity—denotes.

Now for a major presumption—it is my central hypothesis—it's this: Ego Autonomy is enhanced and promoted by such achievements as understanding, honest self-confrontation, and a fuller sense of authentic selfness. In *Psychotherapy,* by coming to know and understand himself better, by becoming more familiar with the full range of his Inner and Outer Reality, and by experiencing himself as a relatively independent and volitional being, my patient will gain in his control and sense of mastery over his experiences and actions. And with this gain will come the "cure."

Thus, the fundamental goal of *Psychotherapy*—and it is also the way I picture the fundamental Therapeutic Process— is the gradual freeing of Ego or Self from the excessive grip of both inner and outer compulsion. More accurately put: the essential goal is to restore and secure an optimal balance between the great agencies that determine and control behavior.

* * * * * * *

Because Ego Autonomy is both its fundamental goal and its fundamental process, *Psychotherapy* has to be for my patient an altogether unique experience. Even if that strikes you as a non sequitor, Simon, you will have to get used to my claim for uniqueness, so seriously do I take it. My patient's therapeutic experience is hardly possible under ordinary interpersonal conditions because, for one thing, he can express himself and can communicate his mind with a kind of freedom that he can hardly have elsewhere.

This freedom—which is both instrumental and purposeful—is rarely if ever an unmixed blessing. There are features of it that can be quite painful and anxiety-provoking, especially during the early phases of treatment. My patient generally does not want the kind of freedom that *Psychotherapy* offers him, and neither does he want the kind of relationship with me that that freedom requires. It requires of me, for one thing, a perfectly non-evaluative attitude, a position of neutrality that is not only unfamiliar but also usually quite unacceptable to him. Before I spell out what that neutrality entails, let me mention two things that it does not: (1) I am not indifferent to my patient and his well-being; (2) I am not his interviewer. Some remarks about the second, first.

It is a feature of its uniqueness that the *Psychotherapy* session is not to be regarded as an interview—at least not by you, Simon, the therapist. Though it has the external form of an interview, there are, as you will come to see very clearly, fundamental differences between a session and an interview. To put it succinctly, to give and get *Psychotherapy* is not to give and get counsel by sharing information (which is a fair definition of an interview). You will scrupulously avoid taking the role of the psychoarcheologist or the benevolent inquisitor—you are not going to be the elicitor of hidden memories or dreaded feelings. And not only will you not probe, you will not pass judgment or evaluate. In these respects, then, you are not an interviewer.

In order to maintain your position as the one who never evaluates—a position that is difficult to achieve and probably never possible to secure perfectly—you must remain both neutral and nonpersonal. This means, above all else, that you are careful that your words and actions should not convey an attitude that directs or constrains your patient. You never scold, never punish; you never praise, never reward; you avoid reinforcing certain kinds of communications and certain kinds of behaviors. To put it into theoretical terms: the therapist eschews any deliberate reliance upon External (or Extrinsic) Reinforcement. He provides no gratification for the patient's need for acceptance or for rejection, for reward or for punishment, for approval or for disapproval, for nurturence or dependency.

Does this mean that you will be indifferent? I don't believe that it does. What follows has some relevance to the question, but it requires more discussion than I want to include in this overview. In a later letter I plan to take up the matter at some length in the context of considering how it is that you can, and must, *care*.

There is one need, and only one, Simon, that you will gratify in your patient—and in yourself too. It is what we Freudians refer to as the Synthetic Function. This takes the form of the need to Understand and to Be Understood. By Understanding is not meant the kind of "understanding" that really boils down to approval or acceptance or exoneration. *Understanding* another person's experiences means to know them—to reconstruct and to articulate them. To gain knowledge about circumstantial and presumedly causal factors is part of the process of Understanding because it can be invaluable for reconstruction and articulation. To know Why is often an important step toward knowing What and How.

The process of Understanding—of knowing—is often referred to by the psychoanalysts as the Analytic Process. So will I refer to it. To analyze is to know—to apprehend and comprehend. And that's the therapist's great function in *Psychotherapy*. Moreover, it is not only to share that Understanding with the patient, but also—and primarily—to facilitate and foster it on the part of the patient—his Synthetic Function. It's one of *Psychotherapy*'s main goals that the patient learn to Be Understood and to Understand.

Now, let me anticipate your reaction to this, Simon. I can imagine you responding by return mail that it all sounds like an intellectual experience—as if *Psychotherapy* embraces everything that's cognitive and excludes what's emotional and affective. Put this way it's obvious that I intend to refute the charge. Still, there is a sense in which it's not far off the mark—but that takes some explaining.

First, a measure of the refutation. You will recognize Intellectualization as a defense (when, and only when, of course, it is one); and you will draw your patient's attention to the fact that he is resorting to intellectual constructions in order to avoid experiencing the full impact of his affects, impulses, and conflicts. If that defense is not implicated, you will try to articulate (and notice that I write "articulate" and not "explain") the affects, impulses, and conflicts. Many of your Interpretations will take the form of, "I think I know what you are feeling" (for example, "You are angry, I believe; but you cannot bear the feeling, and so you . . ."). In this way do you attempt to foster in your patient a readiness to confront and acknowledge his affective experiences, and also to allow such experiences their full effects.

Much of the transaction in *Psychotherapy* commonly has to do with nonintellectual aspects of behavior. At the same time, however, the transaction itself is largely in verbal and cognitive terms. When your patient feels angry you will not give him license to throw ashtrays; instead you will encourage him to talk about it (not, mind you, to talk himself out of it). When he attempts to provoke you into some emotional state, you won't permit yourself the emotion—at least you will not express it to him. Instead you will interpret (again, in verbal and cognitive terms) his intention. Thus, not only is there a steady translation of experience into verbal-cognitive discourse, but you will not engage your patient in anything like a direct encounter.

This flies directly in the face of the popular current that is taking on many properties of a cultural ideology these days. According to it, the patient of the 1970's suffers most from alienation, and psychotherapy must provide him with meaningful contacts with both himself and other people. This requires his therapist to engage him in a relationship that is direct, intense, and genuine, in order to teach him how to overcome his alienation from others.

I suspect that the central difference between Encounter-type therapies and Analytic-type therapies lies in the priority of the two kinds of alienation. In any case, *Psychotherapy* makes the assumption that a person's alienation from himself takes precedence over his alienation from others. And having resolved that alienation—which is conceptualized as Ego Autonomy—the alienation from others can (and indeed, must) be resolved outside of the therapy. But it is undoubtedly not so simple a dichotomy, and at the risk of seeming high-handed about the matter, I will leave it at that for now and return to the question of affect in *Psychotherapy*.

When you conduct *Psychotherapy*, Simon, you don't discourage your patient from experiencing a range of feelings during the session. He may weep or laugh, he may exult or despair, he may feel anger, or desire, or whatever. But the structure of the situation imposes a constraint both on the range of his feelings as well as on the mode of their expression. Verbalization—which includes such things as reminiscence, fantasy and free association—remains the main currency of expression; and this does throw a cognitive cast over things. Moreover, it is also clear that, while he is encouraged to experience affects and impulses, there's an undercurrent in the therapy that flows in the direction of cognitive control over such experiences. The larger goal—while it is plainly not to stifle or to inhibit affects—is to gain a measure of control over them. What it means to "gain control" is a moot point that I'll have to write about later. But please bear in mind that it very often leads to release of affects, to a disinhibition or a freeing of emotions from the grip of cognition.

Let me sum up this overview in the following way. *Psychotherapy* entails the free and untrammeled exploration of a patient's Mind. One of its central goals is that he progressively free himself from the tyranny of inner compulsion and conflict; and this process is achieved within the therapy itself by the therapeutic experience itself. For it is during the therapy sessions that a patient learns how to be free, how to be relatively more autonomous. He speaks to you as freely as he can; he exercises his powers of Will as fully as he can; and he strives for recognition, articulation, and Understanding.

And he gets better!

Your affectionate uncle

Four

Dear Simon,

The psychotherapist's art is made up of three parts: Analysis, Tact, and Technique. I will write about them separately though they are hardly independent of each other. Each resolves to the act of Understanding in the following ways: Analysis is Understanding, Tact entails Understanding, and Technique is knowing how to implement the Understanding. Technique—which is going to be the topic of this letter—is the way we insure and maximize our analytic intentions while maintaining an optimum of Tact. Perhaps it might be more accurate to say, then, that Understanding and Technique are the twin pillars upon which *Psychotherapy* rests.

Technique has fallen on very hard times. Not only has the traditional Technique been roundly ridiculed and caricatured in our contemporary literature and films, many psychotherapists have come to regard the term as a virtual pejorative—"mechanical," "rigid," "inhuman," "cold," are some of the commonly leveled criticisms. And you will hear it widely said that not only does Technique reflect a misplaced emphasis, but it can be a serious hindrance to good psychotherapy. I disagree—strongly. And my disagreement is not over a matter of definition, for I believe that an emphasis on Technique is rarely misplaced, that it is indispensable to psychotherapy, and—most important of all—that good Technique is a requisite for good therapy.

Among those therapists who do not dismiss Technique as altogether irrelevant there is frequently a grudging ambiva-

21

lence toward it. They contend, first, that it is subordinate to Understanding; and second, they take an anything-goes kind of attitude toward it by sanctioning each therapist to find his own methods—as if there were no way in the abstract to distinguish good Technique from poor Technique— what matters only is that each of us do it his own way. They take no such laissez-faire attitude toward Understanding, under the apparent assumption that there is such a thing as true Understanding but no such thing as good Technique. Instead of a judicious "several roads lead to Rome" there is a cavalier "all roads lead to it equally well."

It should be obvious from my form (my literary Technique) that I disagree. There may be more than one road, but there are not so many; some degrees of freedom have to be allowed the therapist, but that isn't the same as no degree of constraint. There is, I admit, an important sense in which each of us does fashion his own form; but good form is not so relative and elastic a matter as is commonly implied. Good Technique, in fact, can be formulated quite objectively and quite independently from different therapist styles and personalities.

Is Technique "subordinate" to Understanding? I think this way of putting it can be seriously misleading. Technique alone, of course, is insufficient—without Understanding it is likely to be empty. But the same can be said of Understanding—without Technique it is likely to be ineffective. There's a sense in which Technique can be said to grow out of Understanding; but it also makes good sense to me to conceive of both of them sharing a common basis—as two aspects of the same underlying process. Moreover, it serves a great practical purpose to maintain a distinction between these two aspects of our art.

Technique, you see, can be objectified in a way that Understanding (Analysis) cannot. While it should not be objectified in the form of rules or recipes, it can be formulated into articulate principles. The same is true, Simon, for an applied art like architecture and for a performing art such as playing the piano; and it applies equally well to games—say chess or tennis. It is possible, you see, to articulate the principles of the good design, the good position, the good move, and the good stroke. And these principles, even though they're based on sensible and pragmatic rationales, are actually quite mechanical—all form and no substance. Furthermore, while you may not become a great architect or a great player by mastering the principles, you can get quite far on technique alone. That fact need not be decried. I'm aware that the truly creative product in art may not reveal its technical underpinning, and there may even be a deliberate negation of technique in the pursuit of the creative. This, however, is rarely the case in the so-called applied and performing arts, where technical skill and facility remain evident. But I'm doing something here I disapprove of, Simon: leaning heavily on analogy for purposes of persuasion (instead of for purposes of illustration). Psychotherapy may not be a creative art, but neither is it a performing art or a game. So let me get back to it.

What do I mean by Technique in psychotherapy? Broadly speaking, I mean the way we conduct it—our form. Technique entails the guidelines, the principles, and the tactics that I rely on in order to implement my intentions. The way I define my role and structure the sessions are matters of Technique; the way I communicate my Understanding—the way I formulate and time my Interpretations—reflects considerations of Technique. By Technique I mean such things as interrogation, ways of dealing with direct questions, with resistances, and the like. When my patient asks how old I am, then I'm faced with a Technical problem—not with a Technical problem alone, to be sure (for the question needs to be Understood), but with a Technical problem also. When he persistently comes late, when he repeatedly denies that my Interpretations have any validity, when he reports a dream, when he falls into silence, when he insists that he needs me to be his friend and counselor, then my responses are determined in significant part by Technical considerations.

Many of the principles I will be promulgating in these letters can be regarded as aspects of Technique. When I write you about Interpretations, for instance, I will propose that they be simple. That's good Technique. Similarly, it's good Technique to interpret the defense before the impulse, to give priority to the here-and-now over the there-and-then, to avoid formulations that are too deep or too shallow. And if you want your patient to become more reflective and self-searching, there are Technical principles you can employ which may help gain that end and avoid ways that may defeat that end. To put the matter succinctly I'll repeat the basic definition: The ways in which a therapist puts his intentions into action are matters of Technique.

* * * * * * *

What I should do now, Simon, is consider in detail and depth what your intentions are to be when you conduct *Psychotherapy*. But that's pretty well what most of my correspondence to you is going to be about. So instead of embarking on that large subject now, let me offer you a number of detailed, concrete examples to illustrate the role and meaning of Technique in *Psychotherapy*. I'm sure you will welcome a respite from generalities and abstractions and rhetoric.

I have to make a decision first: Shall I try to reconstruct actual clinical episodes or shall I simply make them up? My inclination is to make them up because then I can exemplify and illustrate an intended point with greatest economy. If I compose the example with a particular point in mind, then I can keep matters simple and to the point, and there is also less danger of being second-guessed by you. The big disadvantage is that the examples will not be "real"—if they simply emerge from the top of my head they are likely to be contrived. That, however, is not where most of them will emerge from; they will be based to a greater or lesser extent on my actual clinical experience. So my decision is to fabricate.

In the commentaries to the illustrations I will be stating things that I intend to explain and discuss and defend later on. You can count on it, Simon, that every major point is to be repeated and amplified in later letters. My main purpose now is to illustrate the meaning and role of Technique, and at the same time to give you a depiction of what *Psychotherapy* is like—to make concrete what is otherwise abstract and to show you how the methods and principles translate into action.

Example 1

Your patient has regularly been punctual, and today he is 15 minutes late. You have no particular thoughts about the lateness and no reason to believe that it is significant. But the possibility of significance increases because the patient does not make any mention of the lateness. Instead, he begins the session by telling you he's going to recount an event of the day before—"I bumped into my old friend Harry in the library yesterday, and . . ."

You now have three options before you:

Option 1. You can interrupt to inquire about the lateness: "Before you take up what happened in the library, let me ask about the fact that you came late today."

Option 2. You can interrupt to inquire about the fact that the lateness went unmentioned: "Before you take up what happened in the library, let me ask you something about the fact that you were late today. What I'm wondering about is that you have made no mention of the fact."

Option 3. You can remain silent and listen to the event. On Technical grounds alone, you should rule out the first option. Why? For one thing, you would be imposing the topic on your patient. But, you may object, it is his behavior that you are addressing—how does that amount to imposing a topic? In two ways: (1) it is not the topic he has chosen to talk about; (2) you have no reason to believe that it has significance. It's therefore too easy to imagine that the topic could be quite fruitless. Your patient might well respond by saying something like, "Oh, I couldn't get away from work until exactly five o'clock; and then the damn subway stopped for about 15 minutes in the tunnel."

Will you now want to pursue the matter further? Will you ask him to please explain why he doesn't make adequate allowances, or how come he couldn't get away until exactly five? No, you should not want to do any of that. For one thing, you would run the danger of putting yourself in the role of an inquisitor; for another, you are fishing for significance. (Of course, you can easily move into Option 2 at this point, but let me save that for a moment.)

The fact that the conversation you instigate with your question is too likely to be fruitless is the paramount consideration in rejecting Option 1. But there is a further consideration. Let's suppose that, after hearing the patient's explanation for his lateness, you choose not to pursue the matter any further; and since you have no reason to think that his lateness has much significance, you are prepared to accept it as fortuitous. The fact now remains that your having asked the question is likely to have significance.

Say, after his explanation, your patient pauses because he is wondering why you asked. That, after all, is quite reasonable. You should now feel obliged to respond to his answer—whether or not he adds, "Why did you ask?"—and your response would likely have to take this form: "The reason I asked was that I wondered if your lateness might mean that you are having some feelings about coming here." Else why would you have asked? But do you want to introduce this gratuitous note? No, you don't. And the thing to realize is that you have little choice; for once you have chosen to inquire into the (any) matter, you are obliged to answer the spoken or unspoken question, "Why do you ask?" And the answer you must now give is rich with unwanted implications (e.g., "It is a bad thing to be late") and with imposed issues (e.g., "You have feelings about coming"). These are only some of the reasons for avoiding Option 1, and they can be embodied into a Technical principle. (That principle and its rationales will be further explained in my consideration of Option 2.)

Now consider Option 2. Let's suppose that your patient's response is exactly the same as his response to Option 1. You can now proceed as follows: "I see. But I'm wondering why you didn't say that without my having to ask. After all, you have always come on time, so today was unusual in that respect." Where do things stand now? The patient is on the spot for, unlike the subway delay, he was clearly responsible. He could have explained but chose not to, and you are exploring the meanings of that choice.

The exploration may bear fruit or it may not. The Technical principle that guides you here centers on that probability. If, in your judgment, the probability is great, then the unwanted implications and the fact that the issue is imposed can be deemed to have been worth it. True, they will have to be dealt with, and quite soon; but the patient will be well served if it turns out, for example, that he was intending (either knowingly or not) to raise unwarranted questions in your mind, or to keep you in the dark, or whatever. An important Transference issue may be brought to light, or an important fantasy may begin to be examined. So here the probability of such a result is what counts, and you must have some grounds for making an estimate of it.

Not only must you expect a useful result, but you must also be prepared to share with the patient your grounds for it.

Say he responds in a way that dismisses the possibility of any useful exploration. He says, "Oh, I guess it didn't occur to me to explain. You have said that I should feel free to say whatever I wanted here. And I didn't want to make the explanation for my lateness because it just didn't seem important." Now you must be ready—i.e., in the position—to say something like the following, and nothing less: "Sure, I understand; and I'm not questioning your judgment that it may be unimportant. But the reason I decided to raise the issue is this: You've been telling me recently about how your father used to keep you in the dark about what was going on between him and his brother. It seemed to me that you might be doing the same to me by not telling me how come you were late." In other words, you tell him what sort of an Interpretation you had in mind when you raised the issue. That is the best basis on which to answer the question, "Why do you ask?" And the Technical principle is this: *Interrogate only toward an Interpretation.*

If you haven't got an Interpretation in mind you should choose Option 3. (I have learned from experience, Simon, that there's little value and big peril in going on fishing expeditions in psychotherapy unless I can smell the catch.) The third option will not prevent you from bearing in mind both the lateness and the darkness that surrounded it; and you may later on find yourself in a good position to refer back to them. For instance, say he had a conversation with Harry yesterday about therapy; and say he found himself voicing some feelings about being in it that he didn't realize he had. This could provide a basis for explaining his lateness—and you might be able to point that out to him to good effect. Or suppose he talks during the session about his conflicts over telling you everything; and to make matters more simple than they usually are, suppose that Harry is an old friend with whom he used to share his secrets. His encounter with Harry may have thrown him into a conflict of loyalties (with all manner of Oedipal overtones), and that may be the reason he chose not to tell you why he was late.

Suppose, however, that your patient had not begun the session the way he did, but instead he remained silent for a few moments; and say, further, that this is not his usual habit. Is Option 3 still the option of choice? Yes, in my opinion it is. During the initial silence you will probably be thinking about the lateness, and it's a fair assumption that so will he. The question arises: What are his thoughts? Is he wondering whether you will ask why he came late? Is he thinking you are angry, or disappointed in him? or Is he reflecting on how it feels to have come late? Each of these possibilities represents a topic of potential significance. You can explore them by simply asking, "What are you thinking?" (which is a more neutral probe than Options 1 and 2). Unfortunately, there are good reasons not to probe for thoughts during a silence. (One of them is the implication that the patient ought not to be silent; and there are several others I will be writing you about.) So you can choose to wait patiently for him to tell you what he was thinking unless you believe there is a reason you should not. One reason not to wait is that it may imply a collusion on both your parts to avoid the issue. If, say, he subsequently ends the silence by recounting the events of the day before, then the topic of his lateness has been evaded, and you are apparently supporting that evasion. But are you? Is Option 3 potentially an evasion—a cop-out, as your generation puts it?

Let's suppose that your patient was embarrassed by his lateness, so embarrassed that he chose not to mention it. Suppose further that he projects his feelings onto you, by inferring that you too were embarrassed by it and for that reason you remained silent while he proceeded to tell about his meeting with Harry. If so, you can argue, the reason to avoid Option 3 is to show him that you have no special feelings about his having come late—you do not evade it. Or else, under different circumstances, you would be showing him that you regard such incidents as latecoming to be of potential interest and significance. My counterargument is this: such demonstrations are likely to be of limited value. Especially in the context of *Psychotherapy,* their utility is overshadowed by their disutility; your point will have been made at a serious cost to the Therapeutic Process. You see, Simon, if he is projecting, then the most valuable action you can take is Interpretive; if he is assuming you don't care, then you must deal with that assumption not by demonstration (i.e., "I do care") but by Interpretation (i.e., "You need to assume that I don't care").

Moreover, you can often expect to be able to make the same kind of point in a way that does have value insofar as it supports and promotes the Therapeutic Process. Suppose you had chosen to remain silent (Option 3). You may soon be able to observe the consequences of that choice, of not having asked. For example, if your patient begins to have thoughts and feelings that you do not care about him, then you may conclude that that is his reaction to your silence. If so, you can point out to him that your not having asked about the lateness was taken as a sign that you didn't care, or else that you welcomed the shortened hour, or something of the sort. For example:

[PATIENT, after a pause later in the session:] I don't know why . . . it's weird—but I can't shake the feeling that you are not interested in what I am talking about to-day. For some reason it seems to me you don't care.
[YOU:] I have an idea about what may be bothering you. You came late today; it's the first time you ever did; and I didn't ask you how come.

[PATIENT, with a sheepish smile:] That's cool. Yeah, it makes sense. I did wonder why you didn't ask.

[YOU:] And you took it as a sign that I don't care.

[PATIENT:] Whenever I came home from school my mother would always start in with questions—What happened in school? Did I have a good lunch? Was I a good boy?

Now, not only have you shown him that the evasion was his and not yours and that such events as latecoming can serve the interests of useful therapeutic work, but you have helped him gain some Understanding of a significant act. Moreover, you have dealt with him sensitively and patiently, without censure or direction—i.e., with good Technique.

Example 2

Your patient has been talking about her difficulties being alone and doing things alone. This is a long-term problem and it recurred with special intensity the evening before. What happens is that she gets jittery, restless, and vaguely anxious.

While listening to her description of the problem you have the thought that the underlying theme has to do with masturbation. In other words, the formulation forms in your mind that the central dynamic issue has to do with the impulse to masturbate and its associated conflicts. You are tempted to offer the following Intepretation: "I believe that what you are really talking about is masturbation."

You must resist that temptation, because to so interpret would be to violate several Technical principles all at once.

Violation 1. The patient is put into a passive position, insofar as the Interpretation is given to her—again, imposed on her.

Violation 2. She is told that the experiences she was describing are somehow not "real"—as if conscious experience is not to be taken at its face value, as if an underlying theme is more real than its manifest forms.

Violation 3. She may be taken aback or even shocked by the idea. And if it shakes her up too much she will probably fall back on defenses against anxiety, and she will not be able to deal with the theme effectively.

Add to this the possibility that you are assuming the role of the vigilant psychoarcheologist, and it's clear that the Interpretation—even if more tactfully put and carefully formulated—has too many unwanted consequences. So what else are you to do? How can you proceed to implement your intention, which is to explore the role of masturbation?

First of all, you can maintain the theme of masturbation in your mind as a background or context which will play a significant part in the way you continue to listen. You'll be more sensitive to, or alerted to, certain features of your patient's thoughts and experiences. One consequence will be that your remarks to her are likely to focus on those thoughts and experiences that are most germane to the underlying theme. What you will avoid doing is to say anything that might lead her away from the theme, and more than that, find ways of bringing her back to it when she begins to drift away. Your immediate aim is to keep the theme alive and moving and increasingly focused.

Second of all, you can try to bring your patient to the idea of masturbation in a gradual or stepwise way. Your aim is to bring her to the theme rather than bring it to her. One effective way of achieving this is to break your Interpretation down into parts. Whether or not it's useful to conceive of these parts as organized along some dimension of depth, it is useful to think of them as a connected chain of separate Interpretations, for this enables you to introduce them one at a time and thereby gain an important measure of gradualness; and each time you make an Interpretation you can expect her to arrive at the next one by herself. But even if this salutary result doesn't happen, you can judge whether it is appropriate for you to proceed with the next part by observing her reaction to the part you just offered. You can judge whether considerations of Tact can be met, whether the next Interpretation remains valid in the light of her response, and whether it is likely to have a salutary effect. It is important, then, that each of the parts be a complete Interpretation. This is how your Interpretation might be formulated in three parts:

Part 1. "What do you think of the possibility that one of the reasons you feel jittery and restless when you are alone and doing something alone is that there is something else that you want to do—that a part of you, perhaps, is tempted to do?"

Part 2. "I wonder whether it makes you anxious because that something else that you are tempted to do is something you are conflicted about doing, or even something that is forbidden."

Part 3. "One possibility that occurs to me is that that forbidden thing is to masturbate."

Now you have to be patient in two ways. First, you must wait for a suitable "opening" (no pun intended) before you offer the first Interpretation, so that the element of imposition is kept to a minimum. Second, having done the first part, you must be in no particular hurry to get on with the next one. Your patient may need time to deal with each part in her own way. For example, she may digress by considering the form of the Interpretation rather than its substance. She might respond, "That's an interesting idea. It means I get jittery and restless because I don't want to do what I'm doing. I remember when my mother made me practice the viola and I didn't want to, I used to pace around the room while I played. I remember telling my teacher about it, and he said . . . ." If this is indeed little more than a digression, it may be an altogether necessary and useful pause. And if you remain patient, you can usually find an appropriate and tactful way to bring her back to the experience of the evening before. You may be able to point out, for example, that she was doing something the evening before that she didn't want not to be doing; instead, there may have been something else she also wanted to do.

[PATIENT:] Something else? I have no idea what that might be. After all, I was working on a project that I work on a great deal at the office, and I never get restless and jittery there.

[YOU, focusing on an aspect of Part 1:] At the office you are not working alone, all by yourself. I wonder whether the fact that at home you are alone might make some of the difference.

[PATIENT:] I never thought of it that way. What you are suggesting is that being alone makes me want to do something else. But what could that be? When I'm home I usually do some housework, or I might read a book [pause]. I don't read that often either, because that sometimes makes me feel jittery too. Then I have to get up and clean the apartment—that's the only thing that makes the feeling go away.

You now have more information to support your basic Interpretation, but you still have a way to go—several sessions more, perhaps. It may, however, be possible to introduce Part 2 as this session progresses. The difference between reading a book and doing housework might be worth focusing upon in order to develop the "forbidden" aspect of the second part.

But even if it doesn't—even if all of your patient efforts do not suffice and you still believe that it would benefit your patient to acknowledge her impulse to masturbate and examine her conflicts over it—you can make the final Interpretation in the following way.

[PATIENT:] I don't understand what you mean when you say
it may involve the temptation to do something that is
forbidden. What do you mean?

[YOU:] Well, I have several things in mind. There is the possibility, for one, that it may involve something like
masturbating.

Of course, if you had reason to believe that she might be
unduly shocked by this suggestion, you could have stopped
short of introducing the masturbation. You could have responded, "By forbidden I mean something that you would
be ashamed of doing, that you have grown up believing is a
bad thing to do, and you therefore have deep conflicts
about it." But if you decided to raise the theme directly,
then I suggest you pay attention to the way I worded it. For
please note that the patient remains in the position of considering the possibility, and she is quite free to reject it out
of hand (again, no pun). You have shared a thought with
her, and even if it is a shot in the dark, it is only one of several possibilities; and she is invited to think of others. This
way of introducing the theme allows a patient to maintain
the active position—to a significant extent, at least—and
that's good Technique.

Example 3

It is April and you have just told your patient what the
exact dates of the summer vacation will be. After a moment's pause, he asks you quite casually, "Where are you
going on your vacation?" Consider the following two options, each of which is a Technique mistake.

Option 1. The counterquestion, "Why do you ask?"

Option 2. A direct answer giving the requested information.

The first option—it's the standard, if not cliché, thing to
respond—has two main drawbacks. First, it tends to convey

the remonstrative message, "You have no right to ask." Second, it is quite explicitly directive, instructing the patient to consider his motives for entertaining the question. The second drawback is perhaps the more compelling of the two since, if you have carefully avoided this kind of direction up till now, your patient is likely to notice that fact and to wonder, "How come?" He may conclude that this question of his raised a special problem for you insofar as it caused you to respond in a way that you rarely if ever have. (You have never asked, "Why are you thinking about your uncle?" when he was speaking about his uncle. In fact, as I will later have occasion to advise, you have rarely asked him a probing question.) He may therefore quite legitimately ask in return, "Why do you want to know why I ask the question?"—and you cannot respond with anything less than, "Because the reasons behind the question are probably important for us to consider." (And what will you say if he asks what makes you think his reasons are?)

Consider the likelihood that a third option—silence—may not really be different from Option 1, for in the context of such a direct question, silence is also likely to convey a message and a direction. It was not a rhetorical question your patient asked; so a silent response can also convey a "You have no business asking it," or a "Please proceed to examine the meanings and motives behind your question." If this were not so likely, then silence might be the optimal response insofar as it would keep him free to consider the matter however he wanted to—he would not, for instance, feel called upon to examine his motives. Consequently, if you want him to examine his motives, then you must find a response that preserves that freedom. Neither silence nor "Why do you ask?" is likely to do that.

Why is Option 2 a mistake? After all, it not only avoids any withholding that would probably provoke certain feelings in the patient (resentment, for one), but it takes account of the fact that he is asking for something that he has a right to know. Most therapists would agree that a patient should have a way to contact him during any interruptions of the treatment, for there may be an emergency that might require it. So we're dealing with a question that can properly be answered. But when? The time of the example is well in advance of the vacation. The reason you are giving the exact dates now is to allow him ample time to arrange his affairs and make his own summer plans. But for what reasons does he need to know *now* where you will be? So that he can make his own plans accordingly, and perhaps arrange to spend his vacation somewhere close by you? (It is only the rare case where this may be realistically called for.) Otherwise, the only rational reason for knowing is to gain some personal information about you—to find out what sort of person you are in view of the kind of vacation you spend: Are you a world traveller? Do you have a cottage in the Catskills? Do you settle down on Cape Cod with all the other analysts?

In view of the fact that your patient's question has, at this point in time anyway, a personal relevance, you should not answer it. Giving personal information about yourself is proscribed in *Psychotherapy*. Nevertheless, while you should rule out Option 2, some relevant response is clearly called for in the example. You might therefore choose to avoid the implications of the first option by saying, "I will answer your question, but not now." While this achieves one useful purpose, it begs the question, "Why not now?" So another possible variation is to say, "I will not answer your question now because I can't see how the answer would benefit you now." But this, in turn, might be to challenge his judgment—for he may have reason to believe that it would be useful for him to know now—and what might ensue is an argument over the matter. It is rarely if ever our intention to challenge our patient's judgment; that is quite different, after all, from drawing attention to his distortions, misperceptions, and the like. The Technical principle here is a subtle but vital one: *If you must question your patient's judgment, do it without at the same time challenging it;* and an Interpretation is the safest way to avoid the element of challenge.

So where do we stand? We must find an answer that is responsive to his question, that takes into account its legitimate component, that does not gratify its component of curiosity about your personality, that preserves his freedom in the short-run, and that does not convey any criticism or direction. The one answer that does all of this is the following: "I will tell you where I am vacationing and give you the forwarding address (and telephone number) when we stop." That, then, is the Technically prescribed response which best fulfills our various intentions.

Suppose, now, your patient persists and repeats his question—"But where will you be going?" This could serve a variety of functions, and it may represent a kind of challenge to you—perhaps little more than a challenge of your judgment of the appropriateness of waiting until the sessions stop. In any case, you now have a focused intention: to explore the "Why now?" Again, however, you have to navigate the waters of unwanted implications in addition to any defensiveness on your part. You can begin with a tactful, "I take it you understand that I plan to tell you before we stop," which draws attention to the fact that the timing of the answer is at issue. True, you are implicitly asking him to explain why he wants it now, but he can still quite easily avoid it if he wants to—he can respond with, "Oh, yes, I see; I suppose that will be okay." If he chooses to drop the matter there, you will want to remain alert to the issue. But you have not forced his hand; you have maintained Tact; you have not been directive; and neither are you witholding information in an inappropriate way.

If he persists further—"Yes, I understand, but I do want to know now," you can maintain Tact and the rest, but you can hardly avoid saying something like, "Yes, I can see that you do; and what I'm now wondering is why." Or else you can choose to meet his statement with silence. After all, your patient is essentially reflecting on his state of mind ("I want to know") and no longer addressing a direct question. Since it is abundantly clear that you do not intend to give the information now, you can both turn your attention to his state of mind.

Lest you accuse me of having made matters turn out too easy, Simon, let me continue with the scenario in a way that maintains the pressure. You have just said, "Yes, I can see that you do; and what I'm wondering is why."

[PATIENT:] You're wondering *why,* and I'm wondering *why not.* I can't figure out why you make such a big deal out of such a simple question. You'd think I was asking you such a personal question [falls into a petulant, angry silence, and then continues after establishing that you are not going to speak at this point]. I mean, here I am in therapy with you and I don't know a damned thing about you. All I know is where you got your training. Now, I'm not trying to pry into your personal life; I'm not asking you whether you're happily married, or anything like that. So why are you so uptight? Here you tell me when we're going to be stopping for the summer vacation, and I ask you a simple question like one human being to another. It's not such a big thing, is it, to tell me where you're going on your vacation? Why the hell can't you treat me like a human being!

[YOU, suffering a little, but clinging securely to your Technical moorings, remain silent as undefensively as you can.]

[PATIENT:] God, you're impossible! Aren't you going to say something?

[YOU:] All I could say is something you don't need to be told: that you are very angry with me.

[PATIENT:] I sure as hell am! And I think I have a perfect right to be. You make me feel like a nothing, a cipher. If I wasn't your patient you would treat me differently—you wouldn't be so damned detached. A lot of the time that's alright; and I'm not saying you haven't been helping me. But once in a while I wish you would come down off your pedestal and act human [falls silent].

At this point you have two options: (1) you can remain silent in order to let the theme develop further (and notice that it is developing); (2) you can make an Interpretive comment on one or another aspect of what he has just said (he has, after all, provided you with some mill-grist). But, whatever you do, you must avoid acting out of a need to defend yourself from his anger. If you decide to show an interest in his feeling "like a nothing, a cipher" or in his metaphor of the pedestal, you must take pains to make it clear that you are not attempting to deflect his anger. For example:

[YOU:] Without my seeming to imply that you have no right to be angry with me—because I agree that my not answering your question would make you angry—let me point something out. You say I have made you feel like a nothing by not treating you like a human being. And you have been telling me recently how your father used to make you feel small and insignificant—he was always so busy with his work, and didn't have the time to be with you and play with you. That also made you feel "like a nothing, a cipher."

Things might proceed from this in a way that will take
the heat off you. But the Interpretive attempt could also fail
insofar as its intent is quite transparent.

[PATIENT:] Clever! Very clever, doctor! You're a real
    shrewdy! Now I will start talking about my old man,
    and the heat is off of you. It's not you I'm sore at, it's
    really him. Beautiful! But that's got nothing to do with
    what's going on here right now. I don't buy it. I asked
    you a simple question, and got a simple evasion. That's
    why I'm angry.

For you now to remind him that you did say he had reason to be angry with you would be for you to defend yourself and also to scold him for having overlooked your remark. At most, then, I would recommend saying, "I didn't
mean to deny that that is the reason you are angry."

In any case, the situation is now at a point of impasse,
and it is incumbent on you to take steps against it. If you
yourself have become provoked to strong feelings (anger,
defensiveness, or others) you may be unable to think of alternative lines of Interpretation. If, however, you can keep
your "cool" and keep the Interpretive mode in play, then
you might weather the impasse and at the same time promote some worthwhile therapeutic work. One possibility is
to offer an Interpretation that goes beneath the content of
the matter and gets to its form. It might occur to you that
the patient is angry not because you refused to share a
piece of personal information with him, but because he
experienced a powerlessness to affect you, to make you respond to him. So you might offer him an Interpretation that
simply recasts the matter like this: "I think you are angry
because you aren't able to affect me, to move me to answer
a question; that makes you feel 'like a cipher' because you
feel powerless." Or perhaps you might put it this way:

"When I don't respond to you it is as if I am up on a pedestal, out of your reach; then you can't affect me. I think that was what made me think of your father."

Your intentions here are far from simple. On the one hand, you do not want your patient's anger to be dissipated at the expense of therapeutic work and achievement. You must therefore acknowledge the fact that he is angry over an aspect of the therapy that is both real and integral. You must show him in one way or another that his feelings are both acceptable and unthreatening to you—you can take it, and you think he can too. On the other hand, you want him to continue in the therapy. To put it bluntly, you don't want to lose him. Both intentions are best served by your pursuing the Interpretive mode with all due attention to matters of good Technique.

Example 4

Your patient comes to her sessions with a topic apparently prepared in advance, but she has never talked about this habit. Today she begins the session with an opening remark that is typical of her—"I was thinking before I came today about my difficulties getting to know new people. I went to a party on Saturday evening, and had a perfectly dreadful time trying to make conversation with this good-looking man." You can predict that the rest of the session will consist of a systematic consideration of the topic, with all the earmarks of a carefully planned and rehearsed recitation.

Suppose you believe that it would be to her benefit if this habit could—at least occasionally—be broken, if she would allow herself a measure of spontaneity and freedom during the session by permitting the topic to emerge without forethought. The simplest way would be to offer her a piece of so-called procedural advice, "I believe you might benefit more from your sessions if, at times, you tried to refrain from coming prepared with what you will talk about here."

Psychotherapy, however, proscribes all forms of advice. And even if you regarded it as a trivial (or unavoidable) violation of the principle, Simon, you may find yourself loath to open the door to requests on the part of this woman for instructions on how to be a good patient. Furthermore, you may well believe that it would be far more useful for her—and effective for the therapy—if the habit were Understood. The procedural advice, you see, could have the result of forestalling its analysis.

Your goal, then, is to draw your patient's attention to the habit so that it may become the topic. A straightforward way of achieving this is to venture a Confrontation, as follows: "Let me interrupt you in order to draw your attention to something that may be important for you to think about. You say you were thinking about this topic before you came today. Now, it seems to me that this is what you do before almost every session."

Confrontation, if used tactfully and judiciously, can be a valuable therapeutic technique, but it can be dissonant with the spirit of *Psychotherapy* insofar as it imposes a topic on the patient. (To argue that it is not such a serious imposition because it was the patient who introduced the topic with her behavior, is something of a sophistry.) Still, there is no denying that the imposition may at times be effective, if not necessary. So let's consider your patient's possible responses to your Confrontation.

Response 1: Complete Acceptance. "Yes, that's true, and I can see why you are pointing it out to me. I do agree that it could be important for me to consider it, because it is something I always do. I always think about what I will talk about here and make sure to have it all worked out in advance. I don't know why I have to do that, and sometimes it bothers me—it makes me feel kind of guilty, you know. It is as if I were doing something wrong, or even bad. It's a strange feeling. . . . I've been meaning to talk about it, but somehow I always put it off."

Response 2: Complete Rejection. "No, I don't do that at all. What I meant when I said I was thinking about it before I came was that it occurred to me as I walked in here. But I wasn't thinking much about it before that; and I don't usually do that kind of thing."

Response 3: Counterconfrontation. "So what if it is so? Why do you choose today of all days to bring it up? After all, if it's something I have been doing since the start of therapy, you've had plenty of opportunity to draw it to my attention. Why do you do it now when I am about to speak of something that is so important to me?"

Response 4: Perplexity. "What do you mean? Of course I think about what I'm going to talk about here in advance. Isn't that the right thing to do? [pause] But if it were, then you wouldn't be interrupting to draw it to my attention. So I'm puzzled. I assumed that everybody did that before a therapy session. Don't they? Is it a bad thing to do?"

Response 1 is, of course, the ideal one, the one you would most welcome. To expect it, however, is likely to be wishful thinking. Response 2 is alright too, for unless you have reason to believe she is evading the issue, you can now put the matter aside; and this can be useful insofar as it removes a distraction from your mind and will help you listen more attentively to what happened on Saturday evening.

Response 3 is one that you would rather not have to deal with; for your only honest reply might be something to the effect of "Enough is enough!" And that, even with all the Tact you can muster, would inevitably carry with it implications both of advice and of criticism. If you get this kind of response you may have little choice but to focus on her feeling of outrage, and to follow it up with the Interpretation that she is being defensive. For example:

[YOU, in answer to Response 3]: You are feeling outraged,
    aren't you?
[PATIENT:] Yes, I resent your interrupting—because I don't
    understand why you choose now to do it.
[YOU:] It seems to me that if it were only a matter of not
    understanding then you might feel puzzled, but instead
    you feel resentment and outrage. So I wonder whether
    you are also reacting to what I said, and you'd rather
    not have to consider your habit of preparing in ad-
    vance.

She might accept this Interpretation, and things might
proceed as they would after Response 1. Or else the topic
might become her reaction of outrage to the Confrontive
mode. In either case the Confrontation would have been
useful.

Counterconfrontations, however, too often lead to an
impasse. The patient may fall back on her other defenses;
she might retreat to stubborn silence, she might become
more argumentative, she might intellectualize and obfus-
cate. It is pointless (if not self-defeating) for you to pursue
her with further Interpretations or Confrontations in the
face of these defenses. For one thing, they are bound to be
understood by her as little more than criticisms and scold-
ings. It is an important aspect of good Technique that your
interventions, be they Interpretations, Confrontations, or
simple observations, are useful only when they are acceptable to the patient (either at a level of consciousness or to a
part of his personality). Otherwise, you see, she has no useful way to deal with the matter. The same is true for Response 4. You can draw her attention to her perplexity and
mystification, and you can add to this that the reaction
seems defensive; but that too runs the risk of bringing

things to a serious impasse. (And to respond with, "What makes you think I said it was a bad thing to do?" is only to compound defensiveness with more of the same.) So you may have little choice but to fall back on the procedural instruction.

Both Interpretations and Confrontations—but especially the latter—may provoke an argument; and *Psychotherapy* generally eschews that mode. Argument, you see, too often becomes little more than a test of wits, of quickness and facility of thought. It stirs up feelings of contest; it brings into play issues of winning and losing; it is generally to be avoided.

To Response 4, you have the option of focusing on your patient's assumption by saying, "I think there is a reason why you need to assume that everybody does it the way you do." But you must be in a position now to spell out, via an Interpretation, what that reason might be. The Technical principle here is that a therapist makes a Confrontation only when he deems it absolutely necessary, or when there is an Interpretation at hand. In this example it is clear that the former condition does not apply.

Consequently, Simon—in view of the fact that you are too unsure how your patient will respond to a Confrontation, and in view of the likelihood that the Confrontation will quickly require an Interpretation of you—you can well decide to go the route of Interpretation to begin with. And this, let us imagine, is the one that formulates in your mind: "I think you are feeling vulnerable here. You are worried lest something may come to your mind spontaneously that might be upsetting to you, or even frightening. Or else you are feeling as if it was somehow dangerous here because I might say something to you that would upset or hurt you. And for these reasons you need to come to your sessions with something all worked out and prepared in advance, which you can fill up the whole session describing and talking about. This ensures that there will be little opportunity for me to say very much about it. Or, if not that, then having something all worked out may be a way to prevent anything from coming spontaneously to your mind here—something that you would have little control over because it would come as a surprise—and that could be frightening." But you wouldn't dream of saying all that!—and for a variety of Technical (you might be tempted to substitute "common-sense") reasons. Some of them have already been discussed in the foregoing examples. Here, I will focus on the following two reasons:

Reason 1. The Interpretation imposes a number of altogether fresh topics upon the session. If the patient has not already alluded to any feelings of vulnerability, then the Interpretation is a major imposition.

Reason 2. There is far too much in it. Granting that it may all be quite true, what is your patient to do with it? Is she to choose from among the four or five distinguishable ideas the one that she is prepared to deal with?

The Interpretation violates the Technical principle of simplicity and parsimony to the point of caricature. It has at least four major parts to it, and you have delivered them all. What you should do, instead, is to decide which one of them has priority (i.e., the greatest relevancy). Not which part is most true, since we are assuming that it is all true, but which part is most Timely. Is it the feeling of vulnerability? the feeling of fright? the unexpected thought? the unexpected Interpretation?—or is the fear of loss of control the most relevant aspect?

Therefore, if you decide in favor of Interpretation, you must simplify and articulate the Interpretation in your mind, and you must await a suitable opportunity or opening so that the imposition is kept to a minimum. You will not interrupt at the beginning of the session, but will listen to her account in two simultaneous ways: (1) you will attend to the manifest content, listening to Understand and to remember it; and (2) you will listen for some content that you might be able to connect with, or associate to, some aspect of the Interpretation in an appropriate way. This might occur in the following way:

[PATIENT:] I knew I was going to have a miserable time at that party on Saturday.

[YOU, perceiving an opening:] You knew it in advance [said, perhaps, in a half-questioning way].

[PATIENT:] Yes. Parties like that have always filled me with dread.

[YOU:] And I take it that you think a lot about them beforehand.

Notice how this last remark is pivotal. In a certain sense, you are making the opening with a conjecture; but it is neither too farfetched or without Tact. If she says, "No," and then wonders aloud why you made the remark, you can casually deflect it with a remark such as, "I just figured you did that." The temptation should probably be resisted to join the issue at this point by responding, "Because it seems to me that it is what you do before your sessions here." That may be premature.

But let's imagine that you were right, and she responds, "I certainly do that. While I was getting dressed for the party I kept imagining how I was going to have to make conversation with some perfect stranger." Now you can focus on the theme as follows:

[YOU:] Do you find yourself imagining in detail how such a conversation might go?

[PATIENT:] Sort of—not always in so much detail, but I find myself thinking about what I say and what he says, and things like that. This is something I have always been prone to do. Like when I used to go out on dates when

I was younger, I used to figure out things to talk to the boy about. Otherwise it would be deadly.

Now, if you sense that she is returning to her rehearsed account, you can encourage her to continue to explore the habit itself and to focus on the question of why she feels the need to prepare. You can raise the question of the habit's utility, suggesting perhaps that it is less useful than she might believe it to be. Or else you can move directly into the Interpretation as follows: "You know, it occurs to me that this is similar to what you do here. What I have in mind is that you tend to come to your sessions with some-thing figured out in advance to talk about."

And now the desired topic has been raised. Has it been imposed?—not unless your patient now experiences it as an imposition. She may accept the idea as altogether related to the topic she brought in, in which case there has been no violation of her Autonomy. She may, for example, say, "Yes, I guess that's true. I don't know why I should do it here too. After all, it's not as if I felt the same way about talking to you here as I do about talking to a stranger at a party." All is well. You are now in a good position to im-plement one of your Interpretations—not that you should seize the opportunity to deliver it right away. At this point there may be value in forebearance and Tact. It may be sufficient to dwell on the contradiction that she is express-ing, and to allow her a chance to develop the theme of the Interpretation herself.

But what if she does experience an imposition and she denies that there is any connection between the topic she raised and the therapy itself? She responds, for example, "But that's altogether different. It doesn't strike me as simi-lar at all. I'm not nervous about coming here like I am about going to a party. And the reason I think about what I should talk about here is because that's the most efficient way to benefit from these sessions." Now, Simon, you must choose your words carefully, and if you do, then you will most likely respond as follows: "I understand. But I'm wondering whether it might not benefit you to examine that assumption. After all, you say that you still had a dreadful time at the party even though you rehearsed for it beforehand. So perhaps the advance preparation doesn't really help you."

Notice, please, which assumption you have chosen to address. Notice that you chose to retreat, in a way, from the therapy theme and to return to your patient's topic. That is a Technical maneuver serving the interest of Tact. She may not be ready to deal with her advance preparations for the sessions, and you must remain sensitive to that readiness (i.e., Tactful). Thus, after having mentioned it, you can easily shift back to her own topic. Your patient should not be backed into a corner, and should always sense that she has the freedom of movement (if not maneuverment). In this way she does not feel coerced into considering something she does not want to consider at the moment.

Your patient is now free to talk about her habit of preparing for parties or about her habit of preparing for sessions. She can continue by saying, "Well, it's true that I seem to always have such a dreadful time at parties despite the advance preparations . . ." or she can continue by taking up her need to prepare for the sessions by saying, "Well, it may not help much for the parties, but I think it does help for the sessions, because, if I didn't do it, then I would sit here with nothing to say. . . ."

In either event, you are engaged in the implementation of your intentions—and that's what Technique is all about.

Your affectionate uncle

Five

Dear Simon,

The examples in my last letter have evoked a pack of questions from you, and I'm not surprised. I'll save some of them for a later time and try to deal with two now—two which are major challenges actually. You question my stringent views on interrogation, especially in light of the fact that so many traditional psychotherapists make such heavy use of it; and you write, "Is it actually possible to make any Interpretation without at the same time imposing something new on the patient, and also directing him?" (By the way, Simon, the tone of your letter was skeptical, and I must remember to write you about that in a future letter.)

You're quite right with regard to my position vis-à-vis interrogation; it is idiosyncratic. Most therapists lean heavily on the mode. They do a lot of questioning and probing; it's their way of participating in, and maintaining, the flow of the Therapeutic Process. Questions, after all, are a natural means of doing such useful things as focusing, amplifying, and exploring, and they also serve as tangible evidence to the patient that you're paying close attention to him, that you're actively involved. But they achieve this at a substantial cost: they guide the patient, they steer, and they control him; thus, they transform the therapy session into a kind of interview that I believe can be dissonant with the underlying spirit of *Psychotherapy*. I was tempted in my last letter to enunciate a Technical principle that inveighs against the use of questions and probes—such as, *Eschew the interrogative mode!*

51

In most therapy sessions, however, it is not possible to go very long without having to ask a question. For one thing, there will be occasions when you simply haven't understood (with a small *u*) what your patient said or had in mind; for another, you will often find that questions can be helpful in getting him to focus or enlarge upon a theme. In both cases the problem can usually be solved with something other than a question—strictly speaking, you see, "I don't understand what you said, or meant to say," is not a question. Simple observations, or comments, or even Interpretations can sometimes be used for the purposes of focusing and enlarging. But it would be carrying matters to an unrealistic extreme to proscribe all questions. So when I advise against interrogation, Simon, I have in mind any *undue* reliance upon it. For while it is true, as you write, that any and all of the therapist's interventions will exert some control over his patient's behavior, a direct question or probe does it in a way that is more complete. A question demands an answer; an Interpretation doesn't. A probe may leave the patient with fewer options than an Interpretation or observation does.

I regard the two principles that I stated in the last letter to be safeguards against the undue use of questions: (1) *interrogate only toward an interpretation* and *(2) Be prepared to answer the counterquestion, "Why do you ask?"* In most instances, our answer to the counterquestion will contain at least an allusion to the Interpretation; so in this respect they are overlapping principles. But we must allow also for the answer, "Because I don't comprehend what you are saying or meaning to say." All other kinds of answers—for example, "Because I believe the answer might be important," or "Because you are leaving out many of the details," or "Because I'm interested," and the like—are to be avoided as justifications for the asking of a question. I regard this as a particularly important Technical point—for the conduct of *Psychotherapy* at least.

Frequently our problem is not that we haven't understood at all, but that we wish to understand better. So we may want to request some additional information—for example, "How old were you at the time?" Now, that may strike you as altogether sensible and useful. But when you do that, Simon, you will often have to pay a price. The price I have in mind is the consequence of a basic principle of communication in psychotherapy (or anywhere else, in fact). It is this: *Every communication has more than one message or meaning.* The way this applies to the patient's utterances, I will not discuss here. Here I'll consider its application to our remarks, beginning first with the question for information or for clarification.

It seems innocuous enough to ask for information, and often it is; but the principle of multiple messages and meanings is always operating. Take, for example, "How old were you at the time [that the event you are recounting occurred]?" This can convey the following messages to your patient.

Message 1. Age is important.
Message 2. He (the therapist) wants all the facts.
Message 3. I am deficient in my recounting of events.
Message 4. He thinks I am distorting the event (since I was so young at the time it happened).

Say your patient responds to your question this way: "I was only six. But I was a very observant child, doctor. My mother used to call me little nosy because I was always listening to what the grownups were talking about. She used to say I shouldn't because I was too little to understand, and it would just give me all kinds of mixed up ideas. Sometimes she would send me upstairs when she saw I was listening, and I would sulk there for hours." And say he falls into a silent sulk. You must now respond in a way that bares Message 4, as follows: "You are feeling that way right now, aren't you? Partly, I suppose, you're re-experiencing that old hurt. But partly you may also be feeling that I have hurt you in the same way your mother used to, that by interrupting to ask you how old you were at the time of the incident I was implying that you were too young to have understood it correctly."

If those four implications can be raised by a simple question for information, then think of the potential implications of questions that convey the message, "I don't understand what you are telling me." Not that this message is to be avoided when it's necessary; but the full range of its implications must be borne in mind. Every time we make a remark to our patient we must be sensitive to the potential and probable implications of it, to its other (and possibly unintended) meanings. And this applies especially to our questions.

The principle of multiple messages and meanings extends, of course, beyond the matter of questions. It applies with equal force to all of our utterances, and most especially to our Interpretations. An Interpretation that explains, for example, why my patient behaved cruelly to his brother can also serve to exonerate him or else to scold him, even though that was not my intention. When I come round to writing you about Interpretations I will have occasion to discuss this point at length. Briefly: all Interpretations are liable to carry an additional burden of meaning that covers the range from sanction to prohibition. They can imply direction and advice, they can imply a scolding, they can imply forgiveness—and they do. Is there nothing we can do against these implications?

A Behaviorist would answer this way: (1) Reinforcement is indigenous to interventions; (2) It is not only futile to attempt to cancel it out, it flies in the face of therapeutic effectiveness. I agree with (1), but only in principle, and I disagree with (2). We can be alert to the Reinforcement implications and we can articulate them for the patient at

every opportunity. We can—and you should—make it clear
to him that, while they may be unavoidable in principle, we
do not intend them in fact. And in order to make this vivid
to him we must always be prepared to follow up an intervention by drawing his attention to the unwanted meanings
that it conveyed. Let me offer some examples of how this
can be done (I'm not implying that you must necessarily
follow up in this way—only that you be prepared to if you
deem it judicious).

Example 1

Your patient has been criticizing you roundly, taking you
to task for speaking in a pedantic way, for being stiff and
awkward.

[YOU:] It occurs to me that one of the reasons you are criti-
    cizing me may be that you want me to criticize and
    scold you in return.
[PATIENT:] Yeah, that's cool. You're right [grins a sheepish
    grin]. I feel like such an ass.
[YOU:] You're feeling sheepish, as if I actually did scold
    you.
[PATIENT:] Sure! I feel like an ass [pause]. But I also still
    feel sore at you.
[YOU:] It's kind of paradoxical, isn't it? You criticized me
    because you wanted me to scold you, and then, when I
    pointed out that fact to you, it felt like I was actually
    doing it.

Example 2

You have just offered an Interpretation.

[PATIENT:] That makes a lot of sense, what you just said.
    Yes; the reason I was so nasty to my mother yesterday

was that I wanted her to cuddle me like she used to when I was little. So instead I let her have it. That explains why [pause]. Makes me feel a lot better now to know that. What a bitch she is! She really deserved it, didn't she? Treats me like some kind of stranger [falls silent]. You know something? I feel all relaxed now. My stomach is even quiet for a change. You're a great therapist [silence].

[YOU:] You feel warmly towards me right now for two reasons, I think. One is that I helped you understand why you were nasty to your mother yesterday. The other is because the explanation sort of lets you off the hook. It means that I am taking your side against her—maybe also that I am excusing your behavior. [Perhaps it can be added:] In a sense I did what she didn't—cuddle you.

Example 3

[PATIENT:] Men are such chauvinists, and my husband is one of the worst. The minute he gets home from work he wants to be treated like a king. I should serve him, I should comfort him, I should control the kids. Haven't I been working all day too? So of course I exploded when he got sore because dinner wasn't ready. He had no right to get angry [pause]. But I don't know why I exploded as terribly as I did. I didn't really mean to, you know. It was just too much of a tantrum [falls silent].

[YOU:] Perhaps because you had some doubts over whether his anger might not have been justified?

[PATIENT:] Oh, very clever, doctor! So you think I was feeling guilty [bursts into tears]. I'm crying because it's true what you said; I did feel guilty.

[YOU:] That wouldn't explain why you are crying now.

[PATIENT, through her tears]: What do you mean?

[YOU:] I think you are crying because you are angry with me now—because, in pointing out that you may have felt he was justified, I seem to be taking his side against you.

* * * * * * *

When I wrote, at the beginning of this letter, that a question demands an answer and an Interpretation doesn't, that was an overstatement. It's not uncommon for patients to feel that an Interpretation does demand a response from them. Many will feel called upon to deal with the content of your Interpretation; some will feel they have to validate or invalidate it, some will have the need to express gratitude that you gave something, and there are a variety of responses that are evoked. They must all of them be exposed and analyzed because they are unintended and therefore unwanted. What we strive for, you see, is a state of affairs in which our patient feels just as free after an Interpretation as he did before it. That, of course, is one of the unattainable ideals; but it can be approached and approximated.

So my reply to your second question, Simon, is this: There's no denying that every time we speak to the patient we are imposing on and directing him to an extent; but that doesn't render us helpless to take substantial steps against such kinds of influence. Not only can we take active measures to counteract the unwanted consequences, but we can also explain to him that we don't intend any of them. If you take pains to make this point repeatedly and sensitively to your patients, you will find—as I have found—that as the therapy progresses they will respond to your interventions in a way that will convince you that they don't feel imposed upon or directed—or scolded, or exonerated, or advised, and the rest—by you. And if they do, it's a matter of Transference, and can be dealt with as such.

Your affectionate uncle

Six

Dear Simon,

You'll find, if you haven't already, that the didactic literature on psychotherapy is generally composed of three ingredients: Theoretical Conceptualization, Pragmatic Wisdom, and Inspirational Sermon. Identifying these ingredients should be easy, but it isn't. For one thing, they typically occur in mixtures—a formulation is likely to consist of an abstract idea combined with a piece of practical experience, both of them resting upon a hopeful ideal. For another, they're frequently found disguised in each other's garb—a theoretical conception may turn out, on closer inspection, to be little more than Pragmatic Wisdom in conceptual language. This happens, I suppose, because different values and attitudes attach to the three ingredients. Pragmatic Wisdom is nowadays distrusted and depreciated insofar as it makes the abominable Appeal to Authority. Consequently, since Theoretical Conceptualization generally commands the widest respect, the wisdom tends to be woven into theory. Inspirational Sermon is also out of favor, so here too the matter is often cast into quasi theoretical terms (and we get heart-warming theories of the "Man Is Good" variety).

The reason I want to draw your attention to these distinctions, Simon, is that there's a corresponding set of distinctions in what I regard to be the appropriate attitudes with which to approach the subject of psychotherapy. And the reason I want to write you about attitudes is because of the skeptical tone of your questions. Maybe I should have written about this in an earlier letter. I may have been too eager to be finished with the Introductions; or perhaps (because I must inhibit myself from giving any to my patients) I've grown too reluctant to give advice. Anyway, I now want to lecture you.

Consider these three basic attitudes: skepticism, criticalness, and respect. Consider how they aren't equally appropriate for those three ingredients. Pragmatic Wisdom (i.e., practical experience) merits a kind of respect combined with a certain criticalness; but Theoretical Conceptualization calls for a criticalness that is combined with a certain skepticism. Before I try to spell out what I think the differences are, let me exhort you (Inspirational Sermon) to avoid extreme attitudes of any variety when you confront a subject so diverse and multifaceted as psychotherapy. Skepticism in its extreme form can be both paralyzing and obnoxious; and it's both possible and desirable to be critical without at the same time being insufferable. Any formulation, proposition, or rationale can be accepted by us with some conditionality and a degree of uncertainty. An attitude of partiality can be combined with a measure of doubt; and we can also reject things with the same tempered attitude.

Perhaps the common element to all the attitudes is one of searching curiosity. The Scientific approach, however, combines that searching curiosity with skepticism, while the Artistic approach combines it with criticalness. When my teacher tells me how to paint a seascape I don't challenge him with a "Prove it!" When he shows me how to interpret a passage from a Beethoven sonata I don't ask him "How do you know?" The challenge, after all, is altogether unmeetable, and the question is already answered in that I have chosen him as my teacher (and therefore accepted his credentials). This does not mean however, that I fully accept everything he says or does—that I abandon my critical judgment and sensibilities. It means that I don't approach his teachings with an attitude of skepticism. There is, after all, a nice difference between skepticism and criticalness. To emulate the Haggadah:

The Skeptical One replies: "That is very interesting—but what is your evidence? In order to accept your proposition I require it to be based upon adequate proof, upon evidence that is both sound and rigorous."

The Critical One replies: "That is very interesting—but what is your rationale? While it makes a certain sense to me, your proposition does not strike me as altogether sound. It fits in certain ways and not in others. In order to accept it I need to understand how it works and what its conditions and limits are."

Criticalness, you see, is the exercising of the cognitive process of assimilation. The ruling criterion is, "Does this make sense to me?"—"Does it fit with what I know?" Carried to an extreme it of course prevents anything new from occurring under the sun. But the process of accommodation takes care of that possibility. The critical person does more than simply fit everything into his already formed schemas; he also permits his schemas to change and grow—slowly, perhaps, and some more slowly than others. But the twin processes of assimilation and accommodation (and you will recognize Piaget here, but these processes have been described by many psychologists) guarantee that our beliefs and values, our knowledge and understanding, will evolve adaptively. Sometimes our schemas will have to change radically and precipitously, but I doubt whether that adaptive requirement ever happens around the events of psychotherapy.

This question of attitudes has to do with the larger question about psychotherapy: Is it a Science? Is it an Art? Is it somehow Both? or Is it a Technology? Now, personally, I'd opt for Both. And in my estimation most of the contemporary forms of therapy—with the possible exception of Behavior Modification—are more Art than Science. Whether psychotherapy ought to be more Science, or what place Science can and should have in it, is a Big Question. To the extent that it is Art, however, it is Applied Art, more analogous to the profession of architecture than to a Performance Art such as playing the piano. And just as the architect must limit his artistic pretensions to sound principles of engineering and physics, so the psychotherapist must base his practice on sound principles of interpersonal relations and psychology.

Now consider the fact that not every method for promoting behavioral change can be equally effective. Some are bound to be more efficacious, more valid, or more humane than others. The analogy with architecture highlights the fact that a wide range of options remains available given the conditions of material, of social usage, and of habits of living. Psychotherapy too depends upon time and place—it's a cultural enterprise insofar as it is embedded in, and responsive to, social realities. It may be intellectually rewarding for us to search for the common denominator in all forms of psychotherapy, as if cultural and social variables could be partialed out, but practically speaking it is likely to be a futile undertaking. Individual differences tend to remain recalcitrant to every reductionistic attempt at all levels of discourse excepting the most abstract. So it remains practically inevitable that different people, at different times and places, will benefit differently from different forms of psychotherapy.

To the extent that becoming a psychotherapist is similar to becoming an artist, it shares some of the same difficulties and perils. Perhaps the biggest is becoming closed off to new influences—deciding at some point that "I have mastered that Art and I know the Truth." Moreover, just as the surgeon is likely to believe that most patients can best

benefit from his kind of treatment and the architect believes
that most inhabitants will live best in his kind of dwelling,
the psychotherapist is likely to believe that most patients
will benefit from the form of therapy that he practices. That
may be an altogether unavoidable conviction even for those
of us who intellectually acknowledge its basic flaw and who
recognize that Art—especially Applied Art—is essentially
relative. Unlike the poet, we cannot continually suffer the
anguish of pursuing the elusive Muse. There is also a tendency to become complacent and somewhat dogmatic. Most
of us will need to stick to what we know and what we can
do; it takes both effort and courage to change one's basic
way of working. On the other hand, we are also prey to a
temptation to change, to regard the different as the better
and more creative, for there's a tendency in us to believe
that progress is automatically ensured by making changes.
So, Simon, a certain amount of quiet conviction must be
combined with your criticalness; and fickleness is not to be
confused with flexibility.

I write you nothing about how one goes about respecting
Inspirational Sermon. Respect is a subtle, and also a treacherous, attitude. Anyway, I'll assume that that is the attitude
you are taking while reading this letter.

* * * * * * *

I realize that what I'm writing you in these letters sounds
like it comes exclusively out of my own head and experience. That's because I've decided to do without citations
and quotations, so I'm not backing up my beliefs and opinions with the authority and experience of others. But I am
assuming that you're aware of the fact that there is behind
me a rich tradition of Pragmatic Wisdom. I regard pragmatic experience (clinical, naturalistic, and otherwise) as
one of the chief sources of knowledge in the field of psychotherapy. I believe, you see, that the much-maligned

Anecdotal method has a vital place in psychology, and that to wholly dismiss it in favor of methods that are relatively more scientific is an outright mistake. So it matters that a man with the clinical experience of Karl Menninger believes this and that, or that someone with the discernment of a Carl Rogers has abandoned this or that approach. For it's inevitable that our willingness to accept a proposition will depend in part upon the reputation of the one who makes it.

If I chose to be compulsively conscientious in giving due credit for every conception, formulation, principle, rationale, and argument, then not only would I have to reread everything I've ever read on the subject and recall everything I've ever heard, but these letters would be littered with citations and quotations, and they'd get more unwieldy than they already are. And there's another handicap—a psychological one—that's more serious. It has to do with the inevitability of omissions, of failing to give credit where it is due. It's a steady source of potential embarrassment for an author to paraphrase the words of a Menninger or Rogers— if not to quote them directly—while pretending to be their originator. The fact that this can happen quite unwittingly is what makes it so worrisome. As Bakan has pointed out, what scholars suffer from most is a nagging guilt that they are failing in conscientiousness (and do you see how citations work?). Anyway, one has to shake off this worry and proceed with equanimity, facing the likelihood—the inevitability, actually—that a reader will often recognize close paraphrases and will occasionally think to himself, "Why, the scoundrel! He's writing the words of Merton Gill as if they were his own." The only defense is to acknowledge at the outset—as I'm doing it here—that his thoughts, ideas, and opinions are formed out of myriad experiences of having read, listened, and learned. What matters is that he accepts them, not where he learned them. And especially when his purpose is didactic rather than scholarly, the way in which and the extent to which a particular idea is original to him need not be of serious concern to you. That, in any case, is the position I'm taking here. When I get round to giving you the reading list I promised you, you'll see some of the sources of my methods and principles.

* * * * * * *

A further piece of lecturing, Simon. The *reductio ad absurdum* can be a foolish and destructive challenge. It is common in branches of philosophy to put every proposition to the extreme test, to examine it under extreme conditions to see whether it turns absurd. Now, even if it is a cogent way to examine certain kinds of intellectual propositions, it isn't cogent for the kinds of propositions in this correspondence. For one thing, the principles that I am promulgating are not meant to be applied in the extreme; rather, they are meant to be used with balance. Things are relative—or, better put, they are optimal (I have in mind the ubiquitous U-shaped curve for virtually all psychological functions). In psychological matters there are always substantial exceptions; and, since I want to avoid the cumbersomeness of inserting a qualifier such as "relative" or "optimal" every time I state a proposition, I am assuming them. I also want to disavow the relevancy of the extreme case; every principle will be assumed to have its limits and its range of optimal conditions.

While I'm at it, let me say something about the use of analogies and metaphors. The temptation is irresistible to rely on them to help explain and argue matters of therapy, and this temptation is apt to arise when the going gets rough. But we must never lose sight of the fact that they are little more than crude visual aids to help make a point. Analogies and metaphors are rarely to be taken as theoretical models. Even the best of them should be regarded with some suspicion and never taken too literally (or even too seriously). Psychotherapy—and especially *Psychotherapy*—is a unique event. It's not a game, it's not a voyage, it's not a repair job or a hydraulic adjustment, or a diet—or anything other than itself. It isn't that analogies cannot be helpful, for—as you can plainly see—I believe they can. But sometimes the help is illusionary. They necessarily distort the subject, and occasionally they may also misinform. So they should be used mainly for the purposes of illustration and rarely for purposes of persuasion.

And finally, Simon, a plea for tolerance—tolerance for uncertainty and for ambiguity. I'm writing you about a system that is like a dynamically organized set of interrelated parts. But the parts must be presented in a linear way, as if they were connected end to end—I can only deal with matters one at a time. If, at every turn, I have to take into account every question, limitation, and other considerations, then I'll get tied in knots. So you may often have to wait for a future letter to read about something that was germane to the one you are reading. Some repetition is unavoidable, but there is a limit to my willingness to repeat, and often I will forego mentioning something because I intend to mention it later on.

If it sounds as if I don't welcome your questions and challenges, then I am failing to make the point. I do want you to be critical, and I do want your questions; but I also want you to be patient.

Your affectionate uncle

Seven

Dear Simon,

You have no need to apologize. I suspect that I seized on what was only a mild expression of skepticism in order to have the excuse to lecture you. When I work with my patients I also look hard for opportunities, and I sometimes see them where they don't exist. I daresay that when you do psychotherapy you too will lay yourself open to the charge of being paranoid (or, as one of my patients put it more nicely, "You take everything I say so seriously!").

The point I made—that it's practically inevitable that different people at different times and places will benefit differently from different forms of therapy—struck you as heavy with implications for *Psychotherapy*. You wonder what they are. I must therefore write you yet another piece ,of Introduction.

Let me approach the subject obliquely by starting from the fact that no two therapies are ever without important differences. Even two quite similar patients with similar kinds of problems who are in therapy with the same therapist will necessarily experience therapies that are significantly different. That is true, at least, for the traditional forms of psychotherapy; it follows from the fact that the treatment is not the administering of remedies for particular ailments or problems. The psychotherapist does not administer conversation in the way the physician administers medicine. It's quite accurate to say that he provides a treatment that is rather nonspecific to his patient's problem. In an important sense, he treats the patient and not the problem. How shall I explain that sensibly?

I'm skating on some thin ice, Simon. I want to avoid overstating the matter or falling back on some of the fashionable clichés about the "whole person." When I claim that we treat the patient and not his problem, I am obviously tilting with the so-called medical model and its disease concept. As you know, Simon, it has been heavily and validly criticized in recent years; but, like most overdue criticism, it tends to go too far. It begins to sound somewhat gratuitous, if not arrogant, to keep repeating the claim that we psychotherapists treat our patient (i.e., ought to treat him) as an entire person, a living Gestalt. That certainly looks good on paper—but what does it mean in plain fact? Anyway, I doubt whether the implications it has for our work justify the overblown rhetoric. So let me try to formulate the matter more realistically than it's usually done.

I'll begin by making a rather obvious point that may strike you as beside the point. Psychotherapy in general, and *Psychotherapy* in particular, are not suitable methods of treatment for any and all patients who seek the help of a psychotherapist. I'm sure I'll have occasion to amplify on the important qualification that I am now going to write about: namely, that the methods I am describing to you in these letters are not appropriate for all patients. There are those for whom *Psychotherapy* would be quite impossible, or even detrimental. A patient who is suffering an acute depression, for example, can hardly be expected to tolerate most of the requirements, much less benefit from them. Patients who show serious impairment in Reality Testing, who may be borderline psychotic, are not suitable; the same may be true for those with serious character defects (so-called psychopaths, for instance). Moreover, there are patients whose chief need is for medication, or for reconditioning, or for an authentic interpersonal encounter, or for group therapy. But let me not try to list here all the cases and circumstances that would require a different kind of treatment. At a later date I'll write you about the question of modifications, and I'll also consider the situation of the patient who is seeking the removal of a symptom for which an altogether different form of therapy is the most appropriate.

The point I'm leading up to is this: Having come to the clinical judgment that *Psychotherapy* is indeed the treatment of choice (and having made sure that our patient understands what it entails), we proceed without very much regard for his presenting symptom or problem. Instead, we pay attention to a wide variety of aspects of his behavior and experience; we address ourselves to aspects of the patient that may appear to be quite unrelated to that which motivated him to seek the therapy. In this respect the treatment is not specific to his problem, but to the patient himself, to his Mind. Succinctly put: our overriding aim is to provide him with a Therapeutic Experience (and what that is I promise to tell you soon). We work on the assumption—the working hypothesis—that the amelioration of the symptom or problem will occur when he has experienced the processes of *Psychotherapy*.

There's another way to look at it. Our way of treating a patient's presenting problem is to approach it indirectly and from the vantage point of other aspects of his personality. We do not regard the phobia, the obsessional ritual, the paranoid streak, the inability to form intimate relationships as isolated aspects of the patient—as "foreign bodies" in an otherwise healthy organism. If we did, we would try to treat them directly. Instead we deal with a variety and range of aspects of our patient. All of them? The whole patient? That is plainly a fiction. However, insofar as it helps make the basic point, it may be a useful fiction.

It's difficult, if not quite impossible, to do without certain kinds of fictions in talking about psychology and psychotherapy (they are our theories, as Skinner loves to point out). The set of methods that I am presenting to you has to be regarded as an ideal state of affairs that in reality can only be approached or approximated. It is a standard, if not a theory. The especial usefulness of this mode of discourse is that it permits us to formulate principles without having to qualify and hedge at every turn. It's an enormous advantage to be able to speak of the "whole person," of the "average expectable patient," of the therapist's "neutrality and impersonality," and the like; but the advantage is undermined if we lose sight of the fact that these are essentially theoretical fictions. For one thing, such conceptions suggest a high degree of uniformity that can mislead or blind us. Good theory is supposed to help improve our powers of observation and understanding; but sometimes it does exactly the reverse.

Any attempt to present a set of principles and methods for psychotherapy will inevitably give an exaggerated impression of coherence and uniformity that can be quite misleading unless it is recognized that it's always the rationale behind them that counts. I want to stress the primacy of the rationale because I want to disavow the role of rules. The role of rules applies only when it's a game we're playing—and psychotherapy is no game. So I don't want you to regard any of the Technical principles of *Psychotherapy* as rules in any sense, but rather as abstractions or idealizations. Take, for instance, such an apparently simple "rule" as the patient must pay a meaningful fee. Without going into the matter, let me tell you that there are situations in which the rationale underlying the "rule" can better be fulfilled by having no fee paid at all. Furthermore, there are circumstances (more common than the no-fee one, of course) in which the "rule" simply has no significance, so that it doesn't really matter much what the fee is. Every principle, every Technical prescription and proscription, must be critically evaluated by us in each case. Nothing is ever to be applied mechanically or automatically—it's the rationale that rules.

The same applies to the use of *Psychotherapy* as a whole.

Not only must we judge in each case whether or not to use the method, but when we decide to use it we must continue to apply judgment and discretion at every turn. *Psychotherapy* is not so unified that certain parts of it cannot be used without others, or that important modifications cannot be made. I would only advise that such modifications be regarded as deviations from an ideal, so that their implications be understood in the light of the rationales of the method. There is, in my view, an internal consistency to the parts of *Psychotherapy;* but I doubt whether it's of a very high order. How unified, how internally consistent it is, is a matter I do care about. But I care even more that it should be sound, effective, and humane.

Your affectionate uncle

Eight

Dear Simon,

As you will recall, the twin pillars upon which *Psychotherapy* rests are Technique and Understanding. Interpretation—which will be the subject of this letter—is the chief instrumentality of Understanding; it formulates, it articulates, and it communicates Understanding. An Interpretation is a statement that can be prefixed with "I understand"—"I understand what you . . . " and "I understand why you . . . ." It may say what the patient is experiencing or has experienced; it may say why he behaves the way he does—it may articulate his experiences, it may formulate his experiences and actions, and it may explain.

An Interpretation has two major variables: its formulation and its timing—the What and the When of it. I'll have to write separately about these variables, but they are inseparable in practice—the When is determined by the What, and vice versa. In addition, there's a variety of other important variables (or call them considerations) having to do with How: How Much, How Deep, How Followed-up, and the like. It would seem appropriate to begin this letter with a consideration of the more basic question of Why—Why make Interpretations altogether? But I'll take up that question after I've given you my principles of the good Interpretation. Let me just make the claim here that *Psychotherapy* relies heavily on the Interpretive mode. If not for Interpretations, then the uniqueness of the relationship, the therapist's neutrality and impersonality, could cause the

71

treatment to become a mechanical, lifeless, and meaningless ritual—much form and little substance.

In view of the fact that our Interpretations inevitably reflect our way of conceptualizing and Understanding human behavior, it might also be appropriate to begin this letter with a consideration of theory. Again, I'll delay that; and again let me simply make a claim. The principles I present now can be viewed as pertinent to Interpretations in general, and to a large extent, it needn't matter what their particular content is. I don't mean to contend, Simon, that the principles don't imply a theoretical position—for they clearly do. But it's a level of theory that I've already written about— and, if not, I'm sure you will be able to sense it intuitively. So let's proceed.

* * * * * * *

Principle: The Simpler the Better

The good Interpretation is simple and parsimonious; it is focussed and clear—a good Gestalt. It says only that which is necessary for the moment, and no more. It goes to the heart of the matter and doesn't bury that heart with connective tissue.

Consider the following as an example, if not a caricature, of nonsimplicity:

> You feel, as you say, only quite upset about your cousin's rejection of you last week. And yet it was something that you were really dreading a lot. Then when it did happen you had that sleepless night; and since then you've been feeling tired and low. But you're unclear why you've been feeling this way, and you've been wondering whether it might be because of the new diet you are on. But then you say that this never happened before when you went on a diet; so it may not be due

to the diet after all. Now, I think it probably has something to do with your cousin's rejection of you, which you say you feel only quite upset about, but indications are that you are most likely more upset about it than you may realize.

It's bound to be far more effective to simply say, "I believe you may be more upset about your cousin's rejection than you realize."

Obfuscation by overelaboration—a fine obsessional process—is the thing to avoid. Often it will happen, Simon, because you feel a need to sweeten the bitter pill. You may feel that what you have to say may be too painful for your patient; so you soften the blow—and ruin the Interpretation. A therapist naturally applies his characteristic style and defenses to his Interpretation, and obsessional ones are perhaps the most typical. They include such tendencies as circumstantiality, uncertainty, overelaboration, rumination, and the like. For this reason the principle of simplicity is a remarkably difficult one. The experienced therapist not infrequently spoils an Interpretation by violating it, and the inexperienced one can expect to do it frequently. (You will often be exhorted by your supervisor to "Keep it simple!")

Here are some pairs of Interpretations that I have constructed to exemplify this principle for you:

Example 1

[WRONG:] I'm wondering how come you didn't feel elated at the good news. After all, this was something you've been anticipating for weeks now. And you have been so eager for it to happen that you even canceled the tennis game you had set up for last Saturday. So I have the thought that it may have become too much for you to bear, that it was somehow dangerous for you to feel

elated because of how intensely you had been feeling
your eagerness. In other words, to feel so elated had
become, over the several weeks of anticipation, impossible if not dangerous because it had become so intense.

[RIGHT:] I'm wondering how come you didn't feel elated at
the good news. Could it be that to feel so elated had
become somehow dangerous for you?

Example 2

[WRONG:] When you were being so critical of your wife's
cooking, hypercritical as you put it—by not omitting
anything you could criticize, like the table setting and
the lighting and the sauce and even the dessert—don't
you think that you were expressing anger toward her,
that you were taking out on her the anger you felt toward her because she had chosen to invite the Smiths
when you would rather she had invited the Jones?

[RIGHT:] When you were being so critical of your wife's
cooking—hypercritical as you put it—I believe that you
were very angry with her.

Example 3

[WRONG:] When you can't decide whether to go to a movie
or to stay home and study, you do something that
seems to me quite typical of you. You set things up in
such a way that the choice is made for you, and then
you don't have to do the deciding any more. The way
you do this is to find a way to label one of the activities
"good" and the other one "bad"; and then all that
remains for you to do is do the "good" thing. This may
go back to the time you were in Military School, and
perhaps even further back than that. What I have in

mind is the way your father would always arrange
things—both for you and for himself—in such a way
that there was always a right and a wrong action for
every situation. Remember how he used to say that all
you had to do was know which was which and then
you knew what to do?

[RIGHT:] When you can't decide whether to go to a movie
or to stay home and study, you do something that
seems to me quite typical of you. You set things up in
such a way that the choice is made for you. You find a
way to label one of the activities "good" and the other
one "bad"—and then *you* don't have to do the deciding
any more.

In these examples, and especially the third one, the
Wrong Interpretation can be made Right by selecting one
part of it. Because they're too rich, such Wrongs get too
complicated. What usually happens is that—in our uncertainty perhaps—we offer several alternative ideas for our
patient to choose from. While this keeps him in the active
position (always a good thing), it can attenuate his defense
against the unacceptable idea. It is better to let him find the
alternatives. Another cause for the Wrongs is that we may
have in mind a complicated formulation with several
strands of interconnected issues, and we feel the need to
present the whole thing at once. It's generally a better
strategy, however, to break the larger Interpretation into
parts and then to present them one at a time. This touches
on the matter of gradualness, which I'll take up soon in relation to the depth of Interpretations (and you may recall
that it was illustrated in two of the examples in my letter on
Technique).

Among the most effective Interpretations are those that
are very terse and very direct. When they are well-timed,
Interpretations such as the following can have a substantial

effect that takes the form of a sudden release of affect, an experience of insight, and even an alteration of state of consciousness:

—I believe that you are still mourning your father's death.
—You loved your mother intensely, didn't you?
—You must have wanted to kill your brother.
—You believe, then, that you are really crazy.
—So you wanted your father to give you his penis.
—I believe you have felt all your life that things just aren't fair.

Such Interpretations, if poorly timed, can miscarry. (I can still hear a patient of mine bursting into laughter and saying, "Excuse me, but you sounded just like an analyst in a Hollywood movie.") Since they also run the danger of being shocking and tactless, they should be used with utmost discretion. As I mentioned, timing is critical. You must be quite convinced that your patient already knows what it is you are about to put into words, that he is ready for it in this sense. The function of this kind of Interpretation in particular is to articulate clearly what is a fully preconscious idea, or to release an emotion that is straining at the threshold.

Principle: The Interpretation is Offered

Since we want our patient to be as active as possible and not to passively receive our Interpretations, we must try to convey them in an appropriate way. For purposes of illustration (and not persuasion) I'll use a feeding analogy that may also suggest some interesting implications to you. After all, patients quite frequently become preoccupied with how much (how little, that is) they are getting from us; and if we're doing *Psychotherapy* what we give, to a great extent, are Interpretations. Anyway, the principle of simplicity can be illustrated by this analogy as follows. If she wants the child to eat soup, an experienced mother will place soup before him and nothing more, because she knows that if she lays out the entire meal the child will avoid the dish that is most unappealing. The principle before us now inveighs against force-feeding. It claims that it's good practice to offer the Interpretation in the spirit of, "Here, try this if you will; it may be nourishing."

By prefacing it with: "I wonder what you think of this possibility . . . ," you can offer the Interpretation in a way that permits and invites your patient to exercise some activity with respect to it. He is invited to consider the idea, to accept or reject it—optimally, to weigh its relevancy and validity. But more than the words used, it's the spirit and tone that count. To be avoided is the sense of giving something to him that he will reject at his peril. "I'm telling you something now that you must accept if you want to get better," is appropriate to a physician or a politician (and even to a mother), but not to a therapist conducting *Psychotherapy.* "Here's something I believe is true and timely; why don't you take it under consideration and see if it helps." That's more consonant with its spirit.

An important consequence of this principle is that, once offered, the Interpretation belongs to your patient. He is free to do with it what he will, and that freedom entails freedom from Reinforcement. He must neither be punished for rejecting or ignoring it nor rewarded for accepting or using it. The therapist tries to avoid undue involvement in the fate of his Interpretation, and "undue" generally means "personal." A mother whose favorite dish is scorned by her child naturally feels disappointed and perhaps angry; the same holds true for a therapist whose Interpretation is rejected or ignored. But such feelings of disappointment and anger should be kept to a minimum, and they should not be permitted to influence the course of events. This doesn't mean that you will ignore the fate of your Interpretation—far from it. If it is rejected out of hand—and also if it is accepted that way—you will be interested in discovering why. My point here is that your interest should be motivated by a desire to promote the Therapeutic Process (and your patient's well-being). While your personal feelings can provide useful signals to yourself in this respect, they can play no useful role by being conveyed to him. It's one thing to pursue an Interpretive line and to offer further Interpretations regarding his response to it (for example, "I wonder if you need to reject that Interpretation because you are angry with me," or, "I think you feel unwilling to accept the Interpretation because doing so would mean that you'd feel obliged to give me something in return"); it's quite another to level an additional Interpretation out of feelings of pique, or whatever. A patient will quickly learn the lesson that if he ignores an Interpretation or he fails to go through the motions of giving it some serious consideration, then he can expect a subsequent Interpretation on that score. Such lessons are inappropriate to *Psychotherapy*. The basic lesson is Relative Autonomy and Freedom.

Every Interpretation has a degree of tentativeness, and I believe it should be conveyed. I might have included it as a separate principle—titled *The Interpretation is Tentative or Probable*—but it seems to go together with the spirit of offering. None of us is always, or even usually, certain that an Interpretation is valid, and there is no good reason not to convey our degree of uncertainty—"I think it is likely that . . ." or, "It seems quite possible to me that . . . " or even, "I'm not very sure about this, but I wonder if it is possible that . . . ." Morever, not only can it be useful for your patient to know the degree of confidence you have in a particular Interpretation, it can be useful for you too insofar as it frees you from having to be so certain before you choose to offer it.

And styles vary. Some therapists favor a sense of probability; others do not. Some are generally tentative; others are generally confident. And many will vary their style according to their patient's style. There is, I believe, an optimal style for each therapist and each patient, and it gets discovered in the doing. Patients will usually tell us about it at some point; if the therapy is going well then the issue will likely be raised and discussed. My own style, for instance, tends to the tentative side of the continuum, and I expect that my patients will sooner or later talk, if not complain, about it.

Principle: Neither too Deep nor too Shallow

Most therapists have a conception of the depth of an Interpretation. To some of us it has to do with the degree of Consciousness-Unconsciousness (with or without Preconscious as an intermediary level); to others it's the degree of distance from Ego or of dissonance with Self; and there are other ways of conceiving the dimension. But almost everyone agrees, no matter what his conception, that Interpretations ought not to be too deep or too superficial.

Few therapists ever want to make overly deep ones, but they are generally not apprehensive about the possibility. Not so with the overly shallow—this is what most, and particularly inexperienced, therapists dread the most. They dread the squelching rejoinder, "So what else is new?" or, "I know that well enough." (Let me hasten to point out that a response such as "I was thinking that before," is quite different.) In addition to the fact that a genuinely superficial Interpretation is apt to be worthless, it may be detrimental in several ways. It may not only define you as the one who is unhelpful, but it can also reflect a timidity on your part—an unwillingness to go beneath the surface that may communicate the message, "What lurks down there is dangerous and has to be avoided."

On the other hand, Simon, if you spend too much time in the depths you will quickly lose contact with your patient. Bear in mind that a "deep" Interpretation may be nothing more than incomprehensible to him. So, at the very least, an important precaution is to make sure, either before it or after it, that he comprehends. And beware the compliant patient who has to avoid the implication that he's rejecting an Interpretation because he hasn't understood it. He cannot say "I don't understand" for fear of disturbing his compliant self-image or for fear of offending you. Then there's the one who uses "I don't understand" as a defense; he understands well enough but has to avoid the implications either of the Interpretation itself or of having accepted it from you. And yet another way of warding you off is to dismiss your Interpretations as old-hat or as common knowledge.

Appearance can often be quite deceiving on this matter. What may seem superficial, judging by a patient's response to it, often turns out not to be. To make the matter even more complicated than it already is, let me mention still another way that patients react to Interpretations: they receive all of them, no matter how superficial they may actually be, as startling news. That too is a defense. So the most parsimonious conclusion we can draw is one that's widely accepted by therapists: a patient's immediate reaction to an Interpretation cannot be taken at face value as a criterion of its depth (nor, for that matter, of its validity). It is always necessary to wait a while—and sometimes quite a long while—before making any judgment.

It's far from a simple matter to say what the optimal depth of an Interpretation ought to be, and it remains difficult no matter what criteria we use and no matter what dimension we consider. One formulation that I lean toward is to put it in terms of what the patient is ready to deal with. It's not sufficient that he be capable of comprehending my Interpretation, he must also be able to apprehend it—to use it, to assimilate it, to make it his own. For this reason it must not be too Ego-alien, too foreign to him; nor should it be too unacceptable to him, too outrageous, too much at variance with his self-image. Another way to formulate the matter is to say that he must, in some actual sense, already know the Interpretation (it must be Preconscious, in the Freudian sense) so that all you have achieved with it is to push an idea into full awareness—to give the affect, the knowledge, or the experience a different mental status.

Depth is therefore relative to the patient. If he's naive, then something like, "You are trying to get me to praise you," can be deep; if he's not very psychologically minded, then, "You're feeling pleased with yourself" can be deep. So it's always necessary to have a conception of the level at which he is working. This will vary from patient to patient as well as from time to time. It's quite common, you know, for there to be considerable fluctuation of level during the course of a single session.

I recommend to you, Simon, that a useful way to work with the concept of depth is to try to deepen the level at which your patient is working. That is best done gradually. Here are several examples of what I mean. (Notice how the utterances that "YOU" make progressively go deeper and further into the matter at hand.)

Example 1

[YOU:] So you mustn't let yourself feel very sympathetic toward your mother.

[PATIENT:] Yes; I was just thinking that. I used to try to be sympathetic to her, especially when she was in one of her nervous, harassed states, but . . . [etc.].

[YOU:] I wonder whether to be sympathetic toward her is for some reason too dangerous for you.

[PATIENT:] I guess that's so. I can see that it must be sort of dangerous. But I can't see why [pause]. She certainly wanted me to be; and she never did anything that would . . uh, prevent it [pause]. I even remember one time when she was having trouble with my father . . . [etc.].

[YOU:] Well, I have a thought about that. It may be dangerous because it would mean, for one thing, that you are siding with her against your father.

[PATIENT, after a pause:] They had a big argument once, when I was about seven years old. And . . . [etc.].

[YOU:] So being against your father stirs up some old feelings of rage—of murderous rage against him. That seems like the big danger, doesn't it?

Example 2

[PATIENT:] I don't know why, but I'm feeling depressed today [falls silent]. Did you say that our Monday session will be canceled next week, or is it the Wednesday?

[YOU:] Monday. I take it you're unclear about it.

[PATIENT:] No, not really. You said it clearly. I don't really know why I asked.

[YOU, after a silence:] Perhaps because you want to talk about the cancellation.

[PATIENT:] I suppose so—not that I have too much feeling about it. As a matter of fact, it will give me a chance to catch up on my work . . . [etc.].

[YOU:] Do you suppose it's possible that the reason you are feeling depressed today has something to do with the cancellation?

[PATIENT, after a pause:] I was thinking about it last night—thinking about the fact that you didn't tell me

why you had to cancel the session. I tell you everything; and if I wanted to cancel a session I would explain why. But you don't. I don't understand why
not—why you can't. What would be so terrible about
telling me why? [falls silent].

[YOU:] And that makes you feel sad.

[PATIENT, tearfully:] Yes, I guess it does. But I don't know
why.

[YOU:] I think that part of the reason, anyway, is that it
makes you feel angry.

[PATIENT:] Angry? I don't really know. Oh my, I think I'm
going to cry [and does].

[YOU, with some warmth:] You are crying because you are
furious with me.

Principle: Avoid Making Connections and Being Didactic

The neophyte therapist's favorite kind of Interpretation is
undoubtedly the Connection:

> I think that your feelings of resentment against your
> daughter are connected to your feelings of resentment
> against your mother.

> I wonder what you think of the possibility that your
> difficulty working is connected to your reluctance to
> come to your sessions.

> The taxi in your dream may be connected to the
> taxi you took to your girl friend's house yesterday.

> I think what you are saying now is connected to
> what you said at the beginning of the session.

Such Interpretations are sometimes difficult to resist. I
suppose they needn't be avoided too strenuously, but—
especially when they stop there and then—they are a poor
kind of Interpretation and likely to be without much useful effect. For one thing, they generally fail to provide an
explanation, much less an articulation, for the actions or
feelings in question. But even more serious is that they typically feed right into the defense of Intellectualization—and
they do so for the therapist as well as for the patient. Finding connections can too easily become an intellectual sport.

It is, I repeat, a very tempting thing to do. A patient is
often ready to accept the Connection and to believe that
genuine insights are entailed. This is particularly true for
those who are obsessional and paranoid, for whom everything has to be interconnected, and who enjoy the game for
its own sake as well as for its defensive utility. But there are
those for whom the Connection may be a necessary first
step in the direction of Understanding. The hysteric, for instance, who experiences his thoughts and feelings and actions as quite random and coincidental may need to be per-
suaded that things are connected. At best, then, the Connection should be regarded as only a first step—as propadeutic
to an Interpretation—and it's a good idea to have an Interpretation in mind before drawing attention to a possible
connection.

The Connection is first cousin to the Didactic. Many of us
are naturally didactic; we like to teach. But even those who
are not particularly didactic are inclined to be when it
comes to interpreting defenses. At such times we may find
ourselves explaining to our patient how a defense works,
as, for instance, in the following examples:

Sometimes our feelings get too much for us to bear,
and we seek for explanations for them in order to alleviate the feelings. Not that it isn't important to know

why we feel the way we do; but sometimes we use the reason to be rid of the feeling altogether.

When you have a fear of something which you know you really needn't be afraid of, then it may well be that what you are feeling afraid of is actually something else.

There are ideas that a person finds terribly repugnant—highly unacceptable to himself. So what he may do at such times is to erase that idea from his mind; and then it is as if he never thought it.

Sometimes a person cannot bear to accept any blame or responsibility for a particular situation or event. And then he tends to lay all of the responsibility and blame outside of himself so that he feels as if he shared no part of it at all. I wonder whether you think that you may have done something like that yesterday.

Being didactic myself, I am inclined to believe that such lessons are not without value. Still, I must confess to serious misgivings whenever I find myself giving them. At their core, you see, they are really a form of reassurance; they reassure the patient that the behavior in question is natural or normal. So I would suggest, Simon, that you only play teacher when you judge that some reassurance is **called** for. Since reassurance is to be used sparingly in *Psychotherapy*, such lessons should also be used sparingly. Besides, your patient will know when a lesson is being taught, and he may wonder why. At one level, you are merely giving him some information; you may be reminding him of something he already knows, or you may be telling him something quite new. In either case, however, you are not doing your regular thing, and that itself always calls for some explanation. The fair question, "Why are you informing me of this piece of human psychology?" can always be asked. The answer (already contained in the last example) is, "Because it seems to me that you are (or were) defending yourself that way." But if your patient continues by asking, "So why didn't you simply say so without the introductory lesson?" you have little choice but to admit that you thought it might be reassuring.

There's a form of Interpretation which is related to the didactic that I do recommend: addressing the patient as if he were composed of "parts." It pertains especially to the formulation of matters of conflict and ambivalence. Instead of, "You want this, and you want that as well," or, "You are drawn to this, and at the same time you are repelled by it," I prefer to say, "A part of you wants this, and another part wants that," or, "Part of you is drawn to it, and another part is repelled." (It is generally helpful to specify the parts that are involved in the conflict.)

Even if you regard it as poor theory to conceptualize your patient into introjects of various sorts, or to parcel him into personality structures, the formulation can still have a practical utility. I think you will find that it's a way that conflict matters can be articulated so that they are clear as well as acceptable to him. At the same time, however, it can easily become for him a handy way of evading his responsibility. It is tempting, you see, to acknowledge the parties to one's conflicts and ambivalencies because it makes it easier to disown one or more of them; and some patients become too enthusiastic about the formulation for this reason. But it has been my experience that the problem can be dealt with, and my patient can eventually be induced to own all of his "parts."

Let me give you some examples of how the formulation can be introduced.

Example 1

[YOU:] I wonder what you think of the possibility that you

are conflicted about it, that you dread being the center of attraction, but at the same time you also like it.

[PATIENT:] But it makes me so nervous when I am the center of attraction.

[YOU:] Yes; a part of you dreads it. But I have the impression that a part of you wants it.

[PATIENT:] When I was a child I did love it . . . [etc.].

[YOU:] So one way to look at it is this: the child in you still wants to be the center of attraction, but another part, the adult you, does not. Perhaps that's why you get so nervous when . . . .

Example 2

[PATIENT:] Sometimes I love my father, and sometimes I loathe him. That just doesn't make sense.

[YOU, tempted to give a lesson in the psychology of ambivalence, but instead you say:] Does it make sense to you to look at it this way—that a part of you loves him and another part of you hates him?

Example 3

[PATIENT:] Sometimes I wish you weren't so goddam impersonal and professional toward me, that you were more like a friend to me [pause]. But at other times I'm kind of glad that you are. I guess I'm just confused about it.

[YOU:] Perhaps a part of you wants it, and a part of you doesn't. The part of you that experiences your loneliness and need wants me to be close and personal; but the part of you that makes realistic judgments realizes that I can be more helpful to you by remaining impersonal and professional.

(The second part of this Interpretation may strike you as a piece of flagrant propaganda; but it may be little more than a necessary piece of information or rationale pertinent to the therapy's procedure.)

Principle: Listen for the Implied Advice

The proscription against giving advice, which is so central to *Psychotherapy,* is much easier said than done. For one thing, it can be validly argued that advice lies implicitly behind or within every Interpretation. For instance, to point out to your patient that he is behaving cruelly to his brother may be to advise him to stop it, particularly if the cruelty was unrecognized by him. Before taking up this argument, let me review one aspect of the rationale so that the desirability of avoiding advice may be as compelling for you as I believe it ought to be.

Suppose that you had in fact advised against cruelty to the brother. What if your patient again acts cruelly to him? Since he has acted in a way that runs counter to your expressed wishes, he has every reason to expect that you will be disappointed in him. Or say he changes his actions in line with the advice, and he reports that to you. Should he not expect that you will be pleased? Now, your feelings of disappointment, anger, or their opposite are not only without real benefit to him, but are a hindrance. For then you have an actual stake in his behavior, and your special role as his therapist is vitiated. That, in my opinion, is bound to have a number of serious consequences, the principal one being an impairment of your ability to help him Understand.

Still, the fact remains that the Interpretation you gave may imply the advice, and that fact must be acknowledged and dealt with. In practice, it's usually possible and always desirable to undo or erase that implication. Sometimes a patient will make it quite easy to achieve that; so let's begin with the simple instance, which can be exemplified in the following way (bear in mind that you have already informed him that you will not give any advice—you did it in the first session):

[YOU, offering an Interpretation:] I believe you are retaliating against your mother for the fact that she emascu-
lated you, that by not calling her up to wish her a
happy birthday you are punishing her.
[PATIENT, accepting the Interpretation:] I can see that that is
quite true. I thought the reason I was not going to call
her up was that I was afraid of being sucked in again.
But now I realize that I really intend to hurt her.
[There now ensues the pregnant pause, and he recon-
siders the planned action.] So I guess I should call her
up after all, shouldn't I? [looks questioningly at you]
What do you think?
[YOU:] That it's up to you.
[PATIENT:] But if all I'm doing is retaliating for an old
wrong, then I shouldn't do it. Isn't that right?
[YOU:] I take it you want me to advise you what to do, or at
least to endorse your new decision.
[PATIENT:] Yes; what's wrong with your doing that?
[YOU:] It's something that I have said I don't intend to
do—to give you advice or tell you what to do.

You may now want to tell him what the rationale for
your position is. In my experience, it is usually unnecessary
to spell it out; most patients understand it quite intuitively.
But there is no special reason not to explain it, particularly
if he asks for it. So say he does:

[PATIENT:] Okay; but won't you please explain to me what
would be so bad about your saying something like,
"Sure, go ahead and wish her a happy birthday"?
[YOU:] Because then, if you chose not to follow my advice, I
would find myself in the position of being disappointed
in you. Or if you did do it, then you would expect me
to be pleased with you. And those are feelings that I
don't want to have toward you, because that would

mean I was judging you. You see, if I did judge you, or have feelings of disappointment, or anger, or whatever, then that would interfere with my ability to help you to understand your behavior. In any case, I don't think it would be helpful to you to behave in ways that are meant to please me or to displease me.

[That speech can, of course, be delivered in parts.]

But that was a simple instance. It's more typical for the matter to remain covert, and then you must try to make it overt. One way to do this is to be on the alert when your patient reports a significant action that is different or new for him, or is clearly related to a topic of a recent session. That action may have been motivated by a desire to conform or disconform to a piece of advice that was latent in an Interpretation. Such an action is usually reported to us with an attitude that reflects the fact. The patient may tell about it with a note of stubborn defiance, or with an air of resigned compliance, or with something equally indicative of the fact that our reaction is likely involved. At such times, it can be imperative for you to raise the issue—and even if it turns out to be something altogether unrelated, the issue is not without intrinsic value. Say, for instance, that the pregnant pause and everything that followed it in the above example had not occurred. It is the next session, and your patient has just told you, with a note of defiance, that he didn't phone his mother. You should now say to him, "I notice that, when you tell me how you didn't phone your mother, you seem to be feeling defiant about it, or stubborn. I wonder whether that reflects how you feel about her, or whether it has to do with feelings you are having toward me."

If he now acknowledges feelings toward you, then the matter can be pursued directly. You can say that he thought that you had given him advice when you made the Interpretation the session before. Implicitly, or better yet explicitly, you can establish that such was not your intention. But he may miss the point and just acknowledge feelings toward his mother. At such times it can be very useful to spell the point out clearly, as follows:

[YOU:] I am wondering, though, whether your feeling of stubborn defiance isn't also directed toward me. What I have in mind is this: last time, when you were talking about the phonecall and how you didn't want to be sucked in again, I said to you that you were retaliating against her for an old wrong. Now, you may have taken that as a piece of advice, as if I were really advising you to go ahead and phone her. So the fact that you are feeling defiant here today may mean that you thought that I wanted you to phone her up—that I was advising you to do it.

[PATIENT:] Okay; that makes sense. I guess I did think that you were sort of saying, "Go ahead and phone the old lady up."

At this juncture you may deem it more useful to deal with the specific issue and say, "So it may be, then, that part of the reason you decided not to call was that you didn't want to do what I seemed to be telling you to do." Or you may want to clarify the general issue and say, "You know, it's not unreasonable for you to hear a piece of advice when I make an observation or tell you what I think your motivation is. But I really don't intend ever to be telling you what to do, to give any kind of advice. I'd like that to be clear to you." Or you may do both.

Your affectionate uncle

Nine

Dear Simon,

Yes, I know the argument. No matter what we traditional psychotherapists think we are doing, what we're actually doing is providing our patients with Reinforcements. Insofar as we reveal to them the consequences of their behaviors, we are teaching them what is Reinforcing them; insofar as we ourselves respond to their behaviors, we're administering here-and-now Reinforcements. Find out whether the protagonist is a Skinnerian, because their definition of the concept makes it a foregone conclusion. As I understand it, anything and everything that follows an act (i.e., a Response) is ipso facto a Reinforcement for them. For other learning theorists, who subscribe to one of a variety of forms of the classic Law of Effect, a Reinforcement must be perceived as a consequence of the act, and it must have the properties of an instrumental or consummatory goal—it must satisfy a need or fulfil an expectation in order to be effective.

I'll cut through a lot of fine theoretical points here because they occupy a level of abstraction that is not appropriate for psychotherapy. My thesis is that a therapist who conducts *Psychotherapy* takes it as his goal to provide few if any dosages of Reinforcement for his patient. Furthermore, as depicted in a cartoon which appeared in the *Columbia Jester*—two smug rats in a Skinner box, one saying to the other, "Boy, do we have this guy conditioned! Every time I press the bar down, he drops a pellet in."—he does not respond to his patient's efforts to Reinforce him.

What I mean here by Reinforcement is roughly all versions of it except the Skinnerian. My main point is that the gratification of needs, instrumental or otherwise, is uniquely absent in *Psychotherapy*.

That might be putting things too strongly. While I could take refuge in the claim that it's a theoretical principle—therefore an ideal and a fiction, a goal towards which we may strive but can never expect to achieve—it may suffice for me to say that we try to keep Reinforcements at a minimum, and we try to ensure that it is not Reinforcement that is doing the therapeutic work. In any case, now I will try to show you how we do that vis-à-vis our Interpretations.

In a most important sense, Interpretations are also criticisms. I like to think of them as analogous to literary and artistic criticism—that what the good critic does with respect to a work of art is similar to what I do with respect to my patient when I offer him an Interpretation. The giving and taking of criticism, however, is hardly a clear-cut and unambiguous matter. Criticism can cover a wide range from the analysis of intentions and their realization in actions, through moral censure, all the way to hostile attack—and so can Interpretations. We've all grown weary of the social use of psychological interpretations as weapons of argument intended to win points and inflict pain and humiliation. But even so-called constructive criticism can hurt, despite the fact that the critic intends only enlightenment.

Interpretations are likely to hurt; they can be unwelcome news; they are often painful and humiliating. After all, if it bears—and bares—the truth, and if my patient needs the Interpretation because he has for long defended himself against that truth, then it is bound to cause him some psychological suffering. It's one thing to minimize the pain by being tactful and judicious; it's quite another to suppose that it can be avoided altogether. But it is still another thing to claim that not only are we powerless against this effect, but it is this effect that is our main therapeutic instrument. If this were so, how could we square it with our chief goal, which is to promote our patient's Ego Autonomy?

I must now take you on a theoretical digression, Simon, for the concept of Autonomy, and especially my way of construing it, runs head-on into the precept of Determinism. Determinism, which is germane to Reinforcement by way of the elements of criticism and valuation, is, par excellence, a Big Question; and I did promise to spare you from them. But I can hardly evade it altogether, especially now that the matter of valuation is before us. You'll soon see why I think so.

To begin, I remind you that the orthodox Freudian circumvents the problem of valuation by subscribing to a quite simple kind of Determinism. His patients—or anyone else for that matter—behave in ways that are essentially Determined and hence essentially out of their control. Thus, it is nonsense for him to say to them, "But you could have behaved otherwise." It follows that it is equally nonsensical to say, "You should have behaved otherwise." Thus, the problem of valuation dissolves—at least in principle. I don't know whether *Psychotherapy* has to rest upon an altogether different conception of Determinism, but I am certain that it requires us to construe matters differently. For one thing, I cannot see how we can avoid assigning responsibility for his actions to someone who is free—to be free, after all, is to be capable of acting otherwise. For another, it is not enough to limit our Interpretations to explanations of why such and such an action took place as if the conditions forced the action. It's vital to persuade our patient that he in fact chose to behave the way he did, and then to explain why he chose the way he did; and for this it's essential to be able to add, "So you could have behaved otherwise."

If it sounds to you like I am reviving the old concept of Will, you may be quite right. I think I could make a case for a more sophisticated brand of Determinism which would allow for freedom of choice—others more qualified than me have already done it. Anyway, I cannot see how we can avoid a Will-like conception and still have a meaningful and sensible construction of Freedom and of Ego Autonomy. Let me hasten to remind you, however, that not only are they *relative* but they are also *limited*—and these limitations are important to bear in mind if we are to avoid the absurdities of an extreme position. What I mean is that it does not follow that each and every action or experience is equally subject to the charge, "It could have been otherwise." When I am in pain I must cry; when I suffer meaningful loss I must grieve; when I am under attack I must retaliate; when I enjoy relief or victory I must exult. This is not always true, and not for everyone either. The Yogi can choose not to cry, the Stoic can choose not to grieve, and the Saint can choose not to retaliate. So it's both a sometime thing and a matter of individual differences. I should also mention that the Neurotic often suffers from a crippling of Will inasmuch as his range of options (i.e., his Freedom) is constricted. The function of therapy is to enlarge that range and to draw a greater variety of behaviors into its sphere. But at no point do we intend that all and every behavior should become equally exempt from the experience of mustness.

So our philosophical position must at the very least permit us to make the charge, "You *could* have behaved otherwise"—not indiscriminately, but selectively and with all due consideration. Now, how about the next step? Can we go on to charge, "You *should* have behaved otherwise"?

There is at least one sense in which we can take that next step legitimately: "If what you intended was this, then you should have behaved in that way"—but this judgment is clearly not valuation. So if we limit our use of *should* to this kind of construction we face no further problems. The matter can easily be made clear to our patients. It may complicate the matter but not change it significantly if he goes on to ask, "But should I have intended that intention?" To answer that question we need only invoke higher-order intentions. After all, everything is hierarchically ordered—isn't it? It's only when we arrive at the highest order of intentions, when we deal with life's ultimate aims and goals, that we have to invoke faith—but we rarely need to go so high up in therapy.

The other sense of *should* is the clearly valuative one—"Was it bad of me to have stolen the book?" Here the issue is not one of intentions and their realization in actions; it is plainly a moral issue. While it's true that moral issues can be reduced to intentions at the level of Man and Society (i.e., if Man intends to live according to social arrangements that are mutually beneficial then stealing subverts that higher intention, and in that sense it is "bad"), it's also true that such considerations are usually irrelevant to psychotherapy.

When my patient asks me, "Was that a good thing to have done?" he probably wants to know about my moral code; and even if he never asks it outright, he nonetheless maintains a keen interest in it. Within fairly wide limits it is possible for me to keep my moral code altogether private and, more than that, to keep it from influencing my work with him. Moreover, I believe that it is vital for the therapy that I keep those limits as wide as possible. This means that I can tolerate a substantial range and variety of behaviors on his part that violate my own code of ethics and, within those wide limits, I can eschew all valuation. If he steals books, or seduces young girls, or lies in order to get ahead, or whatever, and he does so without scruples or any variety of guilt, then therapy—or at least *Psychotherapy*—if it is to proceed at all must proceed free from the influence of my attitude about the morality or ethicalness of those behaviors.

That's a strong statement—and, for a change, I mean to stick to it. If your patient's behavior is morally offensive to you, and if he is not in conflict about it, then for you to impose your moral code on him is to radically transcend (or depart from) the legitimate role of a therapist. This is true for the one who is conducting *Psychotherapy,* but I would argue that it ought to be true for any psychotherapist. I believe that it is both inappropriate and perhaps also futile to implicate our moral attitudes in therapy; and if we feel we must (because our patient's behavior violates them too much) then our only recourse may be to discontinue the treatment. "That was a bad (or good) thing to do," is a statement we should rarely if ever make. It is a blatant act of Extrinsic Reinforcement that clearly violates a basic premise of *Psychotherapy.* And, just as we eschew all valuative comments (according to the commonly understood meaning of "valuation"), we must never criticize (according to the everyday usage of "criticize"). This means that value judgments based upon moral precepts must never play a significant part in our attitude toward our patients.

I am well aware of the far-reaching implications of such an assertion, Simon. I know that value judgements underlie all of our attitudes and every aspect of our way of living and relating to people. I am also aware of the fact that to say, "This action, either by design or not, leads you into self-destructive ways," is tantamount to saying. "This action is bad for you," which in turn can be little more than saying, "It is bad." (All human behavior reeks not only of meaning but also of value judgments.) But when a person complains that he is being criticized and evaluated, what he generally means is that he is being told that he is bad. On the one hand, the action or feeling in question reflects badly upon him as a person; on the other hand, he not only could have, but should have acted or felt otherwise. It is these assertions that we must avoid.

What I will now recommend to you could have been

subsumed under a further principle of the good Interpretation—titled *Listen for the Implied Criticism.* It is my practice—
and it's one that I strongly advocate—that after I make an
Interpretation I listen hard for my patient's reaction to
its latent or implied criticism or valuation. Particularly if
it's early in the treatment, I want to be able to discuss that
aspect of his reactions and that aspect of my Interpretations.
It's enormously useful to be able to say to him, after the
Interpretation has been offered, "I believe you are taking
my remark as a kind of criticism of you, as if I made a
judgment of you, and had accused you of being an unworthy
person (cruel, selfish, unrealistic, or whatever)." Notice
that this, of course, is a bona fide Interpretation.

Suppose now you have made this Interpretation and your
patient acknowledges the fact, and then he goes on to challenge your contention that you did not mean to criticize or
valuate him. He says, "Sure I feel you have criticized and
judged me. What you said was that I feel envious of my
brother. Now that's a terrible way to feel toward anyone,
especially one's brother. And it makes me a terrible person.
So what you've done is to imply that I am terrible—and
if that's not a criticism and a value judgment I don't know
what is." Now the central issue is joined, and you have an
important opportunity to clarify a crucial distinction. You
must yourself be utterly clear about the matter, and you
must take pains to make it as clear to him. And you mustn't
be too eager to be rid of it either, or even to conclude that
once around is enough. You may continue as follows:

[YOU:] I can appreciate that you hear a criticism and value
judgment when I point out to you that you are envious.
But when I, as your therapist, say you are feeling such
and such a way, I mean only that I believe that it's
true, and that it might be helpful to you to recognize
that truth. I do not mean that it's bad to feel or to act

that way—that it means you are a bad person. That part of it is your own judgment. And it may well be that one of the reasons you have not been able or willing to recognize the feeling of envy in yourself is because you have such a negative value attached to it.

[PATIENT:] Fair enough. But do you mean to say that envy is not bad? It's good then?

[YOU:] I mean to say nothing at all about whether it's good or bad.

[PATIENT:] But surely you recognize that envy is a bad and unworthy way to feel!

Perhaps the most serious error you can now make, Simon, is to say anything about the morality of envy. Some would feel tempted to go into why the patient regards envy as so morally reprehensible, but at this point it would have the clear and undesirable implication that he ought not to feel that way and that you do not share his extreme position. I recommend you say something like this:

[YOU:] I recognize that you regard it as bad and unworthy, and I know that in general people do. So, as a person I have a position about the morality of envy, and a lot of other things too. But, as your therapist and during the therapy, I try to steer completely clear of such value judgments. I try not to let myself have them here, or to let them matter to me. You see, my only aim is to Understand and to help you to Understand. And that precludes passing judgment or evaluating.

[PATIENT:] I understand [pause], but I don't see how that is humanly possible.

To this, you needn't make response, even though it's an eminently fair question. After all, all you could say is, "I do my best"—and that can be taken for granted.

Your affectionate uncle

Ten

Dear Simon,

My discussion of Reinforcement was incomplete in the way that you say it was. Don't I "care" that my patient behaved cruelly to his brother?—am I not supposed to want him to behave maturely and rationally, and in ways that will promote his well-being? Surely I must have desires apropos his well-being that will be affected by his behavior, and they will necessarily be reflected in my responses to him. So if you don't Reinforce, if you show no approval and disapproval, then it is as if you don't give a damn? But of course you do. You will *care* most profoundly for your patient—and some day soon I must write you about that, about the difference between caring and valuating, between caring and Countertransference, and between caring and loving. For now I will approach your challenge by defending the claim that you must care most that your patient should have the best therapeutic experience you can provide for him.

I have already written you about What and How you should speak to your patient; now I must write you about Why and When—and this will be more difficult to do. The four questions are naturally interdependent, but the Why is the most pivotal or central, because nothing less than the fundamental function and process of *Psychotherapy* must be specified in answer to it. So that is what we must now consider.

Consider what is the vital event of the *Psychotherapy* session. It is that your patient express, examine, and communicate his Mind—that he reflect, wonder, recollect, reminisce, take fresh approaches, experience his affects and impulses, explore and examine his inner and outer realities, and Understand. All of that is what I mean by the rather bland term *Therapeutic Process*. It follows, then, that your principal function as his therapist is to establish, to facilitate, and to maintain that Therapeutic Process—and that is my fundamental answer to the question of Why you speak (When, What, and How).

Our guiding principle is this: we say what we say and say it when we say it because, in our best judgment, it will promote—or facilitate, or advance, or improve, or enable, or deepen, or broaden—the Therapeutic Process. Our purpose is not principally to impart information, to give Understanding, and the like; rather it is to allow our patient to speak as openly and freely as he can, and experience his Self as fully and as authentically as he can. The process, you see, is an intrapsychic one, not interpsychic; it entails autonomous action. And at the risk of being tiresomely repetitious, let me reiterate that the basic objective of *Psychotherapy* is that the patient be active, that he actively attain Understanding, that he actively exercise and strengthen his Synthetic Function, and that he thereby secure control and freedom—which is what I mean by Relative Ego Autonomy. Every aspect of the method, every technical prescription and proscription, every theoretical rationale, is based more or less directly on this overriding premise.

I've already written you how this imposes a stringent restriction on your participation in the therapy. It's a restriction that is open both to question and to abuse. The abuse I have in mind is mainly the easy rationalization that is facilitated by the loose way I construe the Therapeutic Process. A wide range of interventions can too easily be justified by an appeal to the state of the Process when that process is too broadly defined. For example, any Interpretation that points out unconscious motivation can be said to deepen a patient's understanding of himself and thus serve the Process. Obviously, that will not do.

For many analytically oriented therapists the principal criterion for speaking (particularly an Interpretation) can be expressed in the question, "Can my patient use this intervention?" Timing is based chiefly on the patient's readiness to comprehend and apprehend. His state of mind, his state of affect and mood, the condition of his Transference and Defenses, and the like, are the relevant considerations. When these are deemed to be optimal, then the time for an Interpretation is right, and there is likely to be little difference between the criterion questions, "Can my patient use this intervention?" and, "Does he need it?"—the latter generally gets taken quite for granted. My main point here, however, is that the second question must not only never be taken for granted, but indeed should be the principal criterion. In order to emphasize what I mean by "need," I would put the timing criterion as follows: "Does my patient need this intervention in order to restore and/or promote his involvement in the work of therapy?" There's the Therapeutic Process again.

Before I take steps to qualify the matter and to remind you, Simon, that I have not contended that this criterion is the exclusive one—just the principal one—let me offer an example. Suppose your patient is dealing with his relationship to his father, and he is talking about his long-standing anger against him; and suppose that he is doing it very well—speaking openly, expressing genuine feelings, reminiscing and recalling, associating freely, sticking to the subject, and the like (a tall order, I admit). Suppose now that you have an idea about how come he's angry with his father; or suppose that you see something important in that relationship that he is overlooking. Suppose, even further, that you have reason to believe that your insight and perception are bound to affect his anger, and perhaps even improve his relationship with his father. Should you offer the Interpretation to him? Should you draw attention to what he is overlooking? No, not necessarily. And why not?— because you don't have the appropriate reason to. That, at least, is the thrust of my argument. The Therapeutic Process is proceeding optimally, and it (as distinct from your patient?) has no need for an intervention.

You may question the efficacy of such a criterion—you may object to allowing an opportunity to pass that may contribute to your patient's well-being. You may also suspect that my formulation may be one that looks good on paper but won't work in practice. Fair enough; let me forge ahead. What I recommend is this: instead of offering the Interpretation, you can say to yourself, "Let him arrive at it himself—let him find out what it is he is overlooking." If he is working as well as he seems to be, there is reason to expect or hope that he will in due course achieve the insight himself or discover what it is he is overlooking. And, if and when he does it, then that achievement is bound to be more meaningful and effective than if it was received passively. In the long run, that may benefit his relationship with his father far more.

You will recognize that this position entails a conviction that the naturally functioning Therapeutic Process will yield the stuff out of which changes in behavior, in attitudes, and in experience will flow. You need not insert your Mind into the process—need not share your thoughts and insights, your Understanding—unless and until the process itself seems to require it; and then you participate mainly by restoring and promoting the Process. It is at this juncture, moreover, that you can use your insights and perceptions. If your patient in the above example were to suddenly run into trouble in the session—if he were to block, experience an impasse, feel anxious, become defensive—then you could effectively intervene: "I think I know why you suddenly blocked," or, "why your thoughts drifted away from what you were talking about," or, "why you feel anxious and defensive." "It is because you came face to face with a painful thought concerning your anger with your father," or, "you may have caught a glimpse of something you had been overlooking. It is this. . . ." An intervention in this form is preferable in an important way to one that begins, "I think I know now why you are angry with your father," or, "I see something that you have been overlooking."

Now, Simon, having stated the matter in such extreme (or pure) terms, let me back off from it. To restore and promote the Therapeutic Process may be our principal function, but that is not the same as saying that it is our sole motivation for offering an Interpretation. That would entail an excessively stringent restriction, and it might even become self-defeating if carried to excess. For one thing, your patient might quickly notice that you offer substantive help only when he does not speak freely. He can learn that to evoke your participation in the ordeal he has only to slip into something impasse-ish. This, I promise you, will happen frequently enough even in the usual course of events, and you will do well to bear it in mind. But if in reality you speak only when he doesn't then that provides him with a powerful incentive to avoid the Therapeutic Process.

I know that it's possible to cast even this consideration into the terms of the fundamental guiding principle in this way: "I offered the Interpretation because the Therapeutic Process needed it in the sense that it would have been negatively reinforcing to withhold it,"—but this way of construing the principle stretches it beyond recognition and may render it so elastic as to be practically useless. So I prefer instead to regard the fundamental timing criterion as my main one, and to allow myself others that I regard as less central or basic. In this way I can maintain a sense of proportion and balance.

* * * * * *

Without trying to cast it into the formal terms of a principle, let me describe to you a kind of general attitude that you can adopt toward your participation in *Psychotherapy*. First and foremost, you should want your patient to be doing the main work; and if that is the case, then you should want to remain as passive as possible. You should, in my opinion, experience a kind of inertia against speaking; your preferred position should be that of the silent and attentive listener. You should feel in your bones that every utterance of yours costs; for every time you speak—be it to state an Interpretation, an observation, a Confrontation, or a question—you are directing your patient and thereby encroaching upon his activity and freedom. Now, such encroachments can hardly be avoided altogether, and they needn't be viewed with special apprehension. (It is not sophistry to argue that short-term restrictions of Freedom can facilitate long-term increments of it.) They can be regarded as a species of necessary evil.

Recall *The Basic Instruction* that I recommend you give at the outset of *Psychotherapy*. "You can tell me the things you want to tell me; it's up to you; I will listen and try to Understand; when I have something useful to say I will say it." This means you will speak when you deem it to be useful, when—and this is the principal criterion again—in your judgment you can advance the Therapeutic Process with some remark. Otherwise you will listen. Therefore, for every remark you make, you must not only be able to answer the question, "Why did I say what I said?" but also, "Why did I choose to speak at this moment?" The answer should optimally have a relationship to the state of the Therapeutic Process—and lest you fall into facile rationalizations, you should bear in mind that it is your patient's activity that counts above everything.

I concede that this leaves matters in a rather loose and

amorphous shape. As I've been saying, the conception of the Therapeutic Process can too easily be stretched beyond useful proportions. Still, while it may not be easy to specify it in all actual instances, it is possible to have a good sense of what it entails. And if I haven't already succeeded in conveying that sense to you, I can only contend, Simon, that as you gain experience you will come to intuit it in your session-to-session work. The same ineffability is true, after all, for all of the other criteria of timing for timing is probably the most difficult of all aspects of Technique to articulate and specify. More than any other aspect of our Technique, it rests squarely on our intuition and sensitivity.

Your affectionate uncle

Eleven

Dear Simon,

You've raised an important point. "What if I find myself in the position of having to say something—for the sake of the Therapeutic Process—but I have nothing particularly insightful to say?" Let me assure you: that awkward circumstance will happen, and quite often. But before I discuss it, I need to take up another important point—a most important one—lest you stay with the impression that all breaks in continuity of the Therapeutic Process merit our intervention in the ways that I wrote about in my last letter. They don't. There's a very important exception.

If your patient suddenly experiences a flush of anxiety, if his thoughts become momentarily disorganized, this can be a signal that something special and crucial is happening. That kind of event could signify an alteration in the Therapeutic Process which it would be a mistake for you to take steps against. To explain what I have in mind (and to make sense out of that last sentence), I have to introduce you to a new concept—the *Analytic Experience*.

During the course of therapy sessions there occasionally occurs a special event of particular importance, which I'll call an Analytic Experience. How to define it for you? Though I have a distinct idea of what it is (having myself experienced it), an Analytic Experience is not easy to define or to describe. It may be one of those experiences you must have yourself before you can fully comprehend it. (Try, for instance, explaining panic to someone who has never been panicky.) But it may not be so difficult to imagine it if I can describe it to you impressionistically and well. So that's what I'll try to do.

Imagine yourself, Simon, in the position of our patient. You have a regular, periodic opportunity to speak your mind to someone who listens closely and maintains an attitude of neutrality. Despite the intensity of his listening he never makes a comment that betrays any valuation of you or any judgment about what you tell him. It doesn't matter to him that you do, think, and feel some shameful things, so he remains free of disappointment in you. He never conveys any satisfaction in how you are doing, either. His only apparent wish is to better understand you so that you can better understand yourself. And he maintains an attitude of respect, of tact, and of some warmth. Now, under these "safe" conditions, you talk steadily. Much of the time you recount your experiences both present and past; you talk about your thoughts, about your feelings; you tell your fantasies, your dreams, your wishes, and your fears. The focus of all attention is on you and your life. You also come to have thoughts and feelings about the person who is listening and helping you to talk and reflect. These thoughts and feelings you can recognize as largely your own products because he remains essentially a stranger to you. In this act of recognition, moreover, comes a profound sense of your inner reality—the range and richness of your Self. All of this paragraph describes the Therapeutic Process, but not the Analytic Experience.

Now, occasionally—repeat, occasionally—something special happens during the Process. It may, but need not, be accompanied by a change in your state of consciousness, perhaps a reverielike or deeply contemplative state of mind. In any event, now you are talking "from the gut" and with feelings that are rare and different. It may be an altogether new feeling for you, or it may be a long unexperienced old feeling, but it feels rare and profound—even shaking. You may be having a new insight into yourself or into what you were talking about when it came on; but it's the sense of revelation that really counts—the sense of something deeply valid and authentic for you. It doesn't have to be so new or so startling; but it does feel rare and revelatory. It's an Analytic Experience.

The experience can be rather brief in duration, and it can be quite difficult for a therapist to see it happening. I make it my business to be sensitive, if not alert, to it. Why? Because, for one thing, I want to be able to identify and articulate it for my patient. He can be deeply frightened by the experience, for it can be an awesome one. It is usually accompanied by a sense of utter defenselessness—it is an experience that feels free from one's usual inhibitions. The patient feels wholly open to his Inner Reality, and for this reason it is likely to be accompanied by apprehension if not anxiety. So it's helpful to empathize with his feelings and also to offer him a measure of support. Usually all that is required is to let him know that I appreciate what he has experienced. Sometimes I will tell him that such experiences in therapy, though painful as well as frightening, can be very beneficial. I may also offer the Interpretation that such experiences are defended against, or if I choose not to say so at the time, later on in the therapy I can usually find occasion to offer the Interpretation that he is defending himself against the recurrence of such experiences.

Analytic Experiences, then, despite their relative infrequency and brevity, are events of critical importance and impact. Some therapists refer to them as Peak Experiences; I prefer Analytic because that emphasizes the fact that they are heightened experiences in Knowing. In my opinion, they are acts of acute Understanding, and therefore likely to have a profound effect. Such experiences are memorable and moving, but also traumatic. They are probably the stuff out of which basic change is wrought and against which major defenses are applied.

* * * * * * *

Now I return to the question you raised. Your patient is not having an Analytic Experience; he is simply experiencing a disruption of the Therapeutic Process. You are experiencing a need to say something, but you have nothing particularly good to say. It may help you to accept this awkward position with equanimity if you appreciate the fact that the correctness of an Interpretation is only moderately correlated with its efficacy. Let me put this another way. There is good reason to proceed at times with relatively little concern over an Interpretation's correctness. Nobody likes to be wrong, especially a psychotherapist who is making an Interpretation. But it is widely agreed that the wrong Interpretation can still have the right effect. It can be incorrect in substance, you see, but still have the desired effect of promoting the Therapeutic Process.

This claim is somewhat too facile and must be qualified. To have interpreted incorrectly is also to have Understood incorrectly, and incorrect Understanding is virtually a contradiction of terms. So I'm not talking of Interpretations that are often—or too often—incorrect. (If that is the case then something important is going wrong.) I have in mind, rather, the single Interpretation that is incorrect in content. It may be helpful to distinguish between correctness and timeliness. My point is that the incorrect Interpretation can still be timely.

It's in the early stages of *Psychotherapy* that this point is most likely to be relevant. When the therapy is young, situations arise when its progress can depend upon your making an Interpretation. For what reason? Because the Therapeutic Process needs it. Your patient may have gotten nothing from you aside from information about how the therapy will proceed, and he has also heard some Technical prescriptions and proscriptions. (I will write you all about this in a later letter, when I tell you in detail how to conduct the

Beginning stage of *Psychotherapy*.) Aside from that, he's had to carry the ball all by himself. He may legitimately come to wonder what kinds of contributions you make to the ordeal; and that wonder can be mixed with some dread. So it may be useful for you to show him. And when you venture an Interpretation at such a time, the correctness of its content may be less important to your patient than its form and its function.

But even later on, the progress of the therapy can at times depend upon an Interpretation—any Interpretation. At such times you can defend it (to your supervisor, for instance) by simply contending, "I felt I had to say something." This has to be done judiciously; it can too easily be misused. I am assuming that you are free from undue Countertransference feelings and are not struggling with conflicts about your passivity.

If you feel the Therapeutic Process requires that you say something, I would suggest that what you say be an Interpretation. The temptation at such times is to ask a question, and that temptation should be resisted. Even if you feel you have little basis for the particular Interpretation you choose to make, there are likely to be substantial benefits to resorting to this mode. Naturally, you will want to convey your uncertainty, and you will take pains to be especially tactful. But you can reassure yourself with the knowledge that incorrect Interpretations are likely to be only relatively incorrect, and that their benefits can far outrun their incorrectness.

Let me seize this opportunity to make another point that sort of fits here insofar as it can be your patient who speaks out of the feeling that he has to say something. First, a cautionary note: In your steady appraisal of the state of the Therapeutic Process you have to avoid setting too high a standard for it. Later I'll discuss the value of your contributing a sense of excitement and aliveness to the process. Here I want to draw your attention to the fact that a considerable amount of therapy time is generally taken up with verbalization that may seem unproductive. What happens typically is that your patient is involved enough in his talk, but you wonder whether it's as "useful" as it could be. Not only may you find nothing useful to say about it, but you may also (or therefore) feel that he is not dealing with important material. Now, without dwelling on what it can mean to judge material as not "important," let me make the point that it's helpful at such times to keep the following assumption—or is it a hypothesis?—in mind: *the mode of therapy has a substantial intrinsic value.*

Even when the material is not vital to a patient, the format of *Psychotherapy* can be beneficial to him. This doesn't mean that you shouldn't make some efforts at vitalizing the material. But such efforts have to be carefully weighed and tactfully made, and—this is my main point—you needn't feel under undue pressure to vitalize the material. If you are convinced, as I am, that the mode and format of *Psychotherapy*—namely, that a patient has a unique opportunity to speak his Mind and his Heart free from control and criticism—has intrinsic value to him, then you will relax and listen when he gets "chatty." Bear in mind that patients need occasionally to rest up. Marking time, treading water, or any metaphor for the respite, is a natural part of the process too. We must allow quite generously for them and not maintain too much pressure to keep swimming against the current, marching into the wind, or whatever the metaphor may be.

Above all, Simon, the Therapeutic Process is a slow one. Despite the contemporary impatience and general sense of frustration with it, *Psychotherapy* takes that most precious of all commodities: time. How much of it? I'll write you about that at another time.

Your affectionate uncle

Twelve

Dear Simon,

Now let's consider another big characteristic of the Therapeutic Process—silence. In the ordinary course of events a psychotherapist is silent often and a patient is silent sometimes. Silence, therefore, is bound to play an important part in the therapy. Its meanings, its functions, and its effects are likely to be both complex and ambiguous; and it usually poses special problems for both parties.

Your silence will have different meanings, different functions, and different effects from your patient's; but there is an area of overlap that's related to The Basic Instruction. Ideally, when you are silent it reflects nothing more than your commitment to that instruction—namely, you are listening and have nothing useful to say. Similarly, your patient's silence may reflect nothing more than his decision to think a while rather than to speak, and it may merely be an exercising of his basic freedom or Autonomy. It's quite rare, however, for the matter to be so simple and so ideal. With the possible exception of the later stages of *Psychotherapy*, it is typical for a host of other meanings, functions, and effects to be attached to silence on both your parts. Silence, therefore, will require careful analytic attention.

The meaning that most typically attaches to our silence is that we are withholding; and it is around this meaning that problems accrue—not only for our patient but also for us. One or both of us feel that the withholding qua silence reflects a lack of givingness or generosity, or disinterest, or inability to understand, or even hostility. The silent therapist, you see, is not ministering to his patient, not feeding him, not comforting him. Similarly, the silent patient may be asking to be ministered to, fed, and comforted. Passivity may be involved, or anger, or a fantasy of silent intimate communion. In short, a variety of meanings and functions can be entailed.

Silence can also convey a directive signal. On your patient's part it may serve to evoke speech from you; on your part it may signal him either to continue with what he was saying or else to change the subject. A patient's resort to silence as a way to stimulate you into speech is sometimes difficult to discern, but when he construes your silence as a signal it is even more difficult. Usually there are few cues that this is happening, and so you run a considerable risk of being dead-wrong when you offer an Interpretation like this: "I wonder whether you changed the subject a moment ago because when you paused I didn't say anything, and that may have meant to you that I wanted you to speak of something else." Of course, you will probably have some basis for expecting that that actually happened—his pause may have been accompanied by an expectant glance at you, or a change of facial expression, and you could intuit that he was waiting for some direction from you. It is easier to detect this phenomenon when the subject has been changed than when it has not; so it is riskier to say, "I wonder whether you are continuing to speak of the same thing because I was silent when you paused a moment ago. . . ."

* * * * * * *

Before pursuing this subject further it may be useful to draw some distinctions. The main one is between a pause and a silence. A pause has the characteristics of a catching of the breath, or better a catching of one's thoughts. One "takes" a pause, but one "falls" into a silence—and the difference is usually sensed with certainty. Patients naturally differ in the tempo and continuity of their speech. For some a five-second interlude is clearly a pause; for others it constitutes a silence. Some speak continuously during the session without even much pausing, and when they fall silent it is unmistakable; others have an uneven flow of speech with frequent pausing, and their silences are more difficult to discern. Still, it is ordinarily quite easy to distinguish when a pause has become a silence and when a silence was only a pause.

Then there is silence and silence. When it endures for no more than three to five minutes it seems to have a quality that is quite different from the silence that endures for twenty to thirty minutes. The one may be a reflective silence, but the second is more likely to be a silence with a different function; the one need not be regarded as a disruption of the Therapeutic Process, but the other usually needs to be so regarded. The one may cause you to wonder what thoughts and feelings the patient is having about the material he was speaking about; the second may cause you to wonder what thoughts and feelings he's having about the therapy and/or about you.

Now, Simon, an Inspirational Sermon. Just as your patient must come to feel comfortable with your silence, so you must feel comfortable with his. The ability to tolerate silence with equanimity, no matter how long it endures, is a necessary one. There should not be any sense of worry or frustration about it. If your patient chooses to stay in a reflective silence and doesn't want to share his thoughts with you, then not only should you accept that decision, but you should experience no particular feelings about it. It helps if you do not regard any and all silences as wasteful of time or as Resistance. You will, of course, want to discern the meaning and function of the silence, but your want should be no different than when it applies to something he is recounting.

The fact that silence can have the same status as verbal utterance has two major implications: (1) it can be subject to Analytic Understanding—its meanings and functions can be examined; (2) it is not the object of proscription—your patient feels just as free to fall silent as he feels to say whatever he chooses. This point is worth elaborating, for many therapists regard a silence as unproductive—as a form of impasse and Resistance—and therefore as an event to be actively dealt with. They will rarely ask, "Why are you speaking of your uncle?" when a patient has been speaking of his uncle, but they will regularly ask, "Why are you silent?" when he has been silent. Thus, silence is not granted the same status as speaking. Silence, of course, does go against the grain of psychotherapy. There can be little question that both you and your patient expect your main method of interaction to be verbal. So it is reasonable and prudent, and even essential sometimes, to regard silences as a significant departure from, or alteration of, the optimally functioning Therapeutic Process. But as I've been stressing, the matter can be complex and subtle, and there are several critical pitfalls associated with it.

The major pitfall is a function of the fundamental role of Autonomy. It is perfectly basic to *Psychotherapy* that a patient should be free to remain silent. That his silences, like his utterances, are the subjects of Analytic Understanding is not at issue. But, like his utterances, they should not be the object of evaluation, judgment, censure, and Reinforcement. Therefore, any implication that they are bad or especially problematic has to be avoided most scrupulously. This pertains to your silences as well as his, and is difficult to achieve.

It is prudent to assume that your patient believes that he ought not to be silent, or that his silences are essentially wasteful of time. So even if you have avoided conveying that judgment, you may have to bring his assumption into the open. Sometimes he makes the task easy by criticizing himself for a silence, or he may apologize for it in one way or another. Let me give two examples.

Example 1

[PATIENT, following a silence:] "I'm sorry. I was thinking about a bunch of things during the silence. One of the things I was thinking was . . . ."

[YOU, interrupting:] I'm interested in the fact that you said "I'm sorry" and therefore you feel a need to apologize for having been silent. That must mean that you feel it is something of a transgression.

[PATIENT:] Well, yes; of course I do. Am I not supposed to talk here?

[YOU:] But your apology suggests that you believe that a silence is bad.

[PATIENT:] Well, it's certainly not good. I'm puzzled by what you're saying.

[YOU:] I'm suggesting that you feel guilty over being silent here.

[PATIENT:] Yes, I do. But isn't it something that deserves guilt?

[YOU:] You mean that we should take it for granted that it is always a bad thing to do.

[PATIENT:] Exactly.

Example 2

[PATIENT:] I don't know why I'm being silent. I'm sorry.

[YOU:] Are you apologizing for not knowing why you're being silent or for being silent?

[PATIENT:] For being silent. Isn't that obvious?

[YOU:] Yes, I did think that that was probably why you said you're sorry. So the fact that you feel a need to apologize means that you regard silence as a bad thing.

[PATIENT:] Of course. Don't you?

[YOU:] I don't evaluate—I try to Understand.

[PATIENT:] But if I stay silent then what is there to Understand?

[YOU:] The silence itself.

[PATIENT:] Oh boy! I walked right into that. Okay, let me put it this way. What good is it for me to be silent here? Surely I will get more out of the therapy if I talk to you.

Now having exposed his attitude toward silence as bad, wasteful, unproductive, you must perforce make your own attitude known to him—and the matter can get quite delicate. Since there is a tacit assumption that he is to speak his mind, and since silence runs counter to that assumption, it is misleading to convey to him that silences are simply alright. At the same time, however, there is an important sense in which it is not misleading—for The Basic Instruction entails a freedom to opt for silence. The line between these two fundamental considerations is a very fine one.

Optimally, the ideal attitude can be expressed as follows: more often than not it is better to speak, and usually it is alright to remain silent. Put another way: insofar as silence may not convey thoughts and feelings, it is relatively less productive than speaking; but there may be occasions when a silence is more authentic than verbal utterance. Silence can serve a positive function for the Therapeutic Process, and it also can signal an arrest in the process—it all depends. The same, after all, is true for speaking. This means, at the very least, that we cannot make any a priori judgments about the value of silence. It is this fact that you can convey to your patient when the issue comes up. Above all, it is important to remove bad-good valuations from your interaction so that these valuations can be clearly located in his conscience (his Superego).

So let's consider how you will continue the dialogue of the two foregoing examples. To Example 1, you can say: "It is one thing for us to try and understand why you fall silent when you do—what it means to you, and so on. It is another thing to feel that it is a bad thing to do. Sometimes you may be using silence as a defense against me or against what you have in your mind. But sometimes you may fall silent because you choose to think rather than speak. In either case, I try not to evaluate, only to Understand." To Example 2, you might say, "Yes, I agree that that's more often than not quite true. But that still doesn't mean that when you are silent you are simply wasting time. It all depends on the reason for your silence, what's going on during it. You may fall silent at times because you need to do something here that you think is bad or that I will regard as bad. At other times your silence can have an altogether different meaning."

A brief digression. My preferred response to most occasions when my patient expresses guilt over some intratherapy transgression is to suggest that he needs the guilt feeling itself. He may need it for the punishment that is entailed; but he may also need it for defensive purposes—to keep from analyzing the behavior in question, the one that elicited the guilt. That, in my experience, is a common function of Superego injunctions, and can be Interpreted as follows: "So, when you punish yourself for doing the bad thing you are somehow free from having to examine and understand it." For some patients there is an act of contrition involved that also serves the purpose of exoneration ("Having punished yourself for the transgression by feeling guilty, you have done your penance—you have somehow exonerated yourself."). But it is usually necessary in the first place to deal with the real question of the behavior's utility or adaptivness. At some point he has the right to know whether his attitude toward the presumed transgression (in this case the silence) is realistic in any part, and it is misleading to suggest in any way that it isn't.

Having made the point to your patient (that there is no

way to judge before the fact whether a particular silence is an impasse or not), you can go on to reaffirm your commitment to The Basic Instruction, especially to your intention to honor his freedom of choice. Thus, by word and by deed, you will regard his silences with the same neutrality and nondirectiveness as you regard his verbal utterances. You will try to Understand and to Analyze them; but these efforts will not differ significantly from those that pertain to other behaviors.

Your affectionate uncle

Thirteen

Dear Simon,

More than any other subject connected with the traditional psychotherapies, silence provokes the most intense controversy and the greatest number of questions and challenges. So I'm not surprised that my relatively brief letter on the subject should have elicited your lengthiest reply. I did plan to write you more about the subject, but not as much as a full response to your letter would require. I will, however, take advantage of your questions in this letter.

I like your metaphor—"Aren't we somewhat in the position of using a flashlight to see the darkness?"—when you point out that silence differs from verbal utterance insofar as its meanings and functions cannot be discerned until after it is over. Often it's impossible to judge a silence while it is in progress—that's quite true—but I wouldn't put it as strongly as you have. Sometimes, you see, we can do it by taking our cue from what has gone before it; and sometimes a patient's behavior during it will provide helpful cues. The one who ordinarily looks at me while he is speaking may avert his gaze during a silence, or vice versa; the one who is usually placid may fidget, grimace, look angry or stubborn, or he may smile foolishly or embarrassedly. These nonverbal behaviors are in themselves important communications, and they can throw light on the silence. Sometimes, I should add, it is even apparent that he is scanning his thoughts in order to decide what to talk about, or else searching out his memories to find the desired one. But you are quite right insofar as it is more typical that you will

121

remain in the dark during a silence—and you must become accustomed to that position.

A silence is often introduced with an "I don't know what to talk about." When it has become clear that it is in progress, you will be tempted to break the silence by making a comment about the introductory remark. Such remarks often convey an important meaning—consider, for instance, "My mind is a blank"—and they generally indicate that the silence is not a reflective one but rather the result of an underlying conflict. "I have nothing to say," for example, is open to a variety of Interpretations centering around the theme of "I have nothing." Before you give in to temptation, however, you should consider two criterion questions: (1) Do I have a timely Interpretation, or line of Interpretation, to offer? and (2) Do I want to play a directive role in my patient's attitude toward silence? If it is late in the therapy and its structure is well established, then the first question is likely to be your main criterion. If it is early and silences are quite new, you may deem it more valuable to deal with the phenomenon itself and to focus attention on your patient's experience of deciding what to talk about. You will also be interested in the consequences of his silence—does it make him anxious, or ashamed, or apprehensive, or what?

I have already exhorted you, Simon, not to yield to pressure from within yourself to break your patient's silences. This, I admit, is much easier said than done, for it can be difficult to shake off feelings of worry ("This therapy is going badly") and self-recriminations ("I am a son of a bitch to let this silence persist"), especially when it is a protracted silence into which he has fallen. These feelings will impel you to intervene by asking, at the least, "Why are you silent?" By now you should have little doubt that I regard this intervention as undesirable, and you should be able to predict that I would advise you, if you want to break your patient's silence, to do it with an Interpretation—"I have a thought about why you fell silent. . . ." Bear it in mind, however, that he may well recognize that your Interpretation was made primarily to bring his silence to an end.

A patient's first silences are often designed to discover what you will do in response to them. How long will you let it go on? Will you sweat it out completely? What will you do to bring it to an end? Sometimes there will be a contest: who will speak first? If it was you who broke the silence, you will want to remain alert to that fact; if it was he but he did it in a grudging and resentful way, you should be quick to point that out. It can be crucial to expose as early as possible the assumptions, attitudes, feelings, and even the fantasies that attach to silence—and it is the overt meanings and functions that must be analyzed long before attention is paid to the convert, latent, or unconscious ones.

Probably one of the commonest functions of a patient's early silences is to break his therapist's silence. And this brings me to two fine questions that you raised in your letter: (1) "How silent should I be?" and (2) "How much control should my patient have over my activity and participation?" These are difficult questions, Simon, and are bound to be answered with a large "It depends." The second goes well beyond the matter of silence, and I will have to save it for another letter. Before I put it aside, however, let me make one point. The maintenance of your own Autonomy serves both as a model for your patient and as a prerequisite for his Autonomy. Thus, both you and he must ideally come to exert relatively little control over each other. (If this statement strikes you as strange, I can only ask you to wait till I get around to discussing and defending it at some future date.) So it follows that you take it as one of your basic goals to maintain independence from your patient's efforts to provoke you to speech. That goal, however, is best achieved gradually, and you must pursue it with Tact and balance (which is, after all, the way you pursue every other goal in *Psychotherapy*). It can be a mistake to institute it stringently from the very start, or to adopt the position without due regard for your patient's capabilities and needs. For one thing, instead of supporting his Autonomy, the experience can instead support his feeling of helplessness. That, of course, must be the focus of analysis (as must all the meanings and functions of silence to break silence), but it takes time. Meanwhile it may be necessary to aim merely for a gradual reduction in his ability to "manipulate." Moreover, Autonomy is ever Relative. The goal is not to eliminate interdependence completely.

Now to the first question: "How silent should a therapist be?" The extreme position is that of some (but by no means all) orthodox psychoanalysts, whose great silence has been the object of professional criticism and the butt of popular caricature. For them silence is an essential instrument of the treatment and an integral part of Technique. Entire sessions—indeed, many sessions—may go by without the analyst uttering a word. There is no denying that this generally has a profound and special effect on the course of the treatment. Aside from its unconscious meanings, from its role in the Tranference and Regression, and from its effects upon a patient's experience of the therapy itself (for one thing, his sense of engaging in an intrapsychic dialogue), one consequence that should not be overlooked or minimized is that an utterance made against the background of great silence is bound to enjoy an impact that is quite special and profound. What is said in breaking a monastic silence is likely to be vivid and memorable. In an important sense, then, the silent analyst stays silent for silence's sake; he regards his silence as serving a number of real and essential functions. So he would answer your question this way: "The therapist should remain as silent as possible."

But I construe the function of my silence in a quite

different way. Perhaps because I don't believe that it necessarily plays a special role in the development of the Transference Neurosis, or that it achieves the desired Regression, I see little merit in being silent for silence's sake. While I don't converse with my patient, and I foster what is essentially a monologue on his part, neither do I take my silence as an objective. Moreover, I believe that if I am listening actively then I will find ample opportunity to speak up. If I find for instance, that entire sessions are going by without my finding any occasion to speak, then I usually suspect there is a problem somewhere. It is improbable that a patient can maintain the level of the Therapeutic Process at its optimum for very long and that I can find no occasions to improve on it.

My chief objection to the silent position is based upon a consideration of my patient's perception of me. I see little merit in his perceiving me as *The Silent One.* Moreover, I can see some real disadvantages. For one thing, it provides him with a model that may equate Autonomy and Freedom with privacy and insulation. My neutrality and impersonality are necessary evils; to add silence to my attributes is to unnecessarily compound evils. It's one thing to be perceived as listening in silence; it's quite another to be perceived simply as silent. The former can often be unavoidable, and patients will appreciate that fact; not so the latter.

Different patients at different times will differently assess and perceive the extent of your silence. For some the passage of five minutes will already constitute a silence, while for others only the passage of the entire session will count. Much also depends on what the patient is saying. If he is recounting an incident, say, then the perception will be of listening rather than of silence. But if he is struggling with intractable thoughts and unidentifiable feelings, then you will be perceived as silent rather than as listening in silence. At such times your silence can take on the properties of nonparticipation and active withholding of help. Your patient may quite legitimately experience a sense of being unsupported, if not abandoned; or he may feel he is on the wrong track, or that his utterances are beyond comprehension. Bear in mind, Simon, that to greet something in silence is often to convey a message about that something.

One interesting connotation of our silence is that it fosters an image of us as the omniscient one. This may seem paradoxical, but it commonly happens. The silent therapist evokes the image of the one who truly understands, but in such a profound and complicated way that the ordinary patient cannot possibly share in it. Only recently has the popular caricature of the silent analyst taken on the characteristics of the one who only pretends to understand but actually is a fool. This mockery still betrays the underlying omniscient fantasy—and silence is one of its principal instruments.

I'll close this letter by repeating something from a few letters ago. Your basic attitude includes the desire for your patient to be active; therefore, you should want to remain as passive—as impassive—as possible. You should experience a kind of inertia against speaking; your preferred position should be that of the active and attentive listener. You should feel in your bones that every intervention of yours costs. At the same time, however, you can hardly expect to remain silent for very long at a time. That would add a dimension to your role which could introduce extraneous factors, one of which is embodied in your being perceived as *The Silent One.* Your aim should be to establish and to maintain the distinction between silence for silence's sake and silence for listening with Understanding's sake. So in my next letter, Simon, I will write you on the subject of listening.

Your affectionate uncle

Fourteen

Dear Simon,

When you're engaged in *Psychotherapy* you spend a lot of time listening. No matter how good at it you were to begin with, you'll have to learn it anew, for the kind of listening we do in our work is an acquired skill, if not an art.

In your reply to my letter on Technique you teased me about the Talmudic style of my examples. Your generation didn't get subjected to Talmud lessons like mine did. Anyway, what stands out for me is the recurring question, *"Mai komashmalon?"* I recall that my teacher (with the beard, the spittle, and the bad breath) translated it as "What does it mean?" It directs the scholar to unravel the multilayered and complex meanings of the text before him. *"Mai komashmalon?"* cannot, however, be literally translated to "What does it mean?" It asks, "What is one supposed to *hear?"* (or, "What is here to be heard, or to be listened to?"). In other words, the scholar is enjoined to listen to the words rather than simply read them; his orienting attitude is to "hear" the meanings in the text. The underlying lesson is that understanding flows from the listening mode—and that, I believe, is even more quintessential for psychotherapy.

Listening, broadly conceived, becomes virtually synonymous with apprehending and understanding. To have heard the rage in a patient's laughter, the yearning for security in his choice of remembrances, the self-depreciation in his account of an argument, is to have understood a great deal. That's what's meant by the *third ear,* and it's what your supervisor will mean when he advises you to "Listen to the

127

music." But how does one listen to music? And how does one learn to listen with his third ear? Obviously not by reading about it. It takes, among other things, practice. Not all practice and experience however, is equally productive (my piano teacher insists that I never learned how to practice); I may be able to make some helpful points in this regard.

To learn how to be a good listener it may be helpful to consider what is a good story-teller. A story-teller builds an event structure over time whose chief function is to control his listener's attention. A good beginning is one that attracts attention, and the body of the story holds it and wards off distraction. A good way of achieving this is to set up anticipations in the listener, who then engages in a process of confirming and disconfirming them; in this way he participates actively. Participation of this kind is what insures attention. A good story-teller also creates surprises and heightens suspense; and that is what enhances attention-holding. A good listener plays his part by forming anticipations, tolerating the suspenses, and relishing the surprises. Finally, the over-all form of the story should eventually come to a closure. The ending connects with the beginning; the structure of the story becomes simplified and unified because the false leads, the disconfirmed anticipations, split away. The listener now understands the story because he apprehends its structure and can review it for himself.

A good listener, you see, duplicates the process of good story-telling by being active in his anticipations. At the same time, however, he has to avoid short-circuiting the process, so he must exercise patience and modulate his need for confirmation-disconfirmation. The suspense must be allowed some play, and the anticipations must remain alive in order for the story to remain vivid. A listener who is too impulsive, who needs immediate confirmation for his anticipations, spoils the story. Tolerance for suspense—which is a variety of tolerance for ambiguity—is essential.

A therapist is, by trade, an interested and attentive listener. He is interested because he wants to apprehend the structure of his patient's account; and he is actively attentive because that is a good way to achieve the understanding. But there is another way too—there is also passive listening. By passive listening I mean being open to a story's structure. A handicap of active listening is that it may not permit the structure to impress itself. Too many anticipations, too many hypotheses, can spoil things. There is a necessary balance between actively figuring things out and passively taking everything in uncritically. Above all, a therapist must strive to hear everything, and that requires a measure of passivity.

When Freud wrote about "free-floating" or "evenly hovering" attention he was advocating a kind of listening that is closer to the passive than the active. This advice is usually taken to mean a kind of reverie-like attention in which we drift along after our patient without much concentration. In this way we allow our own associations and fantasies a free rein, and this allows hypotheses and ideas to come freely to mind. At times this mode can be fruitful—but only at times. For instance, in listening to a dream, such free-floating attention may be effective; but it should not, in my opinion, be applied across the board. The third ear must be used selectively and judiciously; it should rarely be used to the exclusion of our first two ears.

A useful aspect of the Freudian advice is the freedom from inner pressure that free-floating attention entails. No matter where along the dimension of active-passive we are, we must always strive to listen with relaxation and equanimity. We try to remain free from worried eagerness or desperation. A sense of effortless attention and calm interest should be our goal, even while we are empathizing with content that is strained and uncalm. I think the way one listens to music is the best way. Consider that it is only a naive listener who listens just to the melody. Even he, how-

ever, is being significantly affected by the timbre, the har-
monies, and the rhythm. A trained listener hears the whole
thing, and he can discern the significance of every aspect of
the music. Similarly, an experienced therapist hears more
than the verbal account. He hears also the tone of voice, the
choice of words, the use of metaphors, the changes in
rhythm and tempo, the hesitations and pauses—every aspect
and feature of communication. It is not that he listens *for*
them (though he may occasionally do that in order to
confirm a hunch); he listens *to* them. And while it is humanly impossible to be constantly on the alert for these
so-called extraverbal cues, it is not impossible to be always
sensitive and open to them. The more passive modes of listening are usually the best suited to this task.

So we must listen both actively and passively, with three
ears instead of two, to the music as well as the message.
And at all times we try to maintain a balance between the
different modes of listening, judging when the balance
should be shifted in one direction or the other. Moreover,
notwithstanding the fact that all of this is far from easy to
do, we must do it with ease. As I said: it is an acquired skill,
if not an art.

* * * * * * *

What's the proof, the test, the criteria of good listening?
There are two: (1) having Understood, and (2) having
remembered. There's nothing that will convince your patient more that you were listening well than your ability to
remember what he tells you. Not everything he tells is open
to Understanding—that takes time for the accumulation of
information. But, in principle, everything he recounts is
subject to recall; and the experienced therapist, Simon,
remembers. I would go so far as to propose the hypothesis
that *when an account has been well listened to, it is fully
recalled.*

It can be awesome to hear how well an experienced therapist remembers the contents of a session, and every aspiring one has had the awful experience of having totally forgotten a session that took place the day before. This matter of remembering sessions is complicated, however. There occur, even in the hands of experienced therapists, significant distortions and elisions; so a sense of conviction that I have remembered accurately cannot always be fully relied upon. Still, there are wide individual differences in ability to remember, and experience is a major factor. I believe that the way our experience influences our memory lies in the manner of listening. If our listening was active—if it involved appropriate schemas or trace-systems, if hypotheses were at work—then what we heard will be the better remembered. At the same time, however, if there was too much confirmation-discomfirmation, if our listening was without a balance of passive taking in, then much will be forgotten—because that which was relevant to our hypotheses will mainly be remembered.

Our patient too is often impressed with our ability to remember. At best he'll simply take it as evidence that we care; but it's usually not so simple. It's not uncommon for him to develop a number of Transferencelike feelings and fantasies about it. For some, our heightened recall becomes a source of uneasiness or even dread; it may mean we're paying too close attention, which in turn may mean we're getting too close. For some it supports their view of us as the omniscient one, the one with superhuman abilities. And some—who need perhaps to ward off such a fantasy—may accuse us of showing off.

On the other hand, many a patient will assume that we don't remember what he tells us, particularly details such as names of people he mentions only infrequently. While this is always a fair assumption, he may carry it to an extreme. For example, your patient may take pains always to remind you who the person is—e.g., "I was speaking with Peter; he's my brother-in-law," or, "I had a dream about John; he's the guy who works in the office who . . . ." It's usually a good idea to draw his attention to this kind of habit, for it can reveal the assumption (if not the wish) that you do not remember. Sometimes it also serves to avoid the feelings that would be evoked if you had ask him, "Who is Peter?" These feelings (including hurt, embarrassment, anger, and the like) would expose the underlying Transference issue. Some patients will need to avoid any test of your recall; others may need to test it repeatedly. (The same is true, of course, of the second criterion that you are listening well, namely, your ability to Understand.)

Still, it's important to bear in mind, Simon, that your ability to recall what your patient tells you is in fact quite extraordinary. He cannot be expected to realize that your way of listening enhances your ability beyond its everyday levels, so some degree of astonishment and/or doubt is perfectly appropriate—and there is no harm in telling him that it isn't as difficult for a therapist to remember details as he might suppose. At the same time, you must not arrogantly assume that your memory is infallible. It's important to avoid the argument that can ensue when he insists he mentioned something during a session and you don't recall it. It's usually sufficient to say that you don't remember. Of course, if this occurs repeatedly, and if you are reasonably secure about your ability to remember, then you will want to focus attention on the thing.

There can be a temptation on the part of a therapist— particularly if he is keeping notes—to show off his memory. This is no different than a desire to impress his patient with his powers of Understanding (both are apt to be based on a need to demonstrate his potency). Related to this is an unwillingness to ask about something that was forgotten because it may betray the fact. Embarrassing situations can easily arise—"Oh, you have been talking about Peter, not about John," or "But you are mixed up, doctor. I'm talking about Peter my brother-in-law, not John my cousin,"—and they can be avoided if the therapist does not hesitate to ask when he feels any uncertainty. If I find that I repeatedly forget who a certain person in my patient's life is, or about a certain event, then I suspect that there is a reason for it. No matter where that reason resides—and it's not always with my patient—it can be important to uncover.

* * * * * * *

Then there's the feedback—how a listener responds while he is listening. People ordinarily use a variety of interjections to indicate that they are listening and to encourage the speaker to continue—they say "Yes," and "I see," they grunt and "Uh-huh" (that stock-in-trade of the psychotherapist); and there are the nods, smiles, grimaces, shrugs, and the rest. But for the conduct of *Psychotherapy* I advocate eschewing all of the signals of listening—yes, all of them! I am convinced they are unnecessary. In my experience the two criteria of having listened—remembering and Understanding—are entirely sufficient. The signals and gestures are quite dispensable.

Impassive listening is far from easy to cultivate; it takes practice and conviction. The same holds for your patient; even if he learns that you are listening it is often difficult for him to tolerate your impassivity. For these reasons, many therapists feel the effort is not worth it. Furthermore, not only does it raise the issue of the nonresponsive therapist (the "cold," the "inhuman," the "machine," and the like), it seems to deny the fact that communication—that most basic of human needs—needs a range of gratifications. All of us need signals and confirmations that we are communicating, that we are being listened to. Without minimizing the fact, I maintain my conviction. All of this may be true for ordinary communication and ordinary conversation, but *Psychotherapy* is not ordinary—it is, as I have so repeatedly written, unique; and the way communication occurs in it is also unique.

But what are the big advantages of listening impassively? Is it worth it? The fundamental advantage is that it avoids exerting control over what your patient communicates; at the very least, it keeps such control at a minimum. Along with encouraging a speaker to continue, the signals and gestures and interjections encourage him to continue with what he is saying. It's inevitable that the timing or your signals also steers him to go in this or that direction. For instance, if you say "I see" or "uh-huh" when he has uttered a statement about his feelings, this will reinforce such statements —and we know such Reinforcements can be effective in increasing the rate of such statements. In this way the simplest of signals and gestures can exert a significant control over the patient's verbalization, and that is what we must avoid or at least minimize. By now it should be clear to you how basic it is to *Psychotherapy* that the patient experience, if not enjoy, freedom to say what he will.

This freedom takes work; it is hardly an unmixed blessing, and it will be resisted at every turn. You can count on his being conflicted about it, so he will likely try to discover what you want him to talk about and how you want him to talk about it. He may at times ask the question directly —"What do you want me to tell you?"—but even after he has heard your deflecting answer, he will continue by more diverse and subtle methods to ask it. One of the best ways to learn what a listener wants to hear is to pay attention to his responses to what you are saying. Now, there is no denying that any and every time you speak you will also be providing some Reinforcement. Your remarks are not random; and if your patient needs for you to speak, he can quite easily discover what he has to do to prompt a response. Still, as I have already written, you can take steps against the Reinforcement need and effect. On the one hand, you can point out to him that he wants to be steered and controlled and the ways he is trying to achieve it; on the other hand, you can carefully avoid gratifying the need whenever it becomes overt enough. I believe, you see, that you can move against Reinforcement—within wide limits, at least—and I mean to show you how to do it whenever I can.

* * * * * * *

To listen, and to listen impassively, entails substantial passivity; and *Psychotherapy* requires that of us. It's one thing, however, to accept the value of passivity intellectually, and another to feel comfortable and untroubled by it, for the passive position inevitably stirs up deep and conflictful feelings that can make the matter problematic and painful. When that happens, we will, like any human being, throw up defenses against it.

Without trying to specify the variety of forms the problem can take, let me point out that the passive position can threaten our professional self-image, insofar as it has to be reconciled with our role as the helping one, the one who takes care of the other (and giving guidance and counsel, for instance, would be more consonant with that role), as well as our personal self-image, insofar as it conflicts with a set of Ego interests that center around the value of activity as a basic survival process (and manipulation and influence, for instance, would satisfy those interests). In either case, then, passivity is bound to be a problem. It's a problem that we must carefully deal with, and no one of us can expect himself to fully resolve it. Still, it helps to remain vigilant and to be prepared to confront oneself with the challenge, "Did I say that, or do that, in order to be active?" "Was that probe made in order to advance the Therapeutic Process, or was it primarily a way to placate my need for activity?" "Did I ask that question, or embark on that line of interrogation, only because I felt uncomfortable with the silence?" "Was I responding to my patient's plea for active help, to his sense of helplessness, to his need for passivity; and did I do little more than try to gratify him?" We must at the same time be convinced that *Psychotherapy* depends for its efficacy on a patient maintaining the active position, and that that is rarely if ever served by gratifying his passive needs.

Consider the following examples: (1) Your patient says, "I seem to have nothing to talk about," and falls silent. So you ask, "What's on your mind?" (2) He says, "My mind is simply a blank right now." You ask, "Do you have any idea how come?" (3) He says, "I don't know why, but I need for you to ask me questions; for you to help me talk." You respond, "I wonder how come." Each of your responses may seem altogether sound and innocuous—but notice, please, that each one has already fulfilled your patient's request. The first example seems quite clear, but how about the other two? You may argue, Simon, that you are doing more than merely gratifying the need; you are exploring the basis for it. I disagree, you're actually directing him to explore it, saying, in effect, "I think it's important that you now think about the reasons and circumstances." So you're doing two proscribed things: being directive and being supportive.

Suppose he puts it this way: "I know you don't want to tell me what to talk about here, and I understand why. But I find it hard to do without it all the time. Sometimes—like right now—I feel the need for you to help me decide what to talk and think about [pause]. I suppose you think it's important to find out why I feel that way now and not at other times. So that's what I should think about, shouldn't I?" Your response must be deeply ingrained in you the way the fingering for the chromatic scale is ingrained in the fingers of a pianist. Your patient is asking for direction, and you must be habituated and disciplined to appropriate responses to such requests. You may stay silent; you may comment interpretively on the passive wish or the active-passive conflict; or you may simply remark, "If I answered, 'Yes,' then I would be doing the asking, and I would be telling you what to talk about." But you must feel in your bones that to answer "Yes" (or even imply it in some way) is not among your available options.

But why, you may object, not? It seems such a small thing to do, such a minor way in which to play an active part. Similarly, why not occasionally ask a question in order to keep the action going? Must psychotherapy remain so much of a monologue? What is the harm in some occasional interrogation, some discussion, and some dialogue? Surely that degree of activity will not destroy the therapy! Surely it is not such a fragile thing! In other words, must a therapist restrict his activity so exclusively to the formulating and offering of Interpretations?

If you put the challenge that way, Simon, then I have little recourse but to agree—for I do not mean to advocate a rigid policy of impassivity (nor a rigid policy of anything else). There are circumstances that will demand more active participation of you, circumstances in which interrogation is called for, and times when nonresponsiveness can be unnecessarily harsh. And if you feel you shouldn't remain impassive, then you should not. What I do, however, advocate strongly is trying it out—taking it as a goal—and regarding deviations from it as deviations. Deviations and modifications are often called for (and I do plan to write you about them), but they should not, in my opinion, be taken lightly.

Let me end this letter with a flagrant testimonial. When I first embarked on the habit of impassive listening I did it with considerable misgivings. It felt artificial to me, and I wasn't sure I could really do it. Moreover, I didn't believe that my patients would tolerate it, much less benefit from it.

So it came as something of a revelation when I discovered that I could do it quite well enough, that most of my patients quickly accepted it, and—most important of all—it seemed remarkably effective. For one thing, it gave the sessions a quality they didn't have before; it generally made a significant kind of difference in the way my patient spoke. He still spoke to me (and when I felt he didn't, then I was quick to comment on that), but at the same time he also spoke to himself. At times it was as if a part of him was listening in the same way I was listening. At such times there was an almost uncanny sense that there were three of us in the room. But most important of all was the way his Will came to play such an integral part in the session. He was faced with numerous problems of choice; he frequently had to struggle with decisions; and he had to reflect on what he wanted to speak about as well as how he wanted to say it. And so the topic of his sense of volition and his sense of autonomy came up with greater frequency and urgency.

It's easy to suppose that a patient who is faced with an impassive and nondirecting therapist will fall into a kind of detached and uninvolved monologuing. But that needn't happen at all, and most of the time it simply doesn't. The therapist's presence remains integral, and his participation remains vital. The fact that he is ever listening guarantees that the patient too is listening. And the fact that he (the patient) is listening can intensify and deepen the Therapeutic Process.

Your affectionate uncle

Fifteen

Dear Simon,

  You raise a challenge that surprises me only because you didn't raise it sooner. You caution me not to regard it as provocative because you're only "teasing"—but we know better, don't we? Anyhow, I'm provoked enough to pay serious attention to your challenge. You write, "Since he is so impersonal and neutral, could the therapist—in principle at least—be a machine? Perhaps a supersophisticated information-processing memory-banking ultracomputer? The principles of *Psychotherapy* could be programmed into such a marvelous device, from which tape-recorded utterances would broadcast Interpretations to the patient with exquisite timing." In other words: need the therapist be a human person?

  This sort of challenge is likely to be leveled by a critic who believes in the essential humaneness of the therapist's role and who may feel that *Psychotherapy,* as I have so far described it, negates it. But, Simon, I too regard myself as a Humanist, and I too believe in the essential humaneness of the psychotherapist. Moreover, I have little doubt that effective psychotherapy depends on it. I'm convinced, however, that the impersonality and neutrality *Psychotherapy* calls for neither negate nor abrogate it. There's a good deal more to humaneness than the sharing of personal experiences and the making of evaluations. And the same holds, I believe, for all of the constraints that the method places on the therapist. In this letter, then, I'll try to show you the ways in which our humaneness plays a part in this unique

139

relationship. Let me confess in advance, however, that while it plays an important role, it doesn't play a really pivotal one. It's not going to be easy for me to articulate this distinction, but I'll try my best.

The majority of psychotherapists, no matter what their theoretical persuasion, apparently agree that the distinguishing feature of psychotherapy (if not its defining property) lies in the "relationship" between a therapist and his patient. Many go so far as to claim that the "relationship" is the fulcrum for its main effects. Well, I'm in the minority then. Not that I don't like the term "relationship"—it has such a nice warm ring to it; it feels so much more congenial than the cold and impersonal "object relations" which we Freudians use. Moreover, it feels somehow wrongheaded to place our encounter with live people on the same continuum as our dealings with inanimate objects, which is what a true Freudian does. The people may be more gratifying and unpredictable than the objects, but we acknowledge no fundamental difference; we conceptualize the interaction for both in the same terms (with such terms as "introjection," "projection," "identification," and the like). Still, our formulation of "object relations" and our conceptions depicting its processes have an intellectual kind of rigor and specificity which "relationship"—especially when it is left without an adjective—does not have. A global concept like "relationship" too easily becomes an inarticulate and meaningless piece of jargon—almost a gesture, like an act of obeisance to the prevailing temper of our times which places a high premium on the avoidance of alienation.

Therefore, I'll have to forego the claim that a therapist's humaneness is embodied in the relationship he has with his patients. That's too vague for me. Instead, I'll contend that the core characteristic that actualizes our humaneness as psychotherapists is embodied in the concept of *Caring*. Not that Caring is so easy to articulate either—you'll soon see how I have difficulty with it. For that reason I'll begin with a consideration of Tact and warmth, which are easier. They are intrinsic to Caring, and in themselves reflect important aspects of our humaneness (and I'll shortly get round to writing about Caring and Loving proper).

* * * * * * *

As your hypothetical patient said at the end of one of my letters (nine), it may be humanly impossible to be free from value judgments—but we do the best we can. And it may also be quite impossible to make Interpretations without at the same time inflicting psychological suffering—again, we do the best we can. And the way we do our best as therapists can be summed up under the heading of *Tact*.

Anyone in the position of patient is bound to feel vulnerable, and a psychotherapy patient is likely to feel acutely so. He craves assurances that he'll not be hurt more than necessary, that he won't suffer undue shame and humiliation. Now, if you're conducting *Psychotherapy*, you can't offer such assurances in any tangible way. Your attitude of neutrality and impersonality provides little comfort, and for some patients may even heighten the sense of vulnerability. But the method does not prevent you from being tactful. In fact, it's essential that you be so.

To be tactful is what? In a basic sense it is to be sensitive to the other's true feelings. The tactful person is so in tune, so in touch (hence "tactile"), that his behavior quite naturally takes into account the other's feelings and wishes. It follows that the tactful one avoids upsetting others unduly, does not hurt their feelings unnecessarily, and never trespasses on their self-regard in inappropriate ways.

To the degree that Tact is synonymous with sensitivity it goes without saying that you should be tactful. So when I say Tact in these letters, I also have in mind some other considerations. One has to do with shocking your patient. The experience of shock or even of surprise, in itself, has no special value. Some degree of surprise and mild shock may be unavoidable, particularly when new insights are gained; but the experience of revelation needn't involve a sense of shock or of being taken aback—and I can think of several reasons to devalue the experience. For one thing, it keeps the patient in a state of apprehensive expectation; he lives through each session in a state of suspense—and that's bound to interfere. Many people enter therapy with the belief that they are in for rude shocks, and they remain in a state of readiness for them (if not in a state of guardedness). I believe this expectation must be actively explored and discussed with them, for it does anything but promote the Therapeutic Process. And I go so far as to tell my patients, when the opportunity presents itself, that I don't intend to say anything to them that will be shocking.

At the same time, to avoid saying anything that might be shocking runs the danger of being excessively timid, of pussy-footing. So, like in all matters Technical, the crucial variable is balance. Still, if I had to choose between the Scylla of tactless shock and the Charybdis of pussy-footing timidity, I would choose the perils of Charybdis. "Be tactful" sounds like "Be gentle" ("Have mercy on the poor patient!"). But even if it does, it's not such bad advice. Only when it inhibits you from making an otherwise sound and timely Interpretation is it bad; and only then, I would argue, is the issue of Tact misused. Put another way: a sound and timely Interpretation, almost by definition, is rarely tactless. It can hurt, embarrass, shame and anger your patient; but if it did it unduly or excessively, then it was untimely—ergo tactless. The key judgment lies in what is "undue" and "excessive," and this is where experience and sensitivity are likely to count for a great deal. The crucial consideration, which I believe I have already written you about, is that the patient not be thrown into such an upheaval that he can't use, and deal with, the Interpretation itself.

The matter of Tact generally pertains more to our inquiries, probes, and confrontations than it does to our Interpretations. A well-formulated Interpretation, even if it turns out to have been untimely, is somehow less tactless than an untimely confrontation or probe. To probe is to inquire into a feeling that went unmentioned; to confront is to draw a patient's attention to an aspect of his behavior that he is ignoring or misinterpreting. If they are premature then they are tactless, because premature means that he is not prepared to deal with the inquiry and observation, and instead may simply experience embarrassment, shame, anger, or perplexity. That you are convinced you can later make a timely Interpretation about the behavior may not be sufficient, for his initial reaction may interfere with his ability to use it then. In my experience, it is usually better to have offered the Interpretation in the first place and to forego the riskier probes and confrontations.

Let me give an example that has implications which go beyond considerations of Tact alone, insofar as it illustrates what can happen when we have a different view of some aspect of our patient's Reality than he has. Your patient, a nineteen-year-old boy, early in the therapy, says:

[PATIENT:] My father is an inconsiderate and mean man. He treats me abominably. Let me give you an example, doctor. Just because I smashed up his car last year, listen to what the bastard went and did. He had this fancy gadget installed in his new car, and it makes a record of maximum speed. So after I take the car out he can check afterwards how fast I drove it. And he made the rule that I mustn't go any faster than seventy miles an hour. If the gadget shows that I went faster than that then he doesn't let me have the car—for a whole week!

I have purposely composed this to ensure that you will be struck by the fact that his father's treatment of him seems anything but "inconsiderate" or "abominable"—and you will be strongly tempted to say so. Your problem is how you can do it and still maintain Tact.

Notice that you cannot fall back on "I don't understand," for his account is clear enough. What you don't understand is, "What's so inconsiderate about that?" But let's assume that he genuinely perceives his father's treatment to have been unreasonable and malevolent. What effect will it have for you to simply challenge that perception? Do you suppose that he will be obliging and try to explain his rationale? It's more likely that he will feel challenged, if not baffled, and react with embarrassment, or anger, or perplexity, or all three. It is possible, I concede, for you to make the following confrontative intervention in a way that is tactful enough in one sense:

[YOU:] I'm not questioning whether your father is inconsiderate and treats you abominably, as you say he does. But the example you choose for it strikes me as an inapt (or poor) one, for I don't see how his actions with the car are as inconsiderate or mean as you say. Do you see how I would think that?

This way of putting it preserves Tact in that it allows the patient some latitude to pick up the matter however he wants to. Still, if he reacts with perplexity, then the consequence may not only be of no particular therapeutic value but may in fact interfere with therapeutic progress. For example:

[PATIENT:] The example is an inapt one?—a poor one? No, I don't see how you would think that. What do you mean?

[YOU:] Well, it seems to me quite reasonable that he should set a rule so that you don't smash up the new car too. And seventy miles an hour seems quite reasonable.

[PATIENT:] Not to me it doesn't. All of my friends drive faster than that. And what will they think? And how about my date? She'll think I'm a real square . . .

How are you going to respond to this? It's hard to imagine any continuation that will avoid an impasse. And it is likely to be the same kind of impasse that he experiences with his father, for notice how the confrontative mode has put you into the identical position as his father's. You want to behave toward him like a therapist, not a father; so this is likely to be the wrong tack—not only tactless, but fruitless.

Your guiding principle—which is a Technical one really —is this: until and unless your patient himself comes to sense that there is something amiss in his perception of his father's behavior toward him, there can be no good value in your imposing such doubts on him. This does not mean, however, that your independent appraisal or judgment may never play any part in the sessions (into this, I will go later), for a second guiding principle which is germane here centers around the use of the Interpretive mode. Namely, if you can offer an Interpretation, it can go far toward attenuating tactlessness—or at least counterbalancing it with some positive therapeutic value (i.e., making it worth it). So consider one among several possible explanations for the disparity between his example and what he intended to illustrate with it. It could mean that he intends for you to side with his father, and your Interpretation could go like this:

[YOU:] It seems to me that you want me to side with your father against you, and that may be why you gave that example about the car. You could have sensed that I would react to what your father did differently than you did, that I would not regard his installing of the gadget as such as unreasonable and mean thing to do. So perhaps the reason you chose that example was to get me to think about you the same way he does—as an irresponsible and selfish kid.

You may object to my contention, Simon, that this Interpretation is more tactful than the confrontation. Even if you wait for a timely juncture before you make it, you not only implicate your patient's example in much the same way as you did in the confrontation, but you also accuse him of an ulterior motive. Not only do you challenge his judgment, but you catch him at doing something surreptitious (i.e., you "find him out"); so even if he does not react with any perplexity (because the Interpretation is quite correct, let us say), he may react with embarrassment and resentment.

All of that is quite true, I agree—but quite unavoidable. And you should be sensitive to that truth so that you empathize with, and articulate for him, the position that you have put your patient in. I don't mean that you should try to comfort him by conveying something like, "There, there; I'm sorry that I embarrassed you; I wish you wouldn't take it so hard." But you can help him to acknowledge the emotion and to understand what brings it about. (It may also be mixed with feelings that stem from the fact that you haven't sided with his father.) In this way you will have achieved at least two therapeutically important goals: (1) a Transference theme of potential significance will have been brought to the surface (siding with father); and (2) a reaction to an Interpretation will have been experienced and partially explained (embarrassment at having been found out). Such achievements can obviously be worthwhile and can outweigh considerations of Tact alone.

* * * * * * *

Then there's the matter of warmth—perhaps more ambiguous than Tact, but quite closely related to it. Warmth not only means different things but it takes a variety of forms, and it's easier to say which meanings and forms are not available to you when you conduct *Psychotherapy* than to say which are. The former includes the giving of reassurance and comfort (which is generally what we mean when we say someone is behaving warmly toward us). It goes without saying that the giving of affection is also included (i.e., excluded). But, without being affectionate or directly reassuring and comforting, it's possible to be concerned and involved, attentive and interested—and those forms of warmth you must feel and be able to convey to your patients.

Impersonality does not imply coldness, and neither does neutrality. It's possible, within their framework, to have an attitude of warm concern. The concern is reflected in that you strive to Understand your patient, to know what he is experiencing and appreciate the bases and circumstances of that experience. The warmth is reflected in how you relate and respond to him. Warmth, you see, is conveyed by extraverbal communication. It comes in *how* you look at a patient, *how* you listen, and *how* you speak. The way you offer Interpretations, how you phrase them, can make all the difference. Try, for instance, saying such Interpretations as, "I believe that you're worried because I remind you so much of your brother," or, "Do you notice how hostile you are being?" They can be said coldly and scoldingly; but they can also be said warmly and caringly. Therefore, Simon, you'll always have to be sensitive to what you may be conveying by your tone of voice, your manner of speaking, and your choice of formulation. This applies across the board, for the same statement, the same sequence of words, can be rendered with hostility, criticism, and even vindictiveness, or else with concern, with warmth, and even a quality of support.

The danger here is in taking a sanctimonious tone, or even one that's theatrical. Patients are usually sensitive to any phoniness on our part, and "warmth" can be quite artificial. Since I know you to be a naturally warm person, I'm sure you'll have no problem in this area. If you weren't, then I'd advise you not to strive too hard for it because the effort is likely to show. You want to show your patient the warmth you actually feel, not the warmth you think you ought to feel.

* * * * * * *

Now we come to the core feelings we have toward our patients, and I'll begin with what is undoubtedly the greatest emotion of all: Love. The need to love and be loved is unquestionably basic to the human condition, and while it's the most ubiquitous emotion, it's also the most difficult one to articulate and define. I believe this follows from the fact that each of us has a unique and particular experience of the emotion, a complex experience that is formed out of our earliest interactions (i.e., "object relations") and our most primitive needs. More than any of the other great emotions, love is experienced differently by different people, with different shades of feeling, meaning, profundity, and the rest. But I also believe that aspects of love enter into each and every one of our interpersonal relations, and they also play a vital part in intrapsychic relations.

Having written this, Simon, I'm going to make a claim that might seem contradictory, if not outrageous. I'm going to deny that love—in its commonly understood connotations and meanings—plays a significant part in the psychotherapeutic relationship. What I mean is partly this: a patient "in love" with you is suffering from Transference; vice versa it is Countertransference. Insofar as Transferences are aspects of Resistance and Defense, they need to be analyzed away, so to speak.

Now, that was much too facile and doesn't altogether make sense; so I have to fall back on definitions. It's clear to me that my thesis—which is that we must Care but not Love—stands at least on one leg that is entirely semantic. I want to make a distinction between Loving and Caring. By Caring I have in mind the sense in which the Existentialists generally mean it; it's also what the religious teacher means when he exhorts us to love our fellow man. Caring differs from Loving in at least the following kinds of ways. Love embodies the need to possess and to merge; loving entails the parent-child relationship, seeking gratification of the symbiotic need; it functions reciprocally, and it reflects a range of derivatives of the impulse to form a union or to merge ("incorporation"). Caring embodies needs that lie outside of these areas—though there may be regions of overlap. When we Care about our fellow man, we in no way seek to merge with him; we seek instead to co-exist harmoniously with him—for we recognize that his well-being and ours are interdependent. Caring entails not the parent-child relationship, but the tribal relationship; it expresses the need for brotherhood and comradeship, for family and group. All of this is, admittedly, largely semantic; but let me go ahead with it anyway, for I think it's of great practical significance.

Love reflects, if not embodies, the sexual drive in its broadest sense. Whether Caring entails or requires the sublimation of the sexual drive, as many of my colleagues would have it, is a moot point. I suspect that it can gain some strength from such sublimation, but I doubt whether that is its ultimate or main source. After all, kinship relations have as much survival utility as mating relations. My core feelings for my brother are not sexual, and my "love" for him is more akin to what I mean by Caring than what I mean by Loving. Semantics?—perhaps. But it has great significance for the ways I feel towards my patients.

Caring is not reciprocal in the way that Loving necessarily is. Loving involves Being Loved; if that aspect of it is not fulfilled then it will turn to Hate. Not so for Caring. It is possible to continue to Care about someone who does not Care about us. In fact, that may be one of its defining properties. After all, our major need lies in his well-being, and not in what we can get in return from him. This point is crucial for psychotherapy; for it is our patient's well-being that counts above everything, and it is from that well-being that we derive our gratification. We want him to have a good psychotherapeutic experience; we want him to work effectively and productively with his problems, to gain Understanding and control, and the rest—and those wants embrace our Caring attitudes and feelings. Anything more than that—anything that partakes of Loving—may not only be without therapeutic value, but may even be detrimental to the goals and purposes of therapy.

Let me take this matter further and make it even more difficult than it already is. Not only must you Care and not Love, but your caring must be limited to, or focussed upon, the special and unique relationship you have with your patient. This means that your caring must remain relatively restricted to the therapy situation itself. The reason for this limitation is mainly because that is where the caring counts. Outside of therapy you have no real role in your patient's life. You do not give advice, for instance, and therefore have no direct kind of influence on his outside actions and experiences. Not that you remain indifferent to his sufferings and pleasures—of course you care whether he passes the exam, gets happily married, regains his health, loses his friends—but caring, like Loving, is a matter of degree. My point is this: you have to care more about his therapeutic experiences than about his outside-of-therapy experiences. Why so? Because that's where your caring counts—matters.

I'll make an example. Your patient is about to take an exam for which he needs a book he doesn't own but you happen to have on your bookshelf. You decide, let us say, that for you to lend him the book is inadvisable because, in your best judgment, it may jeopardize the Therapeutic Process. Say he reacts to your refusal by contending, "So you don't care whether I pass the exam or not." Is this necessarily true? I think not. There can be substantial validity to your response, "I do care whether you pass or not, but I care more whether my role as your therapist may be seriously undermined by the act of lending you my book."

This question generally arises around issues of advice and counsel. After all, what better way to care is there than to give advice and guidance? At the same time, however, what better way is there to undermine the foundations upon which *Psychotherapy* rests? Does this mean that we must never give any advice—never lend the book? Not at all. We must ever weigh things in the balance. We must always judge between the relative advantages and disadvantages of the differing areas about which we care. Well-being, you see, is always a matter of priorities and hierarchies. I can want someone to eat a hearty dish because I care that he should enjoy the pleasure of it, and at the same time want him not to eat it because it will make him sick. And if your patient in the above example will surely fail the exam if you don't lend the book, and if that failure will have major consequences for his career, then you will not hesitate to lend it. If you put his well-being vis-à-vis his career on one side of the balance and his well-being vis-à-vis the therapy on the other side, you may judge that the former outweighs the latter. After all, if his life depends on a piece of advice that you can give, then surely you must not withhold it!

* * * * * * *

The theme of Caring commonly comes up in *Psychotherapy*, and you will better serve your patient if you are alert to it and sensitive to the wide variety of forms it can take and meanings it can have. It's quite common for the theme to be associated with the professional nature of the arrangement. Your patient may complain that you "care" only because you're paid to, or because you have an intellectual interest in his psychopathology, or because you need the practice. But it's also quite typical for him to feel that you don't Care because you remain so neutral, or so impassive, or so impersonal.

It will often be sufficient for you to bring the theme out of the background and into the foreground. You may say, for example, "The fact that I don't make judgments and give you advice seems to mean to you that I don't really care about you," or, "What do you think of the possibility that part of the reason you are having such feelings about me (resentment, distrust, or whatever) is that you are not sure whether I care about you or not?" or, "I know that you are aware of the reasons behind the fact that I never judge or direct you, but it may be that you can't fully accept it emotionally, and you can't shake off the feeling that I don't care about you."

In any case, that usually has to be the first step in exploring this theme. Subsequent steps are predicated on the fact that you will find, I believe, that the matter is usually more complicated and many-faceted than it may seem at first. It is not uncommon for a patient—or a part of him—to welcome the feeling that you don't "care," for he may not altogether want you to really Care. Patients who take comfort in the thought that you are indifferent may be worried about the implications of loving and being loved, and some defend themselves against much involvement in the Therapeutic Process by clinging to that belief. To experience your concern can be quite threatening to some, and naturally this is something that will be vital to analyze.

Sometimes a patient will set up what amounts to a test of the nature and extent of your caring. Will you lend the needed book? Will you make a change in the schedule to accommodate a personal need of his? Will you maintain the fee in the face of his financial setback? Will you give something of yourself, share something of your own, put yourself out? If you are reasonably confident that the issue is primarily a test, then you can proceed analytically. If you take the test, so to speak, then you won't be able to help him analyze it successfully, or you'll miss the point of the thing altogether. There's a peril here, however. Some therapists see tests and challenges where they don't exist, or else where that aspect is the minor one. They are likely to be especially, if not overly, sensitive to being "manipulated" by their patients; and they're too ready to disclaim, "All you are doing is trying to get from me some evidence that I care." The danger is that they will minimize the reality issue to the actual detriment of the patient. So I would urge you never to lose sight of the fact that your patient's reality needs may matter a great deal. His need for the book, or for the schedule or fee change, or for a piece of advice, or whatever, may be urgent. You must avoid the potential arrogance of assuming that the purity of your analytic role has all of the priority. That it matters is not to be minimized; but if you Care, you'll remain judicious and considerate, and you will maintain the all-important balance between everything that matters to your patients.

Your caring uncle

Sixteen

Dear Simon,

After posting my letter to you yesterday evening I remained preoccupied with the theme of Caring. I felt I had neglected to emphasize how the act of Analyzing can be an embodiment of Caring, and I fantasied sending you a telegram reading, SIMON TO UNDERSTAND YOUR PATIENT AND TO GIVE HIM UNDERSTANDING IS TO NURTURE HIS WELL-BEING STOP. Later, as I lay in bed trying to fall asleep, I had a vivid recollection of an episode in supervision that beautifully exemplified the point. I had to get out of bed and reconstruct it for you.

A case was being presented in seminar under the supervision of a wise-and-experienced psychoanalyst. The patient's wife had undergone major surgery the evening before the session being reported, and the student-therapist began the session by asking his patient how the operation had gone and how his wife was feeling. The members of the class were surprised, if not shocked, by the wise-and-experienced analyst's reaction when he heard about the inquiry—for he gave a big shrug, and his face conveyed, "What did you do that for?"

[STUDENT:] I asked how his wife was.
[SUPERVISOR:] To what purpose?
[STUDENT:] Because I cared.
[SUPERVISOR:] I take it you had some reason to suspect that your patient didn't think that you cared.

[STUDENT:] No, that possibility was not involved; I simply was concerned. And what is the harm in showing him that I care?

[SUPERVISOR:] That question I will be glad to answer. But since when do we justify remarks to our patients on the grounds that they do no harm? Let's first consider whether it serves a useful purpose.

[ANOTHER STUDENT:] I think most of us would have asked the same question if it were our patient. And one reason has to do with the implications of not asking.

[SUPERVISOR:] Alright; what are those implications?

[A STUDENT:] To begin this session like any other ignores the fact that a real event of great importance preceded it.

[SUPERVISOR:] Its importance I do not minimize; and I agree that it must certainly not be ignored. But to not inquire into it is not to ignore it. If the patient begins the session in a way that seems to ignore it, then the therapist will surely want to draw his attention to that fact. If it was my patient, and he began to speak of something that seemed quite unrelated to the operation and the wife, then I would soon make a remark that conveyed that I wondered why.

[STUDENT:] But that takes a business-as-usual attitude. And before any of this can happen, before you can get around to it, the patient may react by unavoidably thinking that you are a heartless, cold, son-of-a-bitch.

[ANOTHER STUDENT:] Exactly! And that would introduce an unnecessary and time-wasting resistance.

[SUPERVISOR:] If it did indeed lead to that kind of resistance, I would hardly judge it to be unnecessary and time-wasting. Quite the contrary: it could be the most important thing to work on during the session. You are assuming, aren't you, that it is rational for the patient to interpret his [the student-therapist's] failure to inquire into his wife's welfare as evidence that he doesn't care whether she lives or not. Why is it any less rational to interpret the therapist's silence as waiting for him to speak of her condition?

[A STUDENT:] Because in the patient's social experience, in his real world, people who care will ask and not silently wait. If they do not ask, then they are ignoring it.

[SUPERVISOR:] True enough. But therapy is another social experience? I take it you greet your patients with a "How are you feeling today?" And if you don't that means you don't care how he's feeling? Or say your patient is an insomniac. Do you begin the sessions by asking whether he slept well the night before? Of course you don't, because if you do that, then, more than conveying to him that you care, you are directing him to think about the way he slept.

[A STUDENT:] But this patient has had an extraordinary event happen. His wife has had a critical operation, and she may now be moribund if not dead. That doesn't happen every day. And it is not directing him because he can hardly be thinking of anything else.

[SUPERVISOR:] That is more than likely true. But what if it happens not to be? Wouldn't that be most interesting and most vital! And what, let me ask, is the danger of waiting a few moments to find it out?

[STUDENT:] The danger of not inquiring is that it may cause the patient to think that I have forgotten about the operation.

[SUPERVISOR:] Yes. That is a good point. It may well be that the reason he needs you to inquire is that he needs proof that you remember. That is something that happens often in therapy, and certainly one of the big ways we care about our patients is that we remember what they tell us. When, at the beginning of this discussion, I asked the therapist whether he had a reason to suspect that his patient thought he didn't care, one of the

things I had in mind was this question of remembering.
So let us accept this assumption for the moment. Say
there had been some reason to suspect that my patient
was wondering whether you remembered that his wife's
operation was the evening before. What meanings and
implications can that have?

[STUDENT:] One is whether you take his problems seriously,
or do you dismiss them between sessions.

[STUDENT:] Another possibility is that he will wonder
whether I pay sufficient attention to what he tells me.
That in turn can raise several questions in his mind.
Am I being distracted perhaps by my own personal
problems? or perhaps by problems of other patients,
about whom I care more? Another possibility is that
I am filled with dread by such problems as the patient
is having, and so I defend myself against them by
evasion and repression.

[SUPERVISOR:] That is an interesting list, and I'm sure we
could easily expand it. You will notice that it does not
yet include the possibility that you are simply an
uncaring person. But even if it is included, the same
conclusion is unavoidable: namely, that all of these
possible meanings and implications can be of vital
consequence for the therapy and for the patient's
welfare. And—and this now is my big rationale against
making the opening inquiry—none of them has a
chance to emerge into the foreground if the therapist
takes active steps to keep them in the background. If
you have not first found out whether or not your
patient needs for you to ask, you will not find out
whether he is wondering if you have forgotten; you
have lost an opportunity to expose any of the meanings
and implications that you have listed. It is your
obligation to allow for the possibility that there is some
significant reason why your patient cannot bring

himself to volunteer the information about his wife.
For if there is, then it is your job to find it out and help
him examine it. That, after all, will benefit him far
more than anything else you can actually do. Your
asking the question will affect neither his nor his wife's
welfare in any real way, and your failure to ask it can
potentially benefit him—and indirectly his wife
too—enormously.

There was a brief pause at this point. Then the
wise-and-experienced one continued.

[SUPERVISOR:] It is true that during times of crisis we may
have to temporarily abandon our analytic posture. If
our patient is in trouble, and we can help with some
information or even advice, or with some reassurance
and support, then we may want to do it. For example,
if his wife developed an edema, or something that was
a consequence of the operation, and he is worried
about it, and if you happen to know that it is little
cause for concern, then you may want to tell him that
to set his mind at ease. But at the beginning of the
session we are talking about now there is no way to
know whether that is the case, whether there is a crisis.
So there can be little harm in waiting to find out. Bear
in mind that it may well be that the operation was a
complete success, and he finds it difficult to tell you
that. The vital question, if so, is Why. And if you have
not allowed him to experience that difficulty, if you
simply make the inquiry about the operation, then the
vital question will evaporate—for the time being at
least. And you Care too much about your patient to
make, if not let, that happen.

The discussion should have rested there, but one student
still felt unsatisfied and a bit desperate. What he cried out

in protest made the rest of us wince. I will include it, nevertheless, because I like the response; it's a fine way to end this letter.

[DISSATISFIED STUDENT:] But it was such a trivial thing to say—to ask, "How is your wife?"

[SUPERVISOR:] An excellent reason to not say it! Trivialities and ordinary social amenities not only serve no purpose in our therapy, but each one detracts from our value to the patient and robs him of a potential benefit to be derived from therapy. It is precisely because I do Care about his welfare that I will preserve my analytic position as much as I humanly can. What better way is there for us to Care than to strive our utmost to Understand? To Understand another person is also to Care most deeply about him. No?

Your affectionate uncle

Seventeen

My dear Simon,

It seems to me that I've covered the main features of *Psychotherapy*. So what I'll do now is start all over again. Don't worry—I don't plan to start repeating myself. All I mean to do is write you about the Beginning stage of *Psychotherapy* and consider it in concrete detail.

You probably know that to divide therapy into three major stages—the Beginning, the Middle, and the Ending—is a didactic tradition. This subdivision, however, is not just didactically useful for us therapists; the stages can be real and meaningful for our patient too. To articulate that aspect of the way he experiences the therapy (for example, "Your recent preoccupation with death is related to the fact that we are now into the final stage of therapy") can be vital; for it's far more than just an assumption that each of the three stages has distinctive characteristics that reflect the evolving process of psychotherapy.

The Beginning can be critical. It's when the form of therapy is established and set into motion, and so it can shape its entire course. The Beginning is when our Technical principles are likely to play the dominant role. Understanding has to wait, for it needs nutriment (information) and therefore time, but Technique needn't. And since Technique can be objectified and articulated in a way that Understanding cannot, it follows that the Beginning is the easiest stage to teach and learn, if not also to conduct. It also follows, Simon, that I'll have more concrete things to write about this stage than I will about the other two.

Let me start with a point that I've made repeatedly: When you conduct *Psychotherapy* you refrain from giving advice, counsel, and direction. But it's only the rare and sophisticated patient who comes into therapy without expecting to be told, in one way or another, what to do. You must therefore make it clear to him as soon as possible that that expectation is false. And it's not sufficient to merely say it—you must also scrupulously avoid doing it. This is always difficult, and sometimes impossible.

Suppose a prospective patient enters your office for the first time and asks, "Where do you want me to sit?" You can hardly answer, "It's up to you." Now, insofar as your room is arranged in such a way that makes it clear which is your seat and which is for the patient, the direction to "Sit there" is already embodied in the furniture arrangement. Consequently, there's a significant difference between the questions, "Is that one my seat?" and, "Where do you want me to sit?" It's pointless (and tactless too) to make an issue of it right at the start. You may, however, while you are responding, want to make a mental note of the way he put the question, in order to remember that you were already put into the position of giving advice.

You are surely wondering, Simon, why I would want to make any kind of point at all about such an apparently trivial detail as saying to a new patient, "Would you please sit in that chair." Can that be of any consequence? Yes, I believe it can; for I am convinced that each and every transaction in *Psychotherapy,* starting at the very beginning of the Beginning, can have significant implications for the course it takes. In this letter I plan to consider some minute details which may seem altogether trivial—and they may well be. I believe, however, that there may be a cumulative significance on the one hand, and that each detail contributes something to the potential uniqueness of the therapy on the other.

With that in mind, let's return to the sitting down. Let me assume that you have—like many traditional therapists—a couch and a chair for the patient. He may ask right at the outset whether he should lie on the couch or sit on the chair. To this you can respond—and I generally do—"It's up to you." It's one thing, you see, to direct him to his place, but another to instruct him to lie down or sit up. And bear in mind that to say, "Why don't you sit at the beginning," can be to have said, "Later on you should lie down." This direction can therefore be avoided right at the start. The patient can (i.e., should) choose his posture.

Now, to start *Psychotherapy* with no instruction whatever is altogether possible, but it carries the principle to an unnecessary as well as potentially tactless extreme. So I make it a practice to give one instruction; it is what I've been calling The Basic Instruction. You'll recall that it goes like this: "You can tell me the things you want to tell me. It's up to you. I will listen and try to Understand. When I have something useful to say, I will say it."

The Basic Instruction (and soon I'll tell you when and how to give it) makes three points: (1) The patient is free to say whatever he wants to; (2) I will strive for Understanding; and (3) I'll speak when I think I have something useful to say. These points will have to be reiterated and elaborated at various times during the Beginning. In addition, there are further pieces of information—which may actually be tantamount to instructions and I don't want to quibble about this—that are important to give in the Beginning. A patient needs information about how the therapy is going to proceed, and some of this information may have to be accompanied by extended explanations. I will discuss them soon.

Many orthodox analysts—and some who aren't all that orthodox—give two so-called procedural instructions. One is that the patient is to lie on the couch; the second is that he's to try and say everything that comes to his mind and keep nothing back. For *Psychotherapy* neither of these instructions is given. Now, Simon, there's much to be said both for and against the couch. To some patients it will matter little whether or not they use it, but for many it will make a significant and substantial difference. What is likely to matter to most patients, however, is your role in the decision—did you direct? For once you've given a direction—and no matter how tactfully and how considerately you did it, that fact will remain, and your patient can legitimately expect further pieces of advice on how he ought to proceed in the treatment. "Shall I tell you all my dreams?" "Should I now reminisce?" "Should I try to cathart?"—i.e., "How does a good patient behave now?"—are some of the requests for direction he can now make. The same is true of the second, the free-association, direction. Furthermore, to free-associate is more like a goal than a method. It has frequently been observed that it's only later in therapy that a patient learns how (as well as when) to do it.

Now for my characteristic retreat! While I don't recommend anything more than The Basic Instruction, I don't think it's a really serious violation to add some instructions about the couch and the censoring (along with other elaborations of procedure). The conversation might go as follows—and you can easily substitute "speaking openly" for "lying on the couch":

[YOU:] It has been my experience that lying on the couch during sessions can be helpful for the therapy. For one thing, it may make it easier for you to talk openly.
[PATIENT:] You mean you want me to lie down?
[YOU:] That's up to you. I mean only to give you some information—that the couch can help.
[PATIENT:] But it seems to me that you wouldn't be telling me this unless you felt that I should.

[YOU:] I can appreciate that that may be true, to an extent anyway, but I still want to leave it up to you as much as possible.

Even if you don't plan to give such an instruction, your patient may force the issue by saying, "I see you have a couch. Should I lie on it?" You can respond by simply telling him it might be helpful, or you can follow my procedure by saying "It's up to you." Let us imagine a very obsessional patient who now continues as follows: "But you wouldn't have a couch in here if you didn't think it was good for your patients to use it. And I have heard that it can be helpful for therapy. Don't you think so?"

[YOU:] You're quite right; I do think it can be helpful.
[PATIENT:] So you want me to lie down, then [half-questioningly].
[YOU:] I take it that you want me to make the decision for you.
[PATIENT:] Yes, I guess I do. I don't know whether I want to or not. But I will if you say I should.
[YOU:] I would rather not tell you what to do. As I've already explained [or if you haven't you can take this opportunity to do so], I will not be giving you any advice or direction.
[PATIENT:] I understand, and I can appreciate your reasons. But your having said that it can be helpful makes it harder for me to decide not to do it, because then I would be putting up a defense against the therapy right away. In other words, I really don't have complete freedom of choice now.
[YOU:] Yes, I appreciate that fact. But you still have a good deal of freedom of choice left, and I would rather not restrict it further by telling you what I think you should do. I may tell you what I think may be helpful, but that is still not quite the same as telling you what to do.

I know there's only a fine distinction between the two, but it's one that I'd like to maintain.

* * * * * *

The opening moments of therapy are ordinarily not the appropriate time to give The Basic Instruction. Can you picture saying, "You can tell me the things you want to . . . ." immediately after the patient has been seated? The most natural opening topic is how and why he has come to you. So some aspects of the Beginning will inevitably be shaped by how and why your patient came to you.

How much you already know about him will be an important consideration. If he was referred by a consultant who conducted an interview, it's likely that the consultant has already told you about the content of the interview and about his clinical impression of the patient. In such instances, if your patient sits down and looks expectantly at you to begin, you may open the initial session by saying, "Dr. So-and-So has told me about the interview you had with him." Or, if he begins by asking, "Has Dr. So-and-So told you about me?" you can respond, "Yes, he did; he told me about the interview you had with him." Now you can tell him what you already know, with the important exception of Dr. So-and-So's clinical impression.

Your patient may simply assume that you know the contents of the interview and not press the matter any further. If, however, he chooses to ask you what you were told, I recommend that you tell some of the particulars. For example, "He repeated to me many of the things you told him. I don't know that I can recall everything; but I remember his describing your problem getting to sleep, the difficulties you are having with your girl friend, and your feeling that your work is going badly. He also told me some things about your past—about your parent's early divorce and about how you moved around a good deal." Some therapists make it a practice to suggest to their patient that he repeat the things he told Dr. So-and-So; or else, after having mentioned some of the things in the manner I depicted above, they suggest that he amplify on them. This, however, violates the principle that the patient is free—from the very start—to say what he wants to. So it should be amply clear to you that I proscribe that kind of suggestion, just as I do the following commonly used advice: "Why don't you tell me about yourself so that I can get to know you better," or any variation thereof.

The opening moments of therapy can be awkward for a patient. After all, he may have been told nothing at all, save where to sit. In my experience the average-expectable patient will begin to speak as soon as it's clear that I intend him to do so, but some will sit and wait for me to begin. Since I find it inappropriate to enunciate The Basic Instruction cold, if there was a referral, I begin as I described before. If I know nothing about him except that he's interested in having therapy, then I can hardly do anything other than begin with some questioning—and the most appropriate questions have to do with his motivation for seeking therapy and his conception of what it will entail.

The opening moments can be awkward not only for your patient but also for you. If you want to avoid stumbling and becoming too self-conscious, you should have a clear conception of how you want to deal with the great variety of possible openings. It is an enormous help to be confident about what kinds of things you will want to say and ask, as well as what kinds of things you want to avoid saying and asking. It also helps to expect some silence during the opening moments and not to feel pressure to maintain a flow of conversation. You may have to carry the ball, but you needn't do it very energetically. Your patient may need your patience right at the start.

Many come with a prepared list of things to say and to ask; they will take the lead at the very outset, and for the

time being you will face nothing problematic. For such patients the problems of beginning often come at the outset of
the second or third session, but some pose the problem right
away. Let me try and fabricate the most awkward or
difficult of possible openings.

[YOU, after a moment or two of silence:] I take it you're in-
    terested in having psychotherapy.
[PATIENT:] Yes, I am [and falls silent].
[YOU:] Could you tell me something about it?
[PATIENT:] Well, John Doe, who used to be a patient of
    yours, works in the same office I do. And he gave me
    your number. [silence]
[YOU, after enduring as much of the silence as you deem
    tactful:] I assume you discussed with him that you're
    interested in having therapy.
[PATIENT nods, but remains silent.]
[YOU:] You seem to be having trouble telling me about it.
[PATIENT:] Yes. What do you want me to tell you?
[YOU:] Whatever you want to.
[PATIENT:] I don't know what to tell you [pause]. I can't
    even tell you what's wrong with me, because everything
    is. My life is just a big mess [and falls silent again].
[YOU:] So you have decided to try therapy.
[PATIENT:] Yes [silence!].

You may have little option at this point but to forego any
attempt at beginning *Psychotherapy,* and instead to conduct
an interview. So you will embark on a course of interrogation to elicit information. There may, of course, be an additional reason for you to do this because you cannot be sure
this prospective patient is a suitable candidate for *Psychotherapy.* But—and this is the point I want to stress, Simon—if an
interview is avoidable at the outset, then my recommenda-
tion to you is against conducting one. This raises a big issue
that I will give less attention to than it deserves.

* * * * * * *

Many therapists believe that diagnosis is the first order of business. I want to avoid a major digression at this point, which is what a consideration of the advisability of a routine diagnostic interview requires. I'm aware that the issue is both an urgent and a controversial one, and that my treating it so summarily may give you the impression that I regard it as unimportant. In the case of a significant number of prospective patients a series of interviews, combined perhaps with psychological testing, is clinically indicated. Even if you choose to do it routinely with all your patients, Simon, you can readily enough make it clear to them that the therapy proper will begin after the interviewing and testing are completed. You can further explain that you won't continue to follow the interview mode after that. This cleavage can be a problem, but I don't believe that it's necessarily an insuperable one.

Okay; having acknowledged that (and I may return to the question of diagnosis when I get round to writing you about modifications and deviations in the method), let me reiterate my belief that in many cases the special diagnostic procedures can be dispensed with. It's usually possible, you see, to glean diagnostic impressions without interrogation, and to base them on observations of the way a patient behaves spontaneously during the initial sessions. In my experience, the first sessions (conducted according to the methods of *Psychotherapy*) will in most cases provide sufficient diagnostic evidence to judge whether any major modifications need to be made or whether a patient needs an altogether different form of treatment. So let's leave it at that and get back to the opening.

* * * * * * *

It's typical for a prospective patient to begin the initial session by offering to repeat the contents of the consultation interview. He may quietly assume that that is what you want him to do, and there's no point challenging this assumption unless he makes it too explicit. He may say, "I am sure you would like me to tell you the things I told Dr. So-and-So," and for you to remain silent could convey an answer of "Yes." What I recommend then is this response: "No; Dr. So-and-So was interviewing you, and therefore he asked questions and wanted you to give him certain information. But we are now beginning your therapy, and in therapy it is important that you feel entirely free to speak about what you want." At this point you may give The Basic Instruction.

The Basic Instruction should be given as soon as it's appropriate. Sometimes it will have to wait until the second or third session, but often it can be fitted in right away. For example:

[PATIENT:] I am sure that Dr. So-and-So told you about me.
[YOU:] Yes, he did.
[PATIENT:] So what do you want me to tell you?
[YOU:] You can tell me the things you want to tell me . . .
    [The Basic Instruction].

He may simply accept it, for the moment at least, and proceed to talk about some matter. Or he may dwell on the Instruction, as follows:

[PATIENT:] I don't understand. Anything I want to talk about? [to which you nod or say "Yes"] But what good would that do? [to which you remain silent, implying thereby, "All the good in the world"] I mean, there must be things that would be more useful for you to know about me.
[YOU:] Maybe so; but it's more useful still if you tell me the things you want to tell me.
[PATIENT, somewhat incredulously:] And it doesn't matter what it is?
[YOU:] It does matter that it's what you want to talk about.

This conversation can now continue in a variety of ways. The patient may balk, by saying, "But I have no idea what I want to talk about," and you will of course resist the temptation to ask the challenging question, "How come?" Instead you may want to offer an Interpretation, saying, "I take it that you came expecting that I would tell you what to talk about, and now that I don't do that you feel at a loss." That remark, like any Interpretation, can be taken as a mild scolding or criticism. If your patient reacts with some sign of anger or defensiveness, or if he responds with "Yes, I did; is that so bad?" you may take this opportunity to acknowledge the implied criticism and say, "I think you are feeling criticized, as if I said to you that you had no right to expect that I would be telling you what to talk about here," (which, in turn, can be taken as a criticism).

Another possibility is that your patient will fall back on a doctor-knows-best position—for example, "But you're the therapist; surely you must know what it would be most useful for me to talk about here." Notice how this challenge has overtones. Your simplest rejoinder would be to reiterate part of The Basic Instruction, sidestepping the doctor-knows-best overtones—"I believe it would be most useful for you to talk about what you want to." But he may persist, "Yes, you said that already; but can't you give me some idea of what I should talk about?" At this point you have two options (aside from the blunt "No" which is bound to be tactless and provocative). One is to say, "I believe it would not be useful for me to do that, because the kind of therapy that I prefer to conduct requires that you speak your mind spontaneously and talk about whatever you want to talk about." A second is to try an Interpretation: "It seems to me that you are trying to get me to tell you what to do, and I wonder whether you are testing me in a way. I have already said that I don't intend to give you direction or advice of any kind. Perhaps you need to find out whether

I will stick to my word, or how far I intend to take it." This kind of Interpretation, despite being quite risky so early in therapy, can be effective.

It's not uncommon for patients to react to The Basic Instruction with embarrassment combined with a sense of helplessness. At such times it can be useful to acknowledge the reaction by articulating it—e.g., "It seems to me that you are feeling embarrassed [or nervous] over the idea that you are to say whatever you want to, that you have to choose and decide." Under no circumstance is it advisable to probe into this feeling, to ask him, "How come?" or "Do you have any thoughts about why?" It's usually best to put the matter in an "understanding" kind of way—e.g., "I can appreciate that I have put you into an embarrassing position. It's difficult for you, particularly right now at the very beginning, to choose what to tell me." It is, after all, a difficult position for him to be in, and you should empathize with his perplexity and discomfort.

* * * * * * *

Now we have to consider what your patient has the right to know, what questions—spoken or unspoken—should be answered. Before I get into this matter let me make a general point about the answering of direct questions. It's a good principle—and so can be put into effect right at the beginning—that before any question is answered its meanings and the motives behind the asking of it should be made as explicit as possible. Bear in mind that it's usually too late to do this after the question has been answered, because then the answer is the focus of attention. Therefore, it's always fair to ask, "Why do you ask?" when the reason for, and the meaning of, the question are not clear enough. This response, however, is virtually a psychotherapy cliche; more important, it is often tactless. It tends to challenge the patient by implying that he shouldn't be asking.

The counterquestion can be put in different ways, and the way that I favor (particularly in the Beginning) is this: "I will answer your question, for you're asking something that you have a right to know the answer to. But before I answer it, I'm wondering what some of your reasons might be to ask the question at this point. It's likely that during these sessions you will occasionally want to ask me a question. Usually I won't answer it right away, because if I did then the reasons you asked it might get lost." If your patient pursues the topic by wondering, for instance, why the reason behind a direct question is so important, you have to avoid implying that it necessarily is. You can say, "It might be," but you're best advised to reiterate part of The Basic Instruction—"I try to understand." The point here is that a question already answered is usually not as amenable to Understanding as one that's still hanging.

Now, what questions should be answered?—in general, (1) all questions having to do with the way the therapy will proceed: its structure and form, its conditions, and its probable duration; (2) no questions of a personal nature about you, with one exception: your credentials as a psychotherapist. I'll begin with the latter.

If you are asked, I recommend that you tell what training you've had and what diplomas you've earned. This should not be followed up by a probe (such as, "Do you have any thoughts or feelings about my credentials?") unless your patient's reaction is noteworthy. If, for example, he frowns, smiles, or stammers when he says, "You're a psychologist, not a psychiatrist," or, "You're still a student," or the like, then the matter can be pursued. Otherwise a probe is likely to be gratuitous. Many patients will not themselves raise the question of credentials. For some the matter will already have been settled with the referring party, or, if not completely settled, it may require no more than some correction and amplification. But for others it will be avoided as if it were a taboo subject; they may simply not want to know it or discuss it. This, sooner or later, will have to become the topic of analysis because it is bound to become an ingredient in the Transference (particularly when you are a student). It is therefore well worth bearing in mind that he never raised the question.

Any other question about you yourself—e.g., your age, your religion, your marital status—need not, and in my opinion should not, be answered, unless, of course, there is a special and compelling reason in the particular case. Most patients will intuitively understand and readily accept the rationale for your impersonality, and so it is usually unnecessary to go into the matter with them. Only occasionally will you have to inform a patient that only he will be personal. If he asks why, you can tell him that it would be of no benefit to him to share in your personal life, and might in fact be a real hindrance.

Direct personal questions at the beginning can be awkward, if not really difficult, to deal with. Some patients would contend—and some therapists would agree with them—that they have a right to know such things as your age, your personal values, whether you practice a religion, and the like. "Are you experienced enough?" "Do you have my values?" "Do you live an appropriate life style?"—these are the basic questions. Now, it's one thing to respond to his question, "How old are you?" by saying, "I believe you are asking me whether I am experienced enough"; but say he agrees, and then persists, "Are you?" Or say he asks a question this way: "I am a radical hedonist who believes that one's own pleasure is all that matters in life. Do you believe that too?" Of course you can still translate the question into its generic form, "You are asking whether I am a suitable therapist for you." But the question still boils down to, "Are you?"

Most personal questions are elaborations on the basic question, "Are you a suitable therapist for me?" A patient may feel he has the right to know your personal attributes in order to be in a position to arrive at that decision himself. In many forms of psychotherapy—the Encounter types especially—that is a valid step for him to take. But in Analytic-type therapies—and *Psychotherapy* especially—it is not so critical. In fact, it is my conviction, Simon, that the therapist's value system (his beliefs, his mores) can—and should —play an insignificant part. So if you believe it, you can take the position that it needn't matter how old you are, whether you're married, or of what religious persuasion; none of these attributes will provide an answer to the basic question of your suitability. If, as I said, you really believe this (and in a later letter, Simon, I'll try to persuade you), you can in good conscience answer your patient's question by saying something like this: "There is no good way of telling in advance whether or not I am a suitable therapist for you. It need not matter how old I am, or whether I am married, or whether I am an Episcopalian or Jew, or whether I am a hedonist like you or not."

If he agrees, but persists in wondering how he will judge your suitability, then you must avoid implying that you alone will be the judge of that. Not only is that high-handed and presumptuous, but it puts him into a passive role with respect to this important consideration; it abrogates to you a most vital decision. What alternatives do you have? One is to suggest to him that the first sessions be regarded as a sort of trial: "The only sure way that I know to find out whether I am the right therapist for you—whether you can work with me, whether I can work with you, and also whether you find my methods suitable—is for us to give it a try and see how it goes. There is always the option of deciding that it would be better for you to have another therapist or another kind of therapy."

Even when the matter is not explicitly stated or broached, it is prudent to regard the early sessions as a kind of trial run. This, however, raises some difficult problems for which there is no ready solution. The chief problem is: How can you give a fair representation of the therapy's course at the very beginning of the Beginning? There are things that can be told and foretold, but there is no good way to give a picture of some of the really critical issues—such as the nature and frequency of your participation, the cast of your Interpretations, the way you will deal with impasses and crises, the full scope of your neutrality and impersonality, your integrity. These are things a patient can only discover when they happen, and by then it may be too late to alter his commitment. It is true that he remains free to discontinue the therapy at any point, but commitment is a complicated matter, and once the processes of therapy are set into motion the decision to discontinue is far from simple. For one thing, both you and he are likely to regard the decision as a manifestation of Resistance; indeed, it frequently is. For another, dependency may have taken root, along with some degree of Transference feelings. So the freedom to discontinue is likely to become less and less actual as the therapy proceeds.

As I said, this is a difficult problem. One way to alleviate it is for you to make an effort during the early sessions to show your patient the full range of your approach and your methods. This can serve to make these sessions a fair sample of the therapy so that your patient gets an accurate picture of it. He is then in a better position to judge for himself whether it suits him. This trial run, if it is to serve its purpose, must occur before he gets too deeply involved in the treatment; for only then will he really remain free to break it off if he decides that either you or your methods do not suit him.

* * * * * * *

Suitability and commitment are related to two business arrangements that must be settled at the outset: the schedule and the fee. Both require a balancing of costs and benefits, broadly conceived. A patient must pay in time and money in some reasonable and realistic amount that strikes a balance between his ability and your requirements. If either of you sacrifices too much or is unduly inconvenienced, the therapy will have to overcome the added burden of these sacrifices and inconveniences. The key judgment throughout is what is "reasonable and realistic."

The schedule and the fee must of course be discussed in the first session. Sometimes a patient will discuss them with you over the phone when he first contacts you, and sometimes he won't even raise the matters during the first session. In either case, it's your responsibility to introduce the subject even if you must interrupt the flow of the session to do it. It's prudent to allow at least twenty minutes, because these matters have to be carefully and fully explored (and sometimes twenty minutes turn out to be insufficient).

The schedule has two parts: how frequently and when. The frequency of sessions is a most important variable, and you may have to convey its importance to your patient. Commonly, it is determined solely by his ability to pay the fee. That, in my opinion, is most unfortunate. Each form of psychotherapy has its optimal frequence/per/week. Daily sessions go with an intensive treatment, while supportive treatment usually requires no more than once or twice a week. The rationale here has to do with the amount of current experiencing (i.e., living) that goes on between sessions and its relationship to the continuity of the Therapeutic Process. If the patient is encouraged to focus on current affairs and not to reminisce or free-associate much, then the space between sessions should be larger; if the therapist is giving advice, then the frequency of the sessions is apt to be correlated with dependency; if the patient is being plunged into a Transference Neurosis, then he may need frequent sessions in order to allow him a daily channeling of the experience so that it does not ruin his entire day. These are just some of the relevant considerations. How about

Psychotherapy? It has been my experience that once a week is insufficient, twice a week is a bare minimum, three times is generally acceptable, and four times a week is optimal.

Now to the when. Setting the schedule commonly takes place at a time when both parties already have a daily schedule. The sessions must therefore be fitted into two already established schedules, and the major problem that arises involves inconvenience. Ideally, they should fit comfortably; in practice, some degree of compromise is necessary. The important judgment is when the compromise becomes excessive. It's not uncommon, you see, for a patient to structure the therapy so that it's a self-punishment, an act of contrition or retribution. An inconvenient schedule (as well as a fee he cannot really afford) is a way to gratify that need. So if he wants to avoid being an accomplice to that gratification, a therapist should take pains to determine how inconvenient the inconveniences are, and to refuse a schedule that is too costly.

The chief guideline is this: The costs of *Psychotherapy*—both in time and money—should not be so exorbitant that they serve as an extraneous (a real) source of Resistance. (Such reality-based Resistances are generally recalcitrant to analysis.) Neither can the responsibility for making this kind of judgment be left to your patient, for the business arrangements are necessarily shared by you. The fee and the schedule are determined by your needs as much as by his. If both of you are unable to find a mutually convenient schedule then you should not embark on *Psychotherapy*.

The same is true for the fee. Just as you will feel obliged to investigate your patient's schedule in order to judge whether the arrangements are not excessively inconvenient, so you will investigate his financial capabilities in order to judge whether the fee is not exorbitant. To have told what the fee is and then to accept his statement that he can afford it is not sufficient. In order to participate in this judgment you should ask him to tell you about his financial position. In most cases the issue is quickly resolved, for patients rarely initiate a contact with us without first knowing what our fee is likely to be, and they've already figured out how they'll pay it. Sometimes, however, the matter becomes a problem; a patient may misjudge or miscalculate, or he may be unrealistic about the matter. Sometime he may assume a heroic (or is it a martyred?) posture by claiming he can live on very little. Unfortunately, there usually is not time enough to analyze the problem because the fee (unlike the schedule) has to be settled so early. Furthermore, it's no good to make a temporary or trial-and-error arrangement— to be adjusted downward later on if it proves too difficult— unless you are fully prepared to make an appropriate adjustment. You must make a commitment to your patient; once *Psychotherapy* is initiated, it should not be discontinued for financial reasons unless his financial condition suffers a drastic change in the interim. (What to do in that extreme eventuality is something that each of us must decide in consultation with his personal and professional conscience.)

What the amount of the fee should be is a difficult question to answer in a general way. It goes without saying that both parties should be comfortable with it, that there should be no guilt and/or resentment at it being too high or too low. It's facile to say we shouldn't overlook the many subtle social-professional factors that become implicated, so let me brush the matter aside and simply point out that most therapists use the "going rate" as their guideline. They set a fee that they judge to be fair both for themselves and their average-expectable patient, and many will consider lowering it for those who can't afford their regular fee.

When the fee has been set and you have told your patient how you expect it to be paid (for example, that you will provide a bill for the month at the end of each month), the matter of payment for missed sessions has to be raised. Perhaps the only policy that is invariantly followed is the obvious: There is no charge for a session that you cancel. A second, which is far from invariant but quite common, is that there is a full charge for a session that a patient misses without forewarning. Otherwise, there's no single policy that can be advocated for all therapists to follow. Each must consider his own circumstances, the nature of his schedule and his practice, and arrive at his own policy.

Let's begin with the accidental missing of a session. If your policy is to charge for them, and if your patient objects that it's no fair for him to pay for a session he missed because of some unavoidable accident, you can point out that you will have to pay for accidents that occur to you; is it fair for you also to absorb the cost of his? When it applies to single missed sessions then the matter is generally unequivocal. It becomes equivocal and problematic, however, when a series of sessions has to be cancelled (when a patient suffers a lengthy illness, goes on an extended trip, or the like). Some therapists, no matter which policy they otherwise follow, make it a practice to share with their patient the cost of an extended series of missed sessions. Charging a half-fee for such sessions is commonly the way they do it. In effect the patient pays something to compensate for the therapist's loss of income and to guarantee that the time will still be available when he's ready to resume.

The circumstance for which there are major variations in policy is when a single session is missed and the patient has given advance notice. It's quite standard then to try and find a substitute hour. Now, if the therapist is the one who's canceling, and if no suitable substitute hour can be found, then there is little if any basis for charging a fee for it. But if it's the patient who needs the cancellation, and no substitute can be found, then the charging of fee becomes a legitimate issue. Under this circumstance there are three policies available: (1) the fee will be charged; (2) the fee will not be charged provided there is sufficient advance notice (for instance, one or two days beforehand); (3) the fee will be charged only if the therapist is unable to use the hour for some other purpose.

I know that the third policy is commonly used, but I don't recommend it—even for the therapist who has an active consultation practice and can frequently use missed sessions for fee-earning purposes. I believe he should opt for the second policy if he feels it's unethical to earn a double fee for an hour. What worries me, you see, is having to say to a patient, "Since I wasn't able to use yesterday's hour I am charging you for it."

To routinely charge for missed hours no matter what their basis and no matter how much advance notice was given (the first policy) may seem unnecessarily harsh, but it has a sound rationale based on two important considerations: your patient should have no extraneous incentive to miss sessions (a saving of money can be such an incentive); and you have made a commitment of time which involves your economic needs. Whether your patient uses the time or not should not be permitted to affect those needs because then you would have a real stake in his not missing sessions. You must care that sessions are missed, but your caring must center on his well-being and not on your own. If, for instance, you choose to challenge his reason for canceling a session, there should be no possibility that it's your own economic welfare that is motivating you. When the fee is at issue, then it's bound to play a part—at least in his view. Furthermore, Simon, it is sensible to regard the contractual agreement between you as a form of retainer. Less like a physician who charges for services rendered, but more like a lawyer who charges for making himself available to render service, a psychotherapist can charge for the time he sets aside in advance. Whether or not his patient makes full use of that time can be regarded as irrelevant to the contractual arrangement. Of course, his full agreement must be secured in advance, and therefore the nature of the contract must be made perfectly clear at the outset.

The same applies to the more lenient second policy. A critical aspect of this policy, and one that is a requisite for

Psychotherapy, is that the reason for the cancellation plays no part at all in the agreement to charge no fee. It's essential that you eschew the role of judge and arbiter, which is what evaluating the cogency of a cancellation would require. So long as your patient has met the condition of sufficient advance notification he is not charged for the session. So far as the fee is concerned, then, it matters not at all whether he is cancelling in order to take an important examination, to attend a cocktail party, or to take a breather from the treatment. If you opt for the second policy you must be prepared to absorb the loss of income that it can entail; otherwise you should choose the first one.

It's easy to suppose that when you choose the second policy—which is the one I generally use for *Psychotherapy*—you are inviting your patient to take advantage. Certainly he is put into the position of temptation to test your integrity. Will you really disregard the reason for the cancellation? Will you actually not punish him for canceling on a whim? You can expect a session or two to be canceled out of such a need to test you, but while it may cost you in the short run, it can serve a valuable therapeutic function insofar as it actualizes an important aspect of *Psychotherapy.* Notice how this policy places the full onus of responsibility on your patient's shoulders, on his conscience. That it gives him a real power over your economic well-being can be regarded as a serious flaw, and for this reason many therapists would argue against it. But I believe this flaw is sufficiently balanced by several important advantages. For one thing, it provides for a certain sharing of responsibility that can actualize and intensify a patient's freedom and Autonomy. If he cancels indiscriminately or excessively, then he has to face the consequences—which can involve feelings of guilt or shame and can raise matters of morality and interpersonal responsibility. If he pays for it financially (the first policy), he can enjoy a certain amount of exoneration; he has, after all, paid a price for his transgression. But if he remains free to cancel without payment (the second), then the only cost is to his own well-being and the only price is intrapsychic.

Most patients will not take unfair advantage of the leniency, but many will be profoundly affected by it insofar as it maximizes the extent to which the treatment remains free from external constraints and Reinforcements. Some will struggle against this freedom like they do against every other aspect of it, and for this reason they will cancel excessively. When this happens it will of course become the focus of attention and thus may be the fulcrum for valuable therapeutic work. Its analysis and resolution will be essential; and if that achievement is not possible, then the treatment as a whole may well be futile.

* * * * * * *

Now we must face that most difficult of issues—the therapy's duration. This is usually connected to the even more difficult issue—criteria for termination. The question, "How long will the therapy last?" can be articulated into two questions: (1) "What will be the criteria for termination? and (2) "How long will it take to achieve the goals of therapy?"

Many patients will not themselves raise this big question, and then you must decide whether you should. In my opinion, Simon, there's no compelling reason why you should feel you must, for it can usually wait until a more propitious time. If your patient needs to avoid these questions, then that need has to take precedence; it will require analysis before any answers can be meaningful. Moreover, the fact that he doesn't raise the matter needn't reflect a need to avoid it; it can merely reflect a realistic uncertainty. After all, it's hardly unreasonable to take a wait-and-see-how-it-goes attitude. I'm not suggesting that it's prudent for both of you to wait and see until the Ending; as I'll discuss later, I regard the Middle stage as generally the most propitious time to consider the matter.

If, however, your patient does raise the question at the Beginning, then you must be prepared to give him an answer. You can delay for a bit in order to learn about his expectations and what they're based on, but the question should be regarded as a legitimate one even without much information. So, for this and for other reasons, you should have a conception of how long a course of *Psychotherapy* generally is. My conception is between two and three years (at a frequency of three or four times a week). The answer I give is this: "In my experience the therapy can be expected to last from two to three years. Of course it isn't possible to predict now whether it might take as much as four years or more, or as few as two, if not less; but I regard two to three years as a realistic estimate."

The estimate I make, though based on experience, is essentially arbitrary. What I believe is not arbitrary, however, is the necessity for us to entertain an estimate, for otherwise we slip too easily into a time-unlimited conception that can affect the course of the treatment—particularly its final stage, the Ending. That stage (as I will have to discuss it at another time) is difficult and ambiguous, and it can be of enormous benefit if the issues and criteria for termination do not arise then for the first time. I'm not suggesting that the criteria be firmly established at the Beginning, only that they be considered and discussed. For one thing, all that can be expected is a rough estimate of them, and circumstances can easily change them drastically; for another, the criteria for termination can be expected to change significantly during the course of the therapy as a consequence of the therapy itself.

The criteria that are not a matter of time alone—namely, the patient's goals in terms of improvement and change—are more difficult to formulate. These comprise his expectations (and yours) about what treatment will achieve for him. It's the rare patient who will avoid that subject altogether during the Beginning, but it's quite common for him to skim lightly over its surface without getting very deeply into it. Nevertheless, Simon, it's my conviction that you need not press the matter. My position on this issue runs counter to the prevailing one—and even if it didn't it would require explanation. Many therapists regard it as essential to explore and analyze their patient's therapeutic goals during the early stage of treatment. My disagreement is only over the timing of this exploration and analysis—I see no merit in doing it very early. Moreover, I believe that if it is done too early, then the achievement will be superficial if not meaningless (or worse). I regard the Middle stage of therapy—particularly the transition between the Beginning and the Middle—to be the best time to do this work. For it is usually then, and not before, that both you and the patient will have sufficient information and understanding to deal sensibly with these most difficult and ambiguous of questions.

* * * * * * *

Now to the question of what and how much a patient should be told about the way the therapy will proceed—its structure and its form. First of all, The Basic Instruction notifies him about the basic form of *Psychotherapy.* Let me remind you that it is important to give the instruction as close to the outset as possible.

A second notification that is important to give at the outset is that he will receive no advice, no counsel, and no direction from you. So important is this that I recommend you be especially alert to the smallest opportunity to give it during the first session, and if none presents itself, I advise simply saying it cold to your patient before the session ends—"I want you to know that I intend to give you no advice or direction; I will avoid telling you what to do or how to decide, either here in the therapy or outside of it." It's usually unnecessary to add the rationale, and I recommend doing so only if he reacts with perplexity or asks, "Why not?" If that happens I recommend as simple an answer as possible—for example, "Because the main way I can be helpful to you is to help you understand yourself; understand your feelings, your actions, and your experiences. If I were to tell you what to do, then that would interfere with my ability to help you understand." If he should persist and want to know why advice would interfere, you can simply say that in your experience it often does. This will usually suffice at the beginning; but the matter typically comes up again later on, and then it may require additional explanation.

Next, I suggest you be alert for an opportunity to tell your patient that you will not evaluate or judge him in any way. Again, the rationale is much the same—it would not be helpful and might hinder the Understanding process. But this is an issue which will reappear in many forms and at many times. A patient may readily accept the fact that his therapist will give him no advice and will remain impersonal, but evaluation is quite different. And so don't assume for a moment that he will really believe you when you tell him you won't judge his actions and evaluate his experiences—he will continue to hear judgments from you and to need and also fear them—and this is an issue that usually persists for a long time in *Psychotherapy*.

* * * * * *

This letter is also persisting for a long time. There's more to be written about the Beginning, but the hour has grown late and I weary. I'll have to postpone it for another day. I look forward eagerly to your reactions and questions to what I have so far written about the Beginning.

Your affectionate uncle

Eighteen

Dear Simon,

The Talmudic form invites the *What-if?*—that's why it begets commentaries on its commentaries. But the four you put to me in reply to my last letter are fine ones, and I'll try to answer them.

What-if? 1.—"What if he asks me whether I'm a student at doing therapy? Does that count as a credential?" Yes, I think so. That fact is bound to play a significant part in the Transference, both Real and otherwise; it will serve as a handy focus for Resistance; and it is also likely to be a sore spot for you—an issue over which you will feel vulnerable. Our patients can be adroit at locating and exploiting our sore spots, whatever they may be. But the fact that you are a student at it does not mean that the therapy will be second-rate or trial-and-error. Your patient will likely need to believe this, but you should be convinced that you can serve him well even under these conditions. You won't have going for you what I have going for me—the element of faith (magic?) that is evoked by my professional status—but you will have a supervisor behind you and a clinic around you, and that will count for something. Above all, you'll have to struggle with feelings of defensiveness when he accuses you of not knowing what you're doing. It may help you to know, Simon, that I too get my share of such accusations.

Being a student entails needing your patient to serve your learning purposes, and this need has to put its special stamp on the treatment. There's a body of opinion that this places a serious limitation on the possibility of therapeutic effectiveness (the same body of opinion makes this claim for so-called didactic analysis too). But it can be argued that this need is no different in principle from a therapist's need for the fee, for in both cases there is a tangible way in which he is paid something economically useful. Bear in mind that I need my patient not only for financial reasons but also to serve my professional needs. There may be a difference in degree but not in kind in the fact that you will need him to fulfil your learning needs. It's quite true, however, that when my patient misses a session I have less need to feel any personal loss than you will have—after all, you have a supervisor waiting to discuss the contents of the sessions, and I don't. It's a safe assumption that your patient will know this; and he may try to use it against you in a variety of ways.

What-if? 2.—"What if the question of confidentiality is raised by my patient? Or shoud I be the one who raises it?" This question does often come up at the beginning, and it's not so simple a matter as it may seem to be. Many therapists promise confidentiality explicitly and most patients assume it implicitly, but it is only the rare therapy that remains completely confidential, even when it's conducted under private auspices. We therapists discuss our patients with colleagues as well as with supervisors, we present them in papers and conferences, and some of us even discuss them with our spouses. So confidentiality on our part is usually only relative and subject to our professional judgment.

Then there's the question of confidentiality on the part of our patients, which is not unrelated to the underlying theme. Most patients feel free to discuss their therapy experiences with friends and family. This is sometimes done to dissipate some of the tension that therapy induces, and sometimes it can assume the proportions of a Resistance. Still, it has to be approached in the same way that any Resistance is—by analysis and not by proscription. Moreover, you should take the same approach to the patient who most scrupulously avoids sharing any of his therapy experiences with others. That too can signal an underlying Transference fantasy worth analyzing.

For these reasons, Simon, I do not recommend that you raise the matter of confidentiality; and if your patient raises it, I recommend a thorough exploration of the matter with him before you offer any promise (i.e., that you'll use your best professional judgment to protect the confidentiality of the therapy). I suggest you accept the working hypothesis that behind this question there lurks a variety of important fantasies that will shape the Transference toward you and the therapy. It's vital to analyze these fantasies as early as possible.

What-if? 3.—"What if my patient, at the very outset, enunciates a clear set of goals, and he goes further by saying that he will consider termination only when these goals have been achieved?" Putting aside for the moment your further question of whether they are realistic or sensible goals, let's consider the position into which you are placed. If you agree with him, either overtly or tacitly, then you have made an important promise—and you must be prepared to keep it. It will be a serious lapse of integrity for you later to contend that you made no such promise, unless you take special pains to make it clear at the outset that you were listening with interest to his expectations and goals but not accepting them as your own too. And that, I believe, will be the most prudent position for you to take.

Do I contend, as I also seem to have in my last letter, that you must make him no promises concerning goals and achievements? And does this also mean that you must avoid making such formulations for yourself? If so, then I'm taking a position that flies in the face of common clinical practice. (You will often be asked by your supervisor, early in the treatment, "What are your treatment goals?") So let me remind you, Simon, that it's about a particular form of psychotherapy that I am writing. This form has a set of fundamental goals about which I have already written you a good deal. My position does not pertain to short-term therapy, or to problem-centered therapy, or symptom-removal treatment. The principal goal of *Psychotherapy* is not the eradication of this or that symptom or the alteration of this or that behavior pattern; it is that a patient experience the full Therapeutic Process with Analytic Experiences. Moreover, *Psychotherapy's* basic hypothesis is that it is from this process and these experiences that whatever eradications and alterations occur will stem. This means that we do not take the latter events as proximate goals; in that sense, you may not make the kinds of promises we are considering.

Can you, on the other hand, share with him our conception of *Psychotherapy's* goals? Should you apprise him about the notion of Freedom, of Ego Autonomy? They are already implied in The Basic Instruction, but the question here is whether they should be directly and fully articulated. My answer is: you can if you want to, but I don't think you should want to. Why not? Because in most instances you'd be engaging in little more than an intellectual discussion about psychological freedom and Ego Autonomy that might even perplex your patient. Soon I will spell out to you a number of items of information about *Psychotherapy's* form and structure that you must be prepared to share with him, but the underlying process is one that emerges with the doing. It can be articulated by you from time to time as it happens, but that's different from explaining it beforehand.

Now I'll return to your further question: "What if my patient enunciates a clear set of goals, and what if they are unrealistic?" Let's suppose he says, "I want to become an altogether different person than I am," and he goes on to specify that this means changing from an inhibited to an uninhibited person, from a withdrawn to an outgoing one, from an insecure and timid to a confident and bold one, or something of the sort. If so, you must deal with the matter, and may have to convey to him that you don't share his optimism. You may also have to tell him that you believe such goals to be unrealistic. Anything short of this, you see, would imply a degree of acceptance which would amount to a promise that may be broken.

It's a touchy matter, this. The simplest way to approach it is to avoid the promise of "cure" or of radical personality changes. Not that such events never occur—trust me, Simon, they do—but it's quite another matter to promise them. The most you can promise is the probability of important changes that are achieved only gradually. You can accept the working hypothesis that the therapy will work—how could you accept anything less?—but also the hypothesis that its achievements are likely to be both gradual and subtle. And when your patient asks, you can tell him that. Bear in mind, Simon, that few people will seek psychotherapy if they are not convinced that it might be effective for them. Moreover, when you embark on the treatment you are clearly implying that you believe it too. So there's little harm in letting the matter stay tacit. Such silence, however, is no longer appropriate when your patient articulates his goals (or clearly implies them) and you have some question about their realistic chances.

One important and commonly encountered instance is when a patient is suffering from a particular symptom—he stutters, let us say, or has a phobia—and his avowed purpose for seeking therapy is to gain relief from that symptom. Twenty years ago you would have had little choice but to proceed with the traditional methods, but today you have a real choice. There are specialized methods for the amelioration of certain kinds of symptoms, and they are radically different from *Psychotherapy*. Besides, even if you are convinced that this patient can benefit from *Psychotherapy*, it is little short of unethical for you to proceed in disregard of his motivation and the fact that he stands to benefit from an altogether different treatment that may be more economical. You must therefore inform him of these alternate forms, explain to him what they involve, and—unless you happen to be qualified to conduct such treatment—make an appropriate referral. We have the obligation, you see, to be abreast of new developments in the field, and to be ready to judge the appropriateness of this or any form of treatment. As I've already written, the initial sessions should be used to determine whether your patient is a suitable candidate for *Psychotherapy*. If you have doubts—whether or not they are based on his motivation for treatment—you should not only be prepared to modify your methods but also to refer him to another therapist for consultation, for another form of therapy, or both.

What-if? 4.—"What if, after I've given him The Basic Instruction, my patient launches into a seamless account of his day-to-day experiences or his past life, or of both? What if he speaks in a steady flow, and he continues this way session after session? Consequently, I will find myself sitting in silence without having the chance to say anything. How long shall I permit this to go on?"

I take it you expect to find yourself dreading the inevitable moment when he stops, looks you squarely in the eye, and says in effect, "What's going on here?" "Is this a treatment?" he asks; "But you are doing nothing!" he charges. And if you respond, "I am listening," he may simply wonder aloud, "What good is *that* going to do me?"

First, let me admonish you, Simon, that this not uncommon course of events is to be regarded neither with contempt nor with worry. When it happens to you, it will be encumbent upon you to endure your enforced silence with equanimity. If it helps you, you can think to yourself, "I wonder how long he can keep this up before he complains about my nonparticipation." And you can also prepare yourself for that moment by figuring out what he has in mind about the therapy. Is he apprehensive lest you say something that will hurt him? Does he believe that eventually you will deliver to him a curative Interpretation or diagnosis? Does he expect you to begin the therapy proper when you have judged that he has told you enough? (shades of *Portnoy's Complaint*)—in other words, what's going on?

So you stay alert for clues, you observe and strive for Understanding, but you continue to listen in silence, and you will not take action unless and until your patient requires it of you. When the moment of truth arrives, as it typically will, you must navigate some perilous waters. To be avoided at all costs is a reaction of defensiveness and criticism on your part—"But you haven't given me a chance to say anything!" is an entirely unacceptable kind of response for you to make. You shouldn't even think that way. You must try your utmost to maintain an empathic and sympathetic attitude, and it can help if you acknowledge to yourself that his feelings are justified—after all, how should he know "what good this is going to do me"? That *Psychotherapy* will be efficacious is your belief; he doesn't even know what the method entails, much less how it actually works. At worst, you will find yourself in the position of having to explain the method (which is different from defending it)—for example, "I can appreciate that you are puzzled about what's going on, because you have been doing all the talking and I have been largely silent. All I can promise you is that, as we proceed, I will find opportunities to say things that might be useful. And I can also say that I believe this kind of therapy will be good for you."

Now, having remained empathic and undefensive, you may want to point out to him that it was he who structured the beginning sessions. He chose to recount his life's story or to tell you about his day to day life; he also chose to do it in a way that precluded your participation. At some level, you see, you can proceed on the working hypothesis that he knew what he was doing. He may object that he didn't—that he believed simply that that was the appropriate thing to do, that it was what he thought you expected—and you must avoid challenging this objection. Still, you may be able to suggest to him that he also enjoyed doing it the way he did, that recounting things to you gave him some satisfaction.

For all this to happen this way it is necessary that you experience no misgivings—that you not suffer his beginning sessions in anxious silence. (As a matter of fact, you must be prepared to suffer entire sessions of relative silence free from guilt or apprehension.) That your nonparticipation will sooner or later be held against you is something that you can not only expect but might even welcome—for it may well provide a valuable opportunity for some important therapeutic work.

* * * * * * *

So much for *What-if's*. I'll continue with the Beginning stage by enumerating and discussing the themes and concerns that are common to patients during it. In this way I can serve two aims: to familiarize you with the expectable themes and concerns, and to offer suggestions on how to deal with them. Before that, a brief editorial.

I present the expectable themes with some trepidation. I believe that we are at an advantage when we are familiar with them—for if we are alert to the expectable, we will more readily hear and Understand. At the same time, however, there is the danger of overalertness and of being too far ahead of our patient. We can err in our perception when it is based too much on our expectations (as well as on our theory) or, if not err outright, be premature in our Interpretations. I may have occasion to discuss this problem in another letter, but I will proceed, as usual, on the assumption that the advantages of knowing outweigh the disadvantages.

The expectable themes fall roughly into two interdependent groups: those having to do with a patient's conception of how *Psychotherapy* works, and those having to do with the meanings of being a patient in psychotherapy. I'll start with those I regard as the simplest and/or most commonly encountered and work my way up.

Theme 1.

"Once you (the therapist) have all the facts you will proceed to straighten me out."

This misconception—frequently it's a wishful fantasy—is practically universal, even to be detected in the sophisticated patient who "knows better." Moreover, it can also be with considerable dread that he anticipates that you'll eventually deliver to him a full-blown analysis and explanation of his problems. The underlying need here is usually a passive-receptive one, and that need will generally recur periodically during the course of the therapy. Still, this is an issue that I recommend you deal with directly at the outset, or as soon as it comes up. Since it involves a conception of how you will operate, I believe you have the obligation to establish its mistakenness. Therefore, when your patient first acknowledges the expectation, you may tell him quite simply that you don't intend to do it. The reason for stating it directly is twofold: (1) the theme can be expected to recur, and when it does it will be easier to deal with the underlying fantasy if it was already established that it's unrealistic; (2) it could, after all, be true—so why not establish the fact right away?

Theme 2.

"I am in for some rude shocks and painful surprises."

Many patients expect that we will tell them the worst and confirm their most dreaded judgments about themselves—that they are cruel, selfish, unworthy, perverted, and the like. Their apprehension at being shocked and hurt by our analysis of them may lend an undercurrent of anxiety and worry that is quite extraneous and unhelpful. Sometimes, of course, it is anything but extraneous insofar as it reflects a central dynamic of their self-image. Nevertheless, it's generally helpful to such patients to tell them directly that you intend to try not to shock and surprise them unduly. Many will continue nonetheless to anticipate the worst, but the shock and surprise aspects of their apprehension will be more readily understood as an intrapsychic matter.

Theme 3.

"So I can't do it myself after all."

For many patients being in therapy is an admission of defeat. Some, even while they may view it as a way to overcome their difficulties, enter therapy with a sense of deep resignation. For some there is an element of shame, since to need it in the first place is to be weak and unable to take care of oneself. Now, the fact that we make it clear from the start we will give no counsel or support can go far toward protecting his sense of self-reliance. But the fact that he needs treatment will remain, and that can be a lingering sore spot. In my experience, this theme must be thoroughly worked through if *Psychotherapy* is to proceed effectively. At times it may be necessary to challenge a patient's overweening emphasis on the value of self-reliance, as if any neediness were a sign of weakness, unmanliness, or whatever. Sometimes this can go right to the core of his problems with respect to his self-image and interpersonal relations.

Theme 4.

"Being in psychotherapy means that I am crazy."

Many of us harbor a secret fear that we don't think and experience things like everybody else does, or that we are really crazy underneath. This idea is likely to run quite deep, so even when it is discussed during the Beginning you can expect it to recur in force during the subsequent stages. Some patients have the fear that treatment will not only expose their craziness, but will result in their becoming overtly crazy. Many give expression to the fear by asking, directly or indirectly, "How abnormal are my problems?" In fact, it's quite typical for patients to seek our professional evaluation of the severity of their psychopathology. They will contend that it is a kind of judgment or evaluation that's quite different from what we said we would not be making—it's a professional opinion, like a medical diagnosis—and this puts us into a delicate and difficult position. In my experience, this can be a most troublesome question to deal with, and the ordinary deflections (based on the rationale that opinions and judgments will hinder Understanding rather than promote it) may not altogether apply to it. Still, my first inclination is to see whether a simple deflection, combined with an appropriate Interpretation, may not suffice. Sometimes the question can be reinterpreted for him as follows: "I believe you are asking me whether your problems (with sex, or obsessional thoughts, or paranoid ideas, etc.) are hopeless, whether there is reason to believe that therapy can resolve them." If his response is, "Yes—so what do you think?" I may answer, "It's always difficult to be altogether sure about these matters, but I do believe there is a good chance that therapy can help." As

with all questions, the underlying concerns and fears and
fantasies must be exposed and subjected to as much analysis as possible before the reassurance—which may ultimately
be unavoidable—is offered.

Theme 5.

"Therapy will make me ordinary—like everybody else."
This one is part of a more general theme having to do
with the unwanted changes that therapy will wring as a side
effect. The artist, for example, may fear the loss of his exhi-
bitionism or ambitiousness. It's often useful to focus on this
theme early in therapy; typically, simply acknowledging the
fear (i.e., informing him that you are aware of it) has the
effect of diminishing it. Whether or not the fear is realistic
cannot be very readily judged, but it is safe to say that it's
generally exaggerated.

Theme 6.

"Does therapy work?"
It's prudent to assume that every patient, no matter how
well motivated and how urgently felt his problems, will
harbor doubts about the efficacy of psychotherapy. Most
directly this will take the form of, "Is this therapy worth it?"
Such a question can, of course, only be acknowledged by
you. It's only the rare patient who will require a defense of
the enterprise. Bear in mind that the appropriate time to
weigh this question is before initiating a contact with you.
So if your patient becomes preoccupied with it some time
after the therapy has begun, he's probably using it in the
service of Resistance.

Theme 7.

"Can I really trust you?"
This can be a most complicated question, reflecting and

concealing a variety of concerns and fantasies. What it means to a patient that you should be trustworthy and dependable can rarely be said in advance. "Trust" in what sense? "Depend upon" how? Sometimes it means little more than to know what you're doing, to be competent and sensitive: "Do you have sufficient experience?" "Do you know what to expect here?" "Do you understand people like me?" But often it means a great deal more. We can usually predict the nature of the coming Transference from the form of such a question at the Beginning. Sometimes it's synonymous with the larger abiding question, "Do you really care?"; and here too the meanings are various and run deep. During the Beginning you can really do little more than make sure the issue becomes explicit. In my experience these kinds of questions usually come up in force during the Middle stage when the major impasses and Resistances occur. In any case, it's important for you to know the ways in which you are trustworthy and dependable; and it's essential that you have a clear conception of the way in which you Care.

Your affectionate uncle

Nineteen

Dear Simon,

There's an eighth theme that belonged in the last letter, but I decided against including it there because my discussion of it must range beyond the focus of the Beginning. As you will soon see, it merits a letter to itself.

Theme 8.

"This kind of therapy is not for me."

That *Psychotherapy* is not appropriate for every patient, and that the judgment must be made in every case, I have already written you about. Here I want to consider the circumstances that arise when your patient makes that judgment, and says in effect, "I don't think this therapy is right for me."

Everyone who enters it comes with ideas about what he needs both from and in the therapy, and he also has ideas about how he wants his therapist to relate to him. Add to this the fact that it's the unusual prospective patient who hasn't gathered information about what he should expect. Our typical patient expects either a silent "uhuh-er," or an implacable taskmaster, or an elicitor of deep emotions and dreadful impulses, or a benevolent inquisitor. It's a safe bet that his expectations and ideas are composed of information, attitudes, anxious anticipations, conflicts, and wishful fantasies; but it is the rare patient who comes expecting and wanting *Psychotherapy* as I am describing it to you. So it will be far from uncommon that your patient balks at one or another aspect of the method. While the same can be said for any form of treatment, it may be that *Psychotherapy* provides him with more to balk about.

When you begin with a patient for whom you judge the method to be appropriate, you can expect to encounter some resistance to its conditions and structure. Your central problem is how to deal with such resistance while remaining within the method. When your patient protests, "This kind of therapy is not for me," you can hardly respond with, "Yes, it is so," without thereby deviating significantly from the method itself. Nor can you simply advise him to give it a try. So your problem—your dilemma—becomes how to advocate *Psychotherapy* while still adhering to its principles that proscribe advice, advocacy, and imposition.

Now, lest I make a caricature of the matter, let me acknowledge that advocacy as well as advice need not be overt and explicit in order to be operative. A patient may legitimately assume that you know what you're doing. So when you make it clear that you're working within a method, he may simply take it that you're advocating that method. In this real sense, then, when you give The Basic Instruction and all the rest, you are saying, "This kind of therapy will be good for you." The issue I want to consider in this letter arises when he responds—either explicitly or implicitly, and either right away or later on in the Beginning—"No, I don't think so." Most frequently this takes the following forms:

Form 1. "I can't just talk and talk without getting more response or more feedback from you. I need for you to talk to me also, to converse with me, to ask me questions, and to make more comments about what I am telling you. It's too unnatural this way."

Form 2. "I need for you to be more actively involved in my life, to tell me what to do and not to do. After all, I came because I cannot manage my life any more. And it's not enough that you will help me find out why I cannot. I need more direct help from you also."

Form 3. "I can't do it this way, with you never showing me how you feel about me. I need your emotional support. I need you to be like a real friend or a real parent to me. That's what I expected you would be, and that's why I'm coming [and paying]."

So what are you to do now? If it occurs after sufficient therapy time has been logged you may still be able to deal with it by the Interpretive mode. But it often occurs too early in the therapy for that, and even if not, it may take on the proportions of a full-blown impasse against which the Interpretive mode can be ineffectual. Your patient may be serving notice that he's unwilling to continue so long as the method, or some aspect of it, is maintained. This puts you in a serious bind—the most serious of all binds—for it threatens a central condition of treatment—namely, that it continue. Since it's a strange victory to have maintained therapeutic purity and to have lost the patient, your temptation will be strong to abandon the method (at least temporarily) in order to save the therapy.

Now, it may be facile to say it first, but let me say it anyhow: It's poor practice to give in to temptation too easily. Experience has taught us that the threat to quit can often be treated as only that—a threat—and that when a patient insists he can't do it, he can so. Okay, having gotten that off my chest let me face up to the problem when it is a real one, for there are also times when the resistance to the method will lead him to quit.

To lose a patient (as the expression goes) is usually cause for some regret and misgiving. It's rare, even for those of us with experience, to dismiss the matter with a shrug and an "It's just as well." Such experiences almost inevitably cause us to embark on a critical review and to ask that most troubling and difficult of all questions, "What did I do wrong?" And even if we cannot find a direct answer, if we can think of nothing we did that may have been an error and a precipitating factor, we will ask ourselves whether there was something we failed to do that might have prevented it. Since such questions can rarely be answered with much assurance, doubts and misgivings will usually linger on. We may be able to accept them with equanimity—after all, we live with them daily in our work (a high degree of tolerance for uncertainty, if not ambiguity, is mandatory for us)—and if we lose only one patient in ten, say, then we may accept that kind of batting average without our faith being shaken either in psychotherapy in general or *Psychotherapy* in particular.

We may want to review the case for what it may teach us about prospective patients' suitability for working with us and our methods, but, since quitting is irrevocable, it calls for no particular action on our part.

But it's quite a different matter when a patient has not quit and is threatening to do so. Now we are still in a position to avoid losing him, and our deliberations are more urgent. Now we must carefully weigh the pros and cons of instituting modifications, and the relevant question has two parts: (1) "If I resist making any changes will he quit?" and (2) "If I make them, and he does not quit, will therapy be effective?" The answers can be based on little more than clinical judgment combined, perhaps, with a measure of faith and conviction.

Probably the toughest decision a therapist has to make is one on which the very existence of the therapy depends. Unfortunately, there are often a number of influential factors that are unrelated to his patient's welfare, and instead have to do with his own personal and professional circumstances. A student therapist, for instance, may dread losing a patient because it might reflect badly on his performance; an independent one may dread it because it will reduce his practice and income. Ideally, of course, these kinds of considerations ought to play no part at all—only the patient's well-being should count—but for them to really play no part requires of us a capacity for honest self-confrontation and integrity. We must be ready to acknowledge that sometimes the necessary modifications are so basic that it is truly in the patient's best interests to quit (or to be referred), for to continue under the modified conditions might be futile if not detrimental. But sometimes, of course, that decision is unwarranted.

Real resistances (with a small "r") to *Psychotherapy* will occur in patients who are otherwise suited for it. Some aspect of the method may be an unsurmountable hurdle because of some idiosyncracy of character, some particular life experience, or some aspect of the neurosis. Such resistances must often be met—temporarily at least—with accession and accommodation. Some are easier to accede to than others. It is relatively easy to ask more questions, to take a supportive attitude, to make more "I understand" comments, and even to show some emotional responsiveness. It may also be possible, in certain cases, to offer some advice and counsel. All of this you should be prepared to do—if you feel you have to. There are, of course, things you should not be prepared to do (such as giving sexual gratification), but these are matters of professional judgment, and I'm sure its unnecessary to try and list for you the things that are proscribed in all cases.

The point I want to emphasize is this: no one of us should feel such a strong commitment to any method or system that he is never prepared to modify it if, in his best judgment, the therapy depends on it. Lest I seem to be doing little more than defending virtue (i.e., flexibility and balance in all things), there is another issue here that I have in mind. Many therapists feel it's a mistake to let their patient "manipulate" them, and it's around the issue of manipulation, not flexibility, that the matter is construed. One can sometimes detect an undercurrent of Countertransference, if not moral indignation, in a therapist's insistence that he will not let himself be manipulated by his patient; and the reflective one should pose for himself the challenge, "Why not?" Is his patient's well-being the paramount consideration, or is he instead protecting his own self-image? The answer to these difficult questions will determine his response to the complaint, "This kind of therapy is not for me."

So let's consider the three forms of modification that our resisting patient has asked for: greater involvement in the therapy (conversation and interrogation), greater involvement in his life (counsel and criticism), and greater emotional support (feelings and warmth). They are, to a significant extent at least, interrelated, so that any one of them must necessarily entail the other two. For instance, when you choose to counsel him (either because he asked you to or because you deem that it is clinically indicated), you will probably find it necessary to do more interrogating and probing and also to make more comments. Chances are that you will need to show your emotional reactions as well. The same is true, though perhaps to a lesser extent, when it is one of the other modifications that is called for. I believe, you see, that all aspects of *Psychotherapy* are of a piece, so changing any one of them will likely require some changes in all others.

The first question that arises when a modification has been instituted is whether it should be regarded as temporary. I believe that—as a working hypothesis at least—it should. This means that I will strive to move back from it to my original position. If this retreat is made gradually and with all due regard for my patient's development, then it may go unnoticed. But even if it shows, and he remarks (or complains) about it, I can explain that my shift is based on the judgment that he doesn't need the modification as much as he used to. Moreover, the timing of his renewed complaint can be instructive. If he noticed the shift at a time when he was dealing with difficult or conflictful material, then I have an opportunity to draw a useful connection between them. Occasionally it will be possible to discover the basis of his need for the modification—to learn what its meaning and function are—by observing at what point he comes to feel it most acutely. It may be, for example, when he is feeling angry that he cannot bear my neutrality, or when he is feeling sexually aroused that he needs to feel close to me, or when he becomes involved in a friendship outside of the therapy that he has the need for my counsel and guidance.

The second question that arises has to do with the fact that my patient has exerted a significant influence on my behavior. That is bound to have a variety of important consequences, some of them reaching deep into his personality. The fact that he has moved me—has experienced a real power over me—will constitute, according to some orthodox analysts, a fatal flaw in the therapy. That it can be serious, I agree; that it's necessarily fatal, I don't. I don't deny that my acquiescence will probably play a most significant role in the Transference, and I admit further that, insofar as it constitutes a Real event, it can render that Transference less amenable to analysis and resolution. This is the point, you see, that provides the main rationale for avoiding any "manipulation."

I have little choice now but to take up with you, Simon, the commonly held hypothesis that any component of the Transference which is based on Reality will be unanalyzable. (And the same I should mention, applies to Resistance.) This hypothesis is based on two interlocking assumptions: (1) the locus for analysis is the patient's Inner Reality; and (2) the entire Transference must be a product of that Inner Reality—it's a whole cloth that must be woven out of pure projection (and you will recognize this as the basis of the so-called "blank screen" formulation of the Transference). Why is this important? Because it's in the weaving and unraveling of that fabric, the formation and the resolution of the Transference Neurosis, that the patient secures a most profound kind of emotional Understanding into the workings of his Inner Reality. Any real strand is a foreign element, and insofar as it is an element of Outer Reality (an artificial one to boot, inasmuch as the therapy is artificial) it cannot be subjected to the same kind of profound Understanding. Now, this is a position that I fully subscribe to—it's a hypothesis that I have seen at work, and it is a powerful one. At the same time, however, I believe it has to be regarded as a theoretical state of affairs—as an ideal that is never to be fully attained in actuality.

After all, isn't it entirely unrealistic to expect that no real events of any consequences will occur in the relationship between a therapist and his patient? Furthermore, isn't it to be taken for granted that not every issue that arises in a treatment will be equally amenable to analytic resolution? So while it may be quite true that a real event (i.e., a product of a patient's Outer Reality) is not analyzable in the same way and to the same extent as an unreal one (a product of his Inner Reality), it does not follow that it's necessarily such a serious mistake to allow such events to transpire in a therapy. We can try to keep them at a minimum, yes, but we can hardly hope to eliminate them entirely.

Consider the question, "Is it ever possible to achieve a Transference that is made up entirely of projections?" I have no doubt that the answer is, "No, of course not." Each of us, after all, is a person with very real characteristics which must influence and shape the Transference even as the patient's Inner Reality does. There are bound to be important points of intersection between his need to project and our own real characteristics, and the problem can become acute when there happens to be a major coincidence between them. Imagine, for example, a patient who needs to project onto me the image of the wise and kindly father figure. If I happen to be youthful looking and not particularly wise in appearance, then the projection will have a better chance of being clearly discerned and therefore better analyzed. But what if I happen to be a wise and fatherly looking man? My patient will find it harder to accept that it is the working of projection rather than my actual appearance and manner. Every therapist should know what his properties are as a stimulus (which is a poor way to put it, but I promise to improve it later on). The fact remains, however, that there are certain ones over which he can have little if any control.

So the fact that our modifications in method introduce properties over which we do have control does not by itself make the critical difference. We will simply have to take them into account in the same way that we take the others. Bear in mind that if I decide to change from a position of relative passivity to one of relative activity, it is not as if I will be doing something I could not have done in the first place. My patient will know that I had chosen to remain passive by design; and if I have reason to suspect that he doesn't know it, I must in any case draw his attention to the fact. It will not be uncommon, Simon, for your patient to perceive your therapeutic posture as belonging to your personality structure. When that happens you must subject the perception to appropriate Interpretations.

So—while it is true that modifications introduce fresh problems in a therapy, these problems are not essentially different from those that may occur in the natural course of events. On the one hand, the best of therapies will contain issues that remain unanalyzed and unresolved; on the other hand, it is overstating the matter to claim that Real events are entirely recalcitrant to analysis and resolution. It is probably—like everything else—a matter of degree. In any and all events, extreme positions (as I once wrote you) are best avoided when you're involved in something so complex as psychotherapy with a fellow human being.

Your affectionate uncle

Twenty

Dear Simon,

When I wrote several letters ago that your personal attributes—your attitudes, your values, your style of life, and the rest—don't have to matter when you do *Psychotherapy*, I thought to myself that you would surely object to this claim. But I was wrong; you questioned it just, and quite mildly too. (I hope you're not merely being "tactful" with me!) The reason I recall it now is because I'm sitting down to write you about *the therapist*.

The therapist—his many and diverse psychological problems, his personal characteristics, the role and function of his needs and emotions, Countertransference feelings, his appraisal of reality and the limitations that the method imposes on his knowledge of his patient's reality—these are the subjects I'll now take up. I won't try to be systematic, Simon; instead I'll indulge my propensity to skip from one topic to another. I've noticed a tendency to go to a topic I regard as easy after I've been into one that's difficult, and vice versa. This habit entails some repetitiousness; I apologize for it. I'll begin now with a difficult one.

* * * * * * *

Just as the physician need not be healthier than his patient and the piano teacher need not be a better pianist than his pupil, so the psychotherapist need not be a better person than his patient—at least, not the one who is conducting *Psychotherapy*. The patient can be smarter, better informed, more emotional, and even better adapted to his reality and more successful in life. None of this need prevent the therapy from being completely effective—so long as the therapist is expert at his craft. Of course, just as the physician must know more than merely how to administer medical treatments (it helps if he knows some physiology, some biochemistry, and the like) and the piano teacher must know music and what it is to play the piano, so a therapist must be more than just an authority on psychotherapy—he has to know something about living, about psychology. But I want to draw the distinction here between knowing and doing—between knowing what the good life is and living such a life. My point is that, within rather wide limits, the quality of his personal life may be substantially unrelated to his skill and effectiveness as a therapist.

There's a commonly encountered characteristic of therapists that is reprehensible. It's the smug, complacent, and conceitful presumption that because he's a psychotherapist he knows best how to live right; he knows how to relate to family and friends, how to enjoy and fulfil himself—in short, he's a superior person. Now, certain professions do mandate a life style. The priest (and I choose this example deliberately) is expected to behave in a priestly way across a wide variety of life situations; he must be a priestly person. But the same is not true of the therapist. There is, however, a big caveat. He must have sufficient control over his personality difficulties and over his mundane problems so that they don't impinge on his work. That he does have conflicts, difficulties, and problems is not the critical fact; that he can keep them from impairing his work is. In the final analysis, this requires a particular judgment in each case. It's difficult, if not hazardous, to look for any general propositions that can be applied across the board.

Still, some general propositions can be hazarded (again, within the context of *Psychotherapy*) that may be useful at least as guidelines. They revolve around two interrelated questions: (1) Are there kinds of conflicts and problems which are more likely to interfere with his effectiveness than others? (2) Are there certain personality traits which will facilitate the work? Both of these questions can be answered with a qualified Yes.

I'll start with the second, because many of the features of *Psychotherapy* that I've already covered have clear implications for the therapist's personality. For one thing, he must be capable of Understanding, and that requires a well developed psychological-mindedness. For another, the ability to empathize is obviously required, and so is the ability to examine his own Mind and Heart and to face the fruits of such examination. Then the requirements of Tact, of warmth, and of Caring have implications that I needn't spell out. And finally, I already wrote how *Psychotherapy* requires of us to be good listeners. That entails a kind of controlled and disciplined passivity. So the therapist must be a person who is comfortable in the passive position. To all of this let me here add a new ingredient: integrity.

This may strike you as sanctimonious, Simon, but I believe a therapist must have great integrity. His dealings with his patients should be honest, in all the common senses of the term. He has to be reliable and trustworthy. His patients must develop Basic Trust in him, and this is built up through a variety of real experiences ranging from such matters as keeping appointments, living up to promises, and giving adequate warning whenever possible of pending cancellations, to admitting errors, apologizing for unintended actions, and acknowledging forgetfulness. Above all, the hallmark of his integrity lies in the extent to which he values his patients' well-being—and, if there's any single way to promote that well-being, surely it's in building the Basic Trust without which psychotherapy cannot be effective. Without integrity there can be little trust.

In case it seems to you there may be a contradiction between the requirements of integrity and *Psychotherapy's* requirements of impersonality, neutrality, and the rest, let me claim that there isn't. Honesty does not entail saying everything one thinks or admitting to one's judgments and feelings. To withhold the truth is no dishonesty, and when it serves a patient's well-being it is anything but a lapse of integrity. It's one thing to answer "No" when a patient asks you, "Are you feeling angry with me?" and another to answer, "I don't believe it is in your best interest for me to answer that question." If you are in fact feeling angry, the first answer is a lie; the second answer's truth value can be independent of whether you are angry or not. And whenever it comes down to a choice between lying and violating any of the principles of the method, then the choice is clear.

Suppose, for example, that you are momentarily distracted by your own thoughts during a session, and suppose your patient discerns that fact and asks, "Are you paying attention? I had the feeling just then that you were thinking about something else." This can be an occasion to make your integrity actual to him, and it may provide an occasion for some useful analytic work as well. You may respond, "Yes, your feeling is accurate. I was momentarily distracted by my own thoughts." If he continues by saying, "I guess I must be boring you," then you can respond, "But I didn't feel bored. Do you notice how your first impulse is to take all the blame on yourself for what was a transgression on my part?"

Or suppose you just made an Interpretation in a defensive way, and he responds with, "Boy, you sound real defensive there!" There can be little to lose and much to gain by acknowledging the accuracy of his perception—"Yes, I guess I did." Moreover, you may now choose to provide him with a model for the analytic method by thinking aloud why you had the need to be defensive—e.g., "I wonder why I felt defensive; perhaps I identified with your mother and experienced some of the force of your attack on her." Or else you can wait to see how he reacts to your admission and to your defensiveness. He may, for example, react with apprehension—"That frightens me a bit. I did actually mean to attack you, so I wonder why it scares me when I succeed." In any case, it is usually possible to maintain the therapeutic work and still maintain your integrity (two birds with one stone).

Forgetfulness is bound to occur occasionally. To assume that it's always on the part of your patient can be a serious mistake. Imagine the following circumstance:

[PATIENT:] I will pay the bill next session, on Wednesday.

[YOU:] Wednesday? But the next session is Monday.

[PATIENT:] I can't come on Monday because I have the English exam. I told you that last week. Don't you remember?

[YOU:] No, I don't.

[PATIENT:] Perhaps then I didn't tell you. But I'm sure I did. That's strange [falls silent].

[YOU:] Strange?

[PATIENT:] It feels strange that I am so sure I told you and yet you don't remember. So maybe I didn't tell you.

[YOU:] The possibility that you did tell me but that I am the one who forgot is a painful possibility, isn't it? That makes you feel strange.

[PATIENT:] The feeling is all mixed up. I guess that's because there's some anger at you in it . . . ."

Suppose that during this exchange you recall that he did in fact notify you of the pending cancellation. You must now avoid protecting your image at his expense. You must bear in mind that *Psychotherapy* at no point is benefited by your projecting an image of infallibility and omniscience. In fact, when your patient perceives you to be that, it can be understood as projection (most typically it is the projection of and idealized Superego figure) which typically serves a defensive function. Furthermore, *Psychotherapy* is enormously benefited by your projecting integrity and honesty, for those are the hallmarks of the therapeutic enterprise. You must therefore find an opportunity to admit to your forgetfulness and at the same time use the opportunity to your patient's advantage. Ordinarily, that can be readily achieved.

* * * * * * *

Now to the first question, "Are there kinds of conflicts and problems which are more likely to interfere with your effectiveness than others?" This raises issues that are more difficult to articulate. Let me begin by repeating the comment I made about our imperfections and personal shortcomings. Unlike the priest whose life has to embody his priestly functions, but more like the piano teacher whose abilities to play need not be noteworthy, you need not be a superior person whose life is a fulfillment of something we may call Mental Health. Psychological problems you may well have, but they need not interfere with your effectiveness as a therapist.

They need not if you can keep them from doing it—and it is prudent to assume that if they exceed a certain level of intensity and compellingness, there may be no preventing them from interfering. The critical variable is control. That, in turn, hinges on two interdependent variables: (1) the severity of the problem, and (2) the condition of the defenses that are available against it. A severe problem, almost by definition, is one that we have little control over. I believe I can spell out some of the fundamental forms that such control takes in the conduct of therapy.

I'll begin by formulating a basic principle. It's this: *the therapist* (and I should again add, who is conducting the form of therapy I'm describing to you) *must not work out any of his personal problems during the therapy. His patient should not be the instrument for the resolution or satisfac-*

tion of his personal needs and conflicts, and neither should the therapy. A therapist should not derive significant kinds of gratification from his patient. Obviously I don't mean that doing therapy should provide us with no satisfactions. I do mean that there are a variety of vital needs and basic conflicts which should not be gratified or discharged or resolved in our therapeutic work.

What are they?—our sexual, our aggressive, and our narcissistic needs—that's about all! And I repeat: that we may have such needs in greater or lesser degrees and with greater or lesser degrees of everyday satisfaction is not at issue here; that our patients do not serve as instruments of their satisfaction is. Now bear in mind, Simon, that all of our basic needs entail a wide variety of derivatives and partial drives, and their satisfaction can take different forms. To flirt, for instance, can be a gratification of our sexual drive. While you may feel no special need for physical sexual contact with a patient, you may feel a need to be seen by him as a sexually desirable person—and that amounts to a proscribed gratification. Similarly, aggressive and narcissistic needs are various and multidimensional. And my point is this: in principle, at least, you must not feel any significant neediness in these areas in the context of your professional work. You must, to paraphrase Freud, be relatively desireless.

Does this mean, as some would have it mean, that outside of your professional work you must be experiencing no frustrations? Or, to put it more reasonably, that you must be living if not a perfect life then a reasonably satisfying one? This is certainly an attractive and tempting proposition to accept, but it strikes me as facile as well as potentially misleading. I don't find it difficult to imagine that a therapist would have the strength and self-discipline to endure frustrations in his life without letting them impinge on his work. It takes integrity, reflectiveness, and certain obsessive-compulsive defenses; but it can be done. And—since no one is perfect—it must be done. Moreover, the proposition can have a deleterious effect. If you believe that your outside life must be exemplary of mental health in order that you may be optimally desireless in your professional life, then you can actually suffer in your effectiveness. You may lose sight of the fact that desirelessness is a fiction, an unattainable ideal; and if you believe you can and ought to attain that state during your work, you may find yourself often feeling self-reproachful and troubled. Any glimmer of anger (or of a need to be loved, or of sexual desire) during a session will be taken as a transgression, and you will feel guilty and worried about it. That in turn will trigger anxiety and its attendant defenses.

It's not uncommon, Simon, for a beginning therapist to be frightened of the feelings that are aroused in him by a hostile or a seductive patient. He will feel under special pressure to deal with those aspects of his patient's behavior, to ward them off or make them stop. This can become a real hindrance to effective therapy. The problem arises typically because he cannot deal with his feelings and reactions, and so he puts the onus on his patient to stop provoking them. And the reason he can't handle his feelings sometimes centers on his conviction that he ought not be having them. You see, if he were leading a good life—so the conviction goes—he would not be having them. It helps if you bear in mind that, while desire and satisfaction are significantly correlated, the correlation is rarely substantial. I can be free of problems over eating, and I can be leading a gastronomically satisfying life, and still be stimulated to appetite by the sight, the smell, and even the verbal description of a succulent dish. The same is true for all the desire affects; stimulated to appetite, yes—but not impelled to act on it. It should not induce in me a ravenous hunger (or anger, or lust, or whatever) that prevents me from thinking or doing anything else. That's the important difference: the feeling should not become so intense as to take control of my thoughts and actions. That's what I mean by control and by not letting the feeling impair the work. To feel sexual desire, to want admiration, to experience anger, to want to inflict pain, are one thing. It's foolhardy to suppose that anyone can be entirely free of such experiences during the course of their work as a psychotherapist—there's too much stimulation, too much empathy, too much going on. But to have control over them is another thing.

I can offer you an illustrative example. Your patient is criticizing your physical appearance, your grooming and dress. He's saying in effect that he does not admire people who look like you look. Let's suppose that this is an area that you happen to be sensitive or conflicted about; it's a source of everyday frustration for you. How can it now impinge on your work?— and, How can you keep it from doing so?

Suppose you experience a sense of personal insult at the hands of your patient (you feel narcissistically wounded, as we say). This can have two contrasting effects. First, it can inhibit you from making a sound and timely Interpretation about the matter. How? You may be apprehensive lest your hurt and/or defensiveness will show; you may not want him to see that he got to you; or else your feelings may prevent you from thinking of the Interpretation in the first place because you're too stirred up to devote yourself to the act of Understanding. So you will stay silent when the Therapeutic Process requires some action from you, and you will have lost an opportunity to contribute to your patient's welfare. The contrasting possibility is that you'll be unable to maintain an impassive silence when in fact that is the optimal action for you to take. You'll feel impelled to make some comment that is neither sound nor timely; you won't be able to let the matter develop without intruding into it. Moreover, there may be a sense of urgency in the way you respond and Interpret that is more a function of how you feel than how your patient is feeling. The message to him might be, "I can't take it," and this will impose a restraint that may be both unwarranted and untherapeutic.

So what is the aroused Simon to do? First of all, he must assess the intensity of his arousal. Second, he must recognize that it's his personal problem (not lay the onus on his patient). Third, he must know himself well enough to be able to judge the effect that his arousal is likely to have on his own functioning at the moment. If he chooses to speak, will his voice convey his feelings? Will his choice of words do it? In fact, would he have chosen to speak if he were not feeling aroused? These are questions that must be answered on the spot. Basically, the question is, "Do I have sufficient control?" If the answer is "No," then the only recourse is silence. The choice between Scylla and Charybdis here is an easy one—better to have lost an opportunity to advance the Therapeutic Process than to have contributed a real source of Resistance to it. (Remember the advice of the sergeant to his police upon hearing the pirates of Penzance singing their imminent appearance on stage: "Hark, hark!/They come in force,/With stealthy stride./Our obvious course,/Is now: to hide!" Or, if not that, then Stuart Miller's favorite advice to the aspiring therapist: "Don't just say something—sit there!")

There's a fourth step too. After the session is over you can do some self-searching; you can ask yourself how come you became so aroused. Some analytic work on yourself is in order, for your effectiveness as a therapist can depend on your ability to deal with your emotions and needs during your work. It may be that the problem is specific to the particular patient, and it may relate to other needs and feelings he stirs up in you. You may, in short, be experiencing a significant Countertransference problem. But I'll postpone the subject of Countertransference for another letter and

return to the subject of which needs and drives should play
no part in our work.

The primary ones (sex, aggression, and narcissism) I've
already mentioned, and now I want to add two secondary
ones: envy and pity. Obviously I'm going to forbid you
from feeling envious of your patient—but what shall I say
about pity? It's such a complicated feeling, and isn't simply
the counterface of envy. Pity relates also the fundamental
Caring attitude. To empathize and sympathize with another's suffering can entail a measure of pity. But we must
be ready to acknowledge that if it grows intense it may be
borrowing some of that intensity from other feelings, including those that grow out of defenses against hostility,
envy, and competitiveness. On a patient's part the need for
pity may be no different from a need for punishment or for
admiration. A craving for pity may be little more than appeal for mercy—"Don't hurt me, don't be angry with me, for
see how pitiful I am." Still, though you Interpret the matter
to him correctly and you do not allow the feeling to inhibit
you induly, you should not be entirely pitiless.

But perhaps I'm overemphasizing the proscriptions in this
letter, and I should remind you that not all of our vital
needs are proscribed. We are, after all, helping a fellow
human, and that provides us with some very basic
gratification. Moreover, there are a variety of so-called Ego
Interests that are freely called into play in our work. Among
them, as I wrote about in an early letter, is the Synthetic
Function—the concomitant need to know and Understand.
That gets a lot of gratification in *Psychotherapy*. Which
brings me to the intriguing subject of voyeurism.

That we psychotherapists are unrestrained voyeurs, that
we freely indulge this need in our choice of profession and
the nature of our work, is commonly assumed. More than
that, it's often claimed that this need should be given free
rein in the interest of effective therapy. I disagree—and my

disagreement hinges on an important distinction between voyeurism and the need to know. I disagree with the hypothesis that the need to Understand and to know is nothing more than a sublimation of the voyeuristic drive. It seems obvious to me that there is in all of us a voyeuristic tendency, which has not been transformed by sublimation but which still rests squarely on the sexual drive, and which moves us to seek out appropriate stimulation. And I believe that as therapists we gain little from this source of curiosity. But more than that: if it becomes a source of special intensity or conflict then it can interfere.

Anyhow, the extent to which psychotherapy provides for the stimulation and gratification of our voyeuristic needs is greatly exaggerated. In this day and age there is ample opportunity for us to gratify them outside of our office. The reason for keeping them out there is the likelihood that giving them free rein will lead us to violate some of the basic principles of *Psychotherapy*. For instance, it may impel us to probe and prod our patient into telling us secrets and intimate details. That we must experience no urgency to hear such things is clear to me—in fact, it should matter to us very little for its own sake. So we should not experience any significant gratification when we do get to peek, nor any significant frustration when things are hidden from us. This means that we must be free from pressures from, and conflicts over, our voyeuristic tendencies—which is quite different from saying that we need to have such tendencies in abundant strength.

I'm reminded here, Simon, of the interest you showed in my remark of several letters ago that some of us discuss our patients with our spouses. You're surprised that I didn't condemn this practice. Well, I don't, and let me tell you how come. For one thing, a wife's desire to know about her husband's work (or vice versa) is not necessarily, or even usually, a matter of voyeurism. For another, imagine the consequences of being married to someone who cannot share with you the nature and content of his work. No intimate relationship can support such a big area of secrecy. And why should it? Of what benefit is it to a patient that only his therapist knows about his therapy? There may be special issues that need not ever be known to anyone else; and certainly we don't have to share everything with our spouses. But to maintain utter secrecy is not only without real benefit to the patient, but it can betray a serious Countertransference (if not marital) problem.

I should add that, like most of the issues I'm dealing with in this letter, the problem often arises from the patient's side. It will not be uncommon for him to become concerned with your voyeurism. This is part of a larger issue centering around his ability to arouse and move you. The withholding of certain kinds of details may be based on a wish to frustrate you, which in turn may be based on an unacceptable wish to excite you. Or else the wish may be played out in the unrestrained sharing of every intimate detail. In either case, you're in a better position to Understand and to help him to Understand the matter if you maintain control over your feelings. If you are to respond effectively to what he is experiencing and needing—and this is the fundamental point of this entire letter—you should feel under no special urgency from within yourself.

So much for your personal problems, Simon. The next topic is logically Countertransference, but I'm going to postpone that topic for now and turn to your cognitive problems in my next letter.

                                        Your affectionate uncle

Twenty-one

Dear Simon,

You and your patient must be strangers who move in different social circles with a minimum of overlap. Why? For a number of interlocking reasons, among which I regard the most important one to be this: the uniqueness of *Psychotherapy* grows out of the fact that your patient's personal world (his Lewinian *Life-space*) becomes known to us only via his experience of it. You will not get to look for yourself at his parents, or his friends, or at his home and work milieu. You will see only what he shows you and know only what he tells you.

Before I take up what the special advantages of this arrangement are let me hasten to point out that you can of course know what his larger social world is like. You may be familiar with its social customs and its cultural types; you may know what his school is like, or the army in which he was a soldier, or the community in which he grew up, and so forth. In fact, it's a big point of contention whether the effectiveness of psychotherapy has to depend upon a therapist's knowing his patient's social and cultural world. Clearly there's a limit to the amount of information that can be given during the sessions, so a therapist who already knows about life in a big city ghetto is likely to understand his patient's experiences there better than one who doesn't happen to know.

But, Simon, if the Charybdis is knowing too little about your patient's larger world, there's a Scylla here too. Knowing too much may lead you to a kind of complacency, a jumping to premature conclusions, to formulations that are more yours than his. You may rely too much on your own knowledge or judgments of his reality; and even if you avoid imposing them on him, you may lack in sufficient sensitivity to his particular judgments and experiences. And here's a further worthwhile point: there can be enormous value for a patient in describing and explaining what he has been taking for granted for years. The act of reconstructing one's past commonly leads to fresh insights, new perspectives, and the useful examination of long-held assumptions.

The main point I want to write about, however, has to do with a patient's personal world—and that you can only learn about from him. When he says, for example, that his father is a cold and hostile person, you can do little else than take his word for it. That does not mean that you have to believe it in the sense that you accept it as an objective fact. In a certain way, you can (and should) suspend any such belief, and instead accept the characterization for what it is: namely, his experience of his father. And you may further limit or qualify your acceptance by taking into account his character structure, his defenses, his conflicts, and the conditions of time and Transference.

I will soon come back to this important issue. First I want to write about a major exception to this epistemological limitation: the person of the therapist himself—your properties as a stimulus.

* * * * * * *

There is one piece of reality that you do share with your patient—namely, yourself. You naturally come to be an important part of his personal world, and that part of it, unlike the rest, you are in an excellent position to know independently. So when he says that you're a cold and hostile person, you can judge the veridicality of that impression independently. You can—and you should—know how accurate the perception is or how much distortion is involved. Therefore, Simon, you have to know yourself—and not only the kind of person you generally are, but the kind of person you are in your therapist role.

That's one of those easier-said-than-done tasks. While we have opportunity enough to learn what impression we convey to people in general, we have relatively little opportunity when it comes to our professional role. To a large extent we must learn it from our patients, and that's far from easy. For one thing, it places the major burden on the first or earliest patients we work with. But we cannot even believe them too uncritically, for they will have to distort no less than our later patients will. When conducting *Psychotherapy*, the problem is substantially reduced by virtue of the constraints the method imposes. Since we never show ourselves personally to a significant extent, our patients have little opportunity to see and learn very much about us. This has two consequences: (1) certain impressions will be quite accurate—e.g., impersonal, thoughtful, serious, controlled, etc.; (2) certain impressions will be significantly made up of projections—e.g., hostile, seductive, inhibited, uninhibited, etc. That much the structure of *Psychotherapy* itself determines.

But within the limits of that structure there is substantial latitude. Warmth, for example, can be conveyed in varying degree; so can such traits as gentleness, directness, calmness, excitability, enthusiasm—all within limits, but there remains a range. You should come to know the kind of person you are in therapy, and you should also be able to modify it within reasonable limits (because some patients need more directness than others, some need more warmth or more reticence or enthusiasm). Don't lose sight of the fact that our faces and postures convey a great deal about us. The ways we smile and the ways we move and sit, no less than the way we speak, all express our moods, temperament, and certain aspects of our personality. And all of this we should come to know as fully as possible, for it's of great value to be able to tease out a patient's distortions and projections from his accurate and sensitive perceptions.

One of the main skills you will need to have is the ability to maintain utter control over yourself while at the same time maintaining utter attention to your patient. This requires a substantial degree of unselfconsciousness along with steady recognition of the kind of self you are and are presenting to your patient. By the way, Simon, this is a skill that you will not have to apply in your personal and social relationships, and you should be able to forego it there and keep it reserved for your work. We all know therapists who are always therapists (like performers who are always "on") and we know how irritating and uncongenial that can get. The therapeutic mode is generally quite inappropriate to the personal and social relationships of both patients and therapists.

* * * * * * *

Let's return to the larger matter of Reality in therapy. I have heard it argued that the major shortcoming of traditional psychotherapy is that we therapists can know only what our patients tell us. (Certain forms of therapy have been designed to correct for it and allow the therapist to be a participant observer.) But I believe that this limitation, fully acknowledged, can actually constitute an important advantage. How so? The fact that our patients have such active control over this aspect of our knowledge is both a feature of its uniqueness and a peculiar strength of the entire enterprise. I'll amplify.

Since we have little choice but to believe the patient, we can therefore suspend the belief mode. This means that whether something is veridical or not remains largely if not wholly within his prerogative. If he says, "My father hates me," we can do little more than accept it as his experience.

Whether it's in fact true or not remains irrelevant until the point is reached when he himself begins to question it. If and when that point is reached, we can deal with the doubt—we can give support to it and even enlarge it—but at bottom we can only avow (to ourself if not to him), "I cannot know whether your father hates you or not; it is a judgment that you alone can make. I can help you by considering your doubts about it, and also by showing you how certain aspects of your personality and your experiences may be misleading you. But whether they are or are not is finally your judgment too."

This doesn't have to apply to matters of fact. If he says he went to the movies yesterday, we will naturally accept it is a matter of fact. But when he is speaking of judgments, evaluations, impressions, and interpretations, then we will accept them as such—as his experience. If he says he was angry, that is taken as his experience; and if he says the other person was angry, then it is taken exactly the same way—as his experience of the other person, not necessarily as the other person's true feeling.

The issue here is not one of lying or of setting traps; nor is it a matter of disbelief. Rather, it's the way that a therapist believes. *Psychotherapy,* you will recall, is Mental. It takes as its main subject the patient's mental events. Actions are taken as reflections of those states, and it's the mental states that we pay particular attention to. So the fact that he experiences the other's anger or hostility is what concerns us. And if you bear that in mind, Simon, you will resist the temptation to offer an Interpretation that takes the form of, "I believe that the reason your brother was angry or hostile is . . . ," for that assumes the veridicality of the brother's mental state in a way that is both presumptuous and potentially misleading.

The fact that you cannot independently appraise your patient's reality further enables you to maintain your position as the nonevaluator, the one who renders no judgments. Whether or not he acted wisely, or sensibly, or well is something you cannot know for sure; and you can rarely judge for sure whether he was good or bad. This forces you to deal mainly with his judgments and evaluations, and it guarantees that he is the only one who makes them. This, once again, is easier said than done, for it takes great self-discipline on your part to abstain from judging (and sometimes, as you'll soon see, we may be unable to avoid making judgments). But even if it is humanly impossible to abstain from having them, it's clearly not impossible to keep from conveying them to a patient. What is less easy is to minimize their influence on your participation in the Therapeutic Process. To a large extent, however, the Technical principles of *Psychotherapy* ensure this achievement.

Patients sometimes want you to help them appraise reality and evaluate their judgments of it. They'll recount an episode, say of their boss's actions, and then ask you whether their experience of his malevolence was valid or justified. Now, of course, you may be able to help such a patient evaluate his interpretation in the light of his needs, his conflicts, and his defenses. You may be able to suggest that he is overestimating (or underestimating) the boss's malevolence because of his own tendency to feel resentful (or guilty) in the face of authority figures (and the same is true if he did not ask for the help). But your temptation, Simon, will be to do more: to make an independent appraisal of your patient's reality (i.e., of the boss's action).

There are circumstances in which you needn't fight the temptation too hard. First, however, let me repeat myself: the fight is a good fight. You should discipline yourself with respect to the fact that you have no special authority or expertise on matters of reality. More than that, you must accept the limitations that therapy imposes on your knowledge of your patient's real experiences—namely, the fact that you know them only through him. My thesis is that such limitations can have a paradoxical effect; they can actually be a source of Technical strength insofar as they force upon you a mode of functioning that is therapeutically more effective than the mode you would follow if you were a participant observer.

Now to the circumstances. There are certain kinds of good Interpretations that can depend upon an independent appraisal of reality on your part—or at least an appraisal that's somewhat different from the one your patient is making. Such Interpretations make no sense without the clear assumption that you suspect that his appraisal of reality is faulty; and your Interpretation offers an explanation for his misappraisal. Such Interpretations must be made with especial Tact and judiciousness. You must be sensitive to two facts: (1) that you are challenging his judgment, and (2) that you yourself are vulnerable to factual error. So you should convey a sense of tentativeness in the first place, and in the second, you must do a careful follow-up.

What I have in mind is that it won't be uncommon for you to arrive at the conviction that your patient is misperceiving another's intentions or feelings. Now, if you believe you know why, you can take the simple course of wondering aloud whether the other person was not feeling or intending such and so, at the same time offering the Interpretation. For example: "From your description I get the impression that your boss was feeling pleased with you, and yet you didn't sense that at all. So I wonder what you think of the possibility that you could not permit yourself to, because of how vulnerable you feel when someone like him—someone who has authority over you—is pleased with you." Having offered such an Interpretation, you should not lose sight of the fact that you have challenged his judgment. This fact may later (or sooner) emerge with significance.

Things can get pretty complicated, however. Matters of judgment and reality appraisal have a way of shading imperceptibly into matters of information (and the reverse is also true). At times it can be unclear whether a patient is misjudging a situation or is simply misinformed about it. If you think the latter is the case then you face the question of whether you should correct him. Of course it will be necessary to explore the reasons why he was so misinformed, for that may lead to important insights, but in order to do that it may be necessary to identify the misinformation as such in the first place. But isn't giving information tantamount to giving advice? And if so, isn't it proscribed? Well, yes and no. Sometimes it clearly is not (for example, if he is planning an action because tomorrow is Sunday when tomorrow in fact is Saturday, then correcting him does not imply any advice about the action per se), and sometimes there is only a fine line between them. But the giving of information can be the equivalent of giving advice, and you should be alert to that truth.

The perils of not correcting, or drawing attention to, a mistaken piece of information are correlated with the blatancy of the mistake. What will it mean to your patient that you did not notice or draw his attention to an error of fact? At times it may be a kind of trap, set wittingly or unwittingly, and designed to discover whether you are listening, or whether you are informed, or whatever. At such times this becomes the main issue. But notice that for it to become the main issue the mistake must be treated as a mistake—the misinformation must be challenged.

The line between information and advice is often real enough, but the line between information and reality appraisal often isn't. Say, for example, your patient is a young woman who lives in a neighborhood that you think is dangerous. Say she reports that she has lately taken to solitary walks near her home in the late evening. You judge that she is risking assault, but she does not mention that fact. Instead she says that she is puzzled by the new habit. Now, ordinarily, when a patient expresses a sense of bafflement about a habit that is relatively innocuous (like a new way of combing hair, or beginning a letter, or the like) you will feel no special urgency to focus upon, or otherwise deal with, the matter. But when the habit can have serious implications for her well-being, then you will; for her well-being may depend upon your informing her of the real danger, or if she already knows it, then to help her understand the habit as quickly as possible in order to gain control over it. In any case, if you judge that there may be a real and substantial danger to her welfare, you have little choice but to raise the issue and focus attention on it. Let's imagine that the conversation goes as follows:

[YOU:] Let me interrupt you, and ask you whether you are aware of the dangers of what you are doing.
[PATIENT:] What dangers? I don't understand.
[YOU:] Well, it seems to me that you may be running the risk of being assaulted.

If this comes as news to her, then things can proceed in the usual way. But let's imagine that she responds as follows:

[PATIENT:] I know that well enough. Why do you feel you need to point it out to me?
[YOU:] Because you made no mention of the danger. So I wondered whether you are aware of it.
[PATIENT:] I didn't think I had to mention it because it seemed so obvious [pause]. Now I'm wondering why you mentioned it.

You should now feel obligated to explain, because you did after all raise (i.e., impose) the issue of the danger. You have two main options. One is to base your explanation on the grounds that you Care, and so you don't want her to be harmed. But that—while it should certainly be true—can usually be left implicit, although sometimes it need not be, and you may have reason to respond, "Why shouldn't I mention it if I think you are acting in a way that is dangerous to you? Do you suppose that I simply don't care?"

Your second option involves offering an Interpretation. It can be a simple one to the effect that the danger may explain the action—i.e., that she intends the risk of harm. It may be incorrect or unfounded and still serve a valuable function insofar as it introduces a mode of explanation that may be useful for other habits. Be that as it may, the option is for you to respond, "Because I had the thought that perhaps one of the reasons you were doing it was because you wanted to invite assault." This kind of Interpretation will also be appropriate for the following two continuations to your having raised the issue of the real danger:

[PATIENT:] Don't be silly. My neighborhood is not nearly as dangerous as people imagine. What makes you think it's so dangerous?

[YOU:] I may be quite wrong, and you are certainly in a better position than me to judge, but that is my impression.

[PATIENT:] Do you think I'm showing poor judgment?

[YOU:] I have no way of knowing for sure. The reason I raised the matter of the danger is that, if there is in fact some real danger in taking these solitary walks late in the evening, that might be one of the reasons you are doing it.

[PATIENT:] Because of the danger? I don't understand.

[YOU:] One possibility is that you want to invite assault.

[PATIENT:] Don't you think I know that well enough? I'm not a baby. I can take care of myself, you know. I carry a spray and a sharp little knife, and I've taken some karate lessons, so why do you feel the need to point out the danger to me?

[YOU:] Because you began by saying you were puzzled by the new habit, and you made no mention of the real dangers and of the precautions you take against it. I wondered whether the fact that it was so dangerous a thing to do might be part of the reason you are doing it.

[PATIENT:] What do you mean?

[YOU:] Well, one possibility is that you want to invite assault.

[PATIENT:] But that doesn't make sense because I take all the necessary precautions.

[YOU:] Yes, I can see that you do. But the possibility remains that you want to be assaulted in order to prove that you can take complete care of yourself.

The judgment about a patient's well-being is not always such an easy one to make, and the degree as well as the nature of the reality risk can vary widely. She may be risking anything from social embarrassment (wearing inappropriate clothing to a wedding reception) to impregnation (having intercourse without contraception). If you use a criterion that is excessively broad, you will too often find yourself giving information and making judgments. You may, for example, find yourself "informing" her how to avoid provoking her boy friend. I believe that we can more securely navigate these perilous waters if we keep close to the principle that a sound and timely Interpretation should be at hand. That, you will by now recognize, is my favorite prescription. In addition, on this matter you have to remain sensitive to becoming overly concerned and worried about your patient and giving in to a need to protect in inappropriate ways. This leads directly to the topic of Countertransference, which I'll again postpone—but only till the next letter.

Your affectionate uncle

Twenty-two

Dear Simon,

To Care for a patient is one thing, to worry about him is another, and the difference comes down to *Countertransference*. Under that heading is included a broad variety of feelings—anger, pride, competitiveness, frustration, love. In one sense, the concept refers to all of our affective responses to our patients; in another, it refers only to those emotions that grow to problem proportions. Countertransference—as you may have surmised from my repeated postponements of the topic—is a difficult subject.

I have little doubt that the concept is an altogether sound and useful one, but it is widely misused and often misapplied. Strictly speaking, it refers only to what is left over after a therapist has fully accepted and assimilated the Analytic position. If he conceives of his primary function as that of maximizing his patient's Ego Autonomy, if he takes Understanding as his chief goal, if he abides by the fundamental instrumentality of the Interpretation, then any and every departure from that position can be laid at the door of Countertransference. A therapist who is following the principles of *Psychotherapy* is concerned about his patient's well-being—he Cares—but otherwise, as I have already written you, he remains desireless.

I have also written how this position is to be regarded as an ideal, for it can never be fully realized in practice. Countertransference transforms this inevitable imperfection into a therapeutic blessing. It not only exonerates the imperfect therapist, it provides a way for him to use his departures from perfection in the best interests of his patients, for just as Transference is a natural and expectable phenomenon that is intrinsic to therapy, so is Countertransference—just as we make important use of the one in gaining Understanding of our patient, so do we make important use of the other. We rely on our feelings and reactions to help clarify the functions and meanings of our patients' behavior—as signals, so to speak. If, for instance, I find myself angry at my patient, I take it to mean that either he is feeling angry or he intends for me to be, or both. If I feel frustrated, or worried, or seduced, then I similarly lay the onus for it on my patient. You see, Simon, it's little more than a form of Externalization of Responsibility or Blame, which in turn is a benign form of Projection, and its value in the therapy is directly correlated with its validity on the one hand, and with the way it is pressed into service on the other.

While the conception has substantial utility, a big danger lies in its use as a purely defensive measure. It can be tempting to loosen control and self-discipline and then to seek refuge behind the claim that, "Countertransference, after all, is quite natural and unavoidable, and it's very useful to boot." So let me exhort: in dealing with our own behavior we must be unflinchingly ready to call a rationalization a Rationalization, a defense a Defense. Despite the fact that Defense by itself does not entail anything maladaptive or neurotic, and despite the fact that we therapists need every defense we can use fairly, we have to remain vigilant to the possibility that they may be contributing a Resistance factor to the Therapeutic Process. The conception of Countertransference too easily becomes a license for license.

* * * * * * *

Consider what are the two fundamental ways a patient can induce in me an affective state: by empathic response, and by reactive response. When he is feeling sad, I feel sadness empathically. Similarly, feelings of happiness and joy, frustration and anger can, to some degree evoke like affect in me. The second way differs insofar as the affect is provoked; not only is the induced feeling more like a reaction to, but it may be quite different from, what my patient is feeling. If he is feeling hostile and I feel guilty, the process is different from empathy. The same holds true if he is despairing and I am resentful, if he feels stubborn and I feel frustrated, if he feels sexually aroused and I feel disgust.

The difference between these two modes makes an important difference in therapy, but it's far from as clear-cut as I've portrayed it. Affective experiences are anything but simple; they typically occur in mixtures and combinations. Hostility may be mixed with guilt, despair with frustration, sexual arousal with disgust, and so forth. And so I may be empathizing with only one aspect of my patient's total experience. Some therapists go so far as to contend that their affective responses are always empathic in this way. Thus, when they experienced guilt in the face of the patient's hostility, they were actually sharing (empathizing with) an aspect of his total experience. This, you see, is the special value of their response, since it enables them to point out to the patient the component of guilt in his hostility, a component of which he may be otherwise unaware. Now, I don't want to imply that this doesn't occur in therapy, or that it is rare, and that it cannot be valuable. At the same time, however, I think we delude ourselves if we believe that it always happens this way. That is high-handed, at best. It's equally high-handed to contend that the only other possibility that remains is that the patient intended for us to react with guilt—that this was the function or a determinant of his hostility. That, of course, also happens often enough.

What also happens frequently is that we are provoked to a feeling that is quite different from our patient's and was

not intended by him. In my opinion, it's important to acknowledge this possibility and to recognize such occurrences
as something other than Countertransference. Otherwise we
run the danger of imposing our personality (if not our problems) on our patients. It should go without saying that we
therapists are capable of feelings that are a function of our
own makeup and have little useful bearing upon our patients, and we should have sufficient self-awareness and integrity to make such important distinctions.

There are several Technical principles that serve to insure
that the phenomenon is used in the patient's best interests.
The chief one is that *countertransference should never be
given affective expression, only verbal expression.* Another is
that when you speak of your own emotional responses you
make sure to integrate them into an Interpretation *about
your patient.*

Let's consider, by way of example, what is perhaps the
commonest of Countertransference affects: anger. Among
the ways a patient can both express his anger and make you
angry some are obvious (such as heaping insult and abuse),
some are less obvious (such as coming late to sessions or
missing them altogether), and many are subtle (such as repeatedly getting into reality difficulties or even simply showing no improvement). Sometimes he intends to make you
angry, and sometimes that is actually not his intention. No
matter which it is, you should not express any anger. "You
mean to make me angry," can be a sound and timely Interpretation; "I am feeling angry with you," is not only not
an Interpretation, but it's inadmissible.

Before I take up the rationales for this injunction, let me
point out that, just as a patient can express anger in a variety of subtle and not so subtle ways, so too can a therapist.
If you bear in mind that most Interpretations are likely to
be criticisms, you will be alert to the fact that they can be a
vehicle for anger. An interpretation can be a scolding—and

potentially a pernicious one insofar as the scolding may be disguised and unacknowledged. You are familiar, I'm sure, with the use of psychological explanations as a weapon of argument—as a way of scoring points and discharging anger. The guiding principle to respect is: *never interpret out of anger* (or, at least, *try* not to).

Suppose you offer the following Interpretation based on your Countertransference feeling: "I wonder what you think of the possibility that one of the reasons you come late to your sessions is that you believe it makes me angry." Suppose, further, your patient responds, "Yes, I agree—I guess I do want to make you angry. But tell me, does it make you angry?" Consider the value of a substantive reply—i.e., "Yes, it does," or "No," or "A little." Such replies, of course, do little more than acknowledge the feeling and are quite different from expressing it. But what function do they serve beyond informing him that his actions do in fact affect you? And if you regard that function as a potentially valuable one to articulate to him, then why not articulate it directly? The matter can readily be put to him in the following way: "I don't think it would benefit you to have me answer that question. Instead, let me suggest that the reason you ask it is to find out whether you can affect me. If you cannot make me angry, then that could mean to you that you are powerless to move me." Or suppose he has said, "I think that it really does make you feel angry." If you believe that remaining silent would be equivalent to a tacit Yes, you might respond, "Without my saying whether I am angry or not, let me suggest the possibility that you may need to believe that I am angry because otherwise it would mean that you are powerless to affect me." And you may already know enough about him to add to this Interpretation— to point out perhaps that he has mixed feelings about the matter, that it makes him anxious in certain ways, and so forth.

"All well and good," I can hear you saying to me, Simon. "But what does it add to the force of the Interpretation to conceal the affect—to withhold the emotional reaction?" I'll answer by first considering what it might add to its force (or to your patient's well-being, or to the Therapeutic Process) to acknowledge it—to begin the Interpretation by saying, "Yes, your coming late does make me feel angry." One of the benefits that I recognize is that his action is made more real and more vivid; it takes on a quality of effectiveness that can make it more salient to him. By communicating to him that his behavior does make a difference to you, you help remove it from the realm of pure cognition—to move it out of the pale shadow of thought. Against this advantage, I can pit a number of disadvantages. The fundamental one is this: to the extent that his behavior really affects you, his Autonomy and Freedom are restricted. Once the behavior has attained the status of a real effect it must bear the burden of real responsibility that that effect entails. If his coming late makes you angry, then that constitutes a reality consideration that, like all Reality considerations, lies external to him. He must bear the onus for your feelings, and that necessarily constrains him. It's clear that you don't enjoy being angry, so by saying, "Yes, it makes me angry," you may also be saying, "Please stop doing it." Or, if his behavior makes you glad, then the message is to keep it up. In short, it is an Extrinsic Reinforcement if not implicit advice.

But I'm overstating my case. There may be circumstances in which you might deem it useful to acknowledge the fact that his actions do have an impact on you. You may have reason to believe that for this particular patient it will be more meaningful to deal with a real reaction instead of one that is merely verbalized. So you might answer, "Yes, of course it makes me feel angry. What did you suppose—that your actions have no impact on others?" At the same time that you take this position, you can take steps to reduce the

I. H. Paul

constraints that this admission imposes on him. You can,
for example, show him that you have sufficient control over
your anger—you do not fly into a rage, nor do you punish
him in any way. Instead, you clearly convey the message: "I
can handle my feelings." This means that you are putting
little if any pressure on him to stop it for your sake. Moreover, by helping him to recognize that his actions have real
consequences you may spur him on to a better Understanding of the actions.

Some patients regularly need—and most need at least
occasionally—to test out whether they can have a real effect
upon us—whether they can move us to anger, lust, sympa-
thy, laughter, contempt, disgust, worry. Like every other
aspect of our interaction, this needs to be Understood, and
sometimes—repeat, sometimes—the process can be promoted
if we first acknowledge the real effect. More often, in my
experience, the process of Understanding is better promoted
by withholding the effect. Bear in mind that the typical patient runs this kind of test with distinctly mixed feelings. He
may anticipate your emotional reaction with anxious dread
and be considerably relieved that you don't share that reaction with him. His relationship with you can then remain
uiniquely free in a way that optimally serves the Therapeutic
Process. Let me amplify, perhaps gratuitously.

The essence of a mature interpersonal relationship is
what?—mutuality. As we grow we learn how to take the other's feelings and needs into account; we discover not only
the ways in which we are affected by him but also how we
affect him. When, in our interpersonal relations, we share
our problems and our feelings, we do it with inevitable
consequences. When I tell of my sorrow and pain to a good
friend or close family member, I cause him to feel some of
my sorrow and pain; if I exult, then he too shares some of
that feeling. These consequences can (indeed, should) make
a difference in any decision to share my feelings. Suppose

further that my friend or family member is competitive with me; then exulting over my success may run the danger of making him feel envious. Or suppose he is very sympathetic to me; then sharing the full force of my despair with him runs the danger of plunging him into equal despair. These consequences must surely influence, if not constrain, my behavior.

In short, if the person responds feelingfully to me, I must be influenced one way or another by that fact. It constitutes a significant factor in the act of relating to him, and it does it to a greater or lesser extent (and in subtle and complex ways) in every relationship I have. Encounter-type therapies make this the focus of attention by realizing it—i.e., making it real—within the therapeutic relationship. But Analytic-type therapies focus attention on it in a different way— and *Psychotherapy* does it in a radically different way. Here the relationship is kept unreal; it remains uniquely different from ordinary relationships. The chief reason is so that the patient need not feel contraints of the ordinary sort. He is free to wallow in despair without risking a response from his therapist of either matching despair or of reactive contempt; he feels free to admit to his childish and grandi-ose fantasies without evoking derision; he can boast of his triumphs without provoking envy or pride; he can admit to hostility without courting punishment or disapproval.

Let me construct a kind of test case. Imagine a patient who is a long-time masturbator, who is deeply ashamed of the habit and wants desperately to be rid of it. During the course of *Psychotherapy* he attains some Understanding of the habit, succeeds in working the problem through and, much to his satisfaction and gain in his self-esteem, stops masturbating. Then, one day, the habit reappears; he mas-turbates again. Now is a critical juncture. Does he feel so ashamed of himself, so guilty and embarrassed, so worried about what you will feel when you hear of it, that he cannot bring himself to tell it to you? He should not. This is not to say that he should feel no shame and no blow to his self-esteem, but he should be fully aware that those feelings originate from within himself. You will not receive the bad news with disappointment or disapproval, just as you did not receive the good news with any show of affect. Thus your reaction will not contribute to his feelings of shame and disappointment. He will have maximum freedom from external constraint, and any misgivings he experiences about telling you of his masturbation (feelings of guilt, shame, and disappointment) will be recognized as his own.

All very intriguing, you may say. But isn't it so unrealistic—so perfectly unique—as to make it useless for his everyday relationships, if not detrimental to them? Are we merely teaching him an antisocial lesson: to forget about the other person and to behave in an utterly egocentric way? Are we producing a shameless monster? (We've often heard the criticism levelled at the psychoanalyzed person that he is smug, self-indulgent, and insufferable.) That there is here a real and important danger I neither deny nor minimize, and you should be alert to it every step of the way. The possibility that a patient is generalizing from *Psychotherapy* to his real relationships in a way that is inappropriate and potentially maladaptive must be borne in mind. More than that, you must take pains to make sure he understands that the therapy is unique, that it is unrealistic to expect anyone else to relate to him the way you do. Most patients come to understand this well enough, but a few do not—and they will betray their misunderstanding in one way or another. For example, one will proudly tell how free and uninhibited he has become in his everyday relationships. When you hear this you should explore the matter carefully, asking yourself these questions: Is he being indiscriminate and self-centered? Is he taking *Psychotherapy* as the model for life? Is he playing the role of patient (or, for that matter, of therapist) outside of the sessions? Sometimes that amounts to Acting Out, and as such it is a genuine Resistance. But sometimes it is little more than an uncritical generalization, and it merits at most a correction.

When you conduct *Psychotherapy,* Simon, you focus on your patient's interpersonal relationships too, but you do it from the outside, so to speak. (Even Transference issues are, in this sense, considered from the outside.) I am convinced that this outside position will not seriously hamper your effectiveness—and the advantages can be enormous and profound.

Your affectionate uncle

Twenty-three

Dear Simon,

So you've caught me in a contradiction, eh? (I'm far from surprised.) Here I tell you that it's inadmissible to say to a patient, "I am feeling angry with you"; several letters ago I advised you, in the interest of integrity, to own up to such things as forgetfulness, distraction, and even defensiveness. And from me you expect, at the very least, consistency! I could, I suppose, take refuge behind Emerson's dictum that consistency is the hobgoblin of small minds—but I feel inclined, instead, to retract my strong "inadmissible," to retreat to a weaker position (and also to remind you that I admitted to circumstances that can warrant the confession of anger or of any other Countertransference feeling).

To your request for an explanation of what I meant when I wrote you that even Transference issues are "considered from the outside," I'm tempted to paraphrase Browning who, when he was asked to explain a line of his poetry, said something like, "When I wrote it, God and Browning knew what it meant; now only God knows." In other words, I'd rather not go into that subject right now. Instead, I'll continue with the affect-laden topic by taking up the main question you've put to me.

You raise a good and difficult point. In view of the fact that it can be vital for a patient to experience a range and depth of feelings during the therapy sessions, and considering that we may evoke feelings in him with our Interpretations, might it not work better if the Interpretation is made from feelings? You wonder whether your dispassion is likely to be an advantage or a disadvantage in this respect, and you ask, "Is an Interpretation likely to be more effective or less if I offer it while I am affectively aroused?"

This kind of question is one that seems destined to defy a simple answer, and one intuitively predicts an "It depends." But I can think of some relevant considerations that will shape and weight the answer. Let me introduce them by telling you of a recent experience I had—not in the conduct of therapy, but in the course of taking a piano lesson. So this is going to be an analogy.

It happens I'm taking piano lessons again. Recently, I was playing a passionate passage of a Beethoven sonata, and though I could ordinarily manage the passage well enough, my performance of it fell completely apart. "What happened?" I cried out to my teacher. "What did I do wrong?" "Quite obvious," he replied with a reassuring smile. "The only thing you did wrong was that you let yourself be carried away by the music." This explanation came as a surprise, and my first thought was that he was teasing me. But he's a good teacher, and a good teacher—like a good therapist—doesn't tease. So I protested, "Am I not supposed to let the music carry me, move me? Isn't that the whole idea?"

His reply was most instructive. "Spoken like a true amateur! My professional pupil would never make that claim. It is the listeners he wants to move, and to do that he must remain in full control. Don't you know [and at this point he took unfair advantage by adding, "as a psychologist"] that strong emotion can interfere with the execution of a task that requires delicate and difficult motor coordination—that requires executing a carefully worked-out plan of action?" What did I believe, he continued, that a Serkin or Horowitz experienced and felt during a performance of music that's filled with passion and pathos—the full force of the passion and pathos? "That would be most risky and endanger the performance itself." It was when he studied the music in the privacy of his studio that he sought to experience its emotional impact, and that guided him in working out his "interpretation." There he planned how to best play the piece so that its passion and pathos would be fully expressed and conveyed. It was this plan that influenced his solution to the "technical" problems (the fingerings, phrasings, pedaling). Having worked all of that out in preparation, during the performance he devoted his attention mainly to the elements of the interpretation as embodied in the technical solutions, his tempi, his dynamics, his pedaling. He thought ahead to what was coming, so that what he was playing had the proper relationship to what he would soon play. What's more, he conserved his strength (at times, for instance, deliberately relaxing his wrists and fingers). Now, through all of this hard work, he had to remain relatively dispassionate and in control in order to enhance his ability to play the piece the way he had practiced it—so that he could convey to us the full force of the music's passion and pathos.

At the risk of being carried away again—this time by the analogy itself—let me pursue it a bit further. There's a question of balance and proportion here too. While he needs to maintain self-control and dispassion, the artist also needs to feel the music in order to prevent his performance from being mechanical and flat. My teacher went on to discuss this consideration, and he pointed out to me that there are wide individual differences here. Some pianists he knows play everything safe and allow the music no impact at all upon them; others (more experienced ones, perhaps) can allow themselves to feel without risking disaster. In any case, the issue is not necessarily one of no feeling at all, but rather of a degree that will enhance but not impair.

The point, then, is this: a too strong emotional reaction on the part of a therapist can interfere with his effectiveness. This doesn't mean, however that he needs to insulate himself from all feelings—and even if he could do it it would not automatically improve his effectiveness. There is a point at which he needs feelings not only in order to Understand what his patient is feeling, but also to communicate that Understanding. Just like the affectless performing artist, the affectless therapist runs the risk of being mechanical and flat. This can be translated into a limitation of his ability to Understand as well as to communicate his Understanding.

We have to allow ourselves a measure of affective response to our patients. We mustn't be carried away, but neither should we remain frozen and insulated. There's an optimum range that is sensed intuitively, and we will each differ on where our own best level falls. The level will also differ for different patients we work with, and perhaps also at different times during the course of therapy. And this, at the very least, is why the answer to your question must be "It depends."

It depends also on the particular affect that's involved. Obviously it makes no sense to say to a patient, "You are feeling angry," angrily. Neither do I see any advantage in conveying anger while saying, "As you recount the experience you had with your father, I feel myself getting angry; I wonder whether you too are feeling it." Will that add to the force of the Interpretation? I doubt it. In fact, the impact may actually be diminished if he experiences your anger—or, if not diminished, then deflected. (The pianist who emotes all over the keyboard distracts the listener from the music.) Your patient's experience is what counts. Your goal is not to induce it in him by way of empathy from you, but rather to release it from his defensive confines. The same is likely to be true for affects such as anxiety and guilt, as well as for the drive-associated affects such as hostility and lust. It's also a clear fact that to give the Interpretation with utter coldness can be equally distracting to a patient.

Let me sum it up this way: while you will need to react feelingfully to your patient because it will promote your analytic abilities—insofar as your feelings may inform you about what he is experiencing and intending—you're best advised to use this information no differently than you use other information you glean from him, namely, in the interest of his Understanding. This means that you will generally not express and convey your feelings directly, but instead will integrate them into your Interpretations. At the same time, to communicate them effectively will require a measure of feelingfulness—bearing in mind that an excessive show of feelings will distract and deflect him, and so will an excessive absence of feelings. What is required of you is a capacity for both empathic and reactive responsiveness to a wide range of different feelings and the ability to contain and control them appropriately. It's a professional task that's specific to the professional psychotherapist.

Still, your control can not be perfect. No therapist can expect himself to always remain free of manifest affective response. You may be able to withstand verbal insults, but how about vivid accounts of extreme brutality? Say your patient describes an exquisitely erotic episode, or say he recounts a humorous incident in a genuinely funny way—can you remain overtly unmoved? It's inevitable that there will be circumstances that will evoke a strong affective response in you. While it's easy to advise you to keep your response in some degree of check and maintain self-control, it's foolhardy to expect you to be able to show no feelings no matter what. Certain kinds of strong emotions must necessarily be shared and shown. If the humor is funny enough, then you'll laugh; if the brutality is moving, then you'll flinch and grimace; if the sex is erotic enough, you may flush. Even if you are out of his sight, you may be unable to conceal the affect in your speech. Sometimes it's a patient's intention to evoke a response from you that he can see; sometimes it isn't, and sometimes he may take special pains to prevent such a thing from happening, so he avoids details and much graphic depiction. In any case, the matter frequently takes on importance in the therapy, and you have to be sensitive to its vicissitudes. Your sensitivity will be heightened if you can allow yourself to react without anxiety and defensiveness, if you are not alarmed by an uncontrollable show of feelings. This usually requires of you a sufficient measure of self-control in the first place so that you can regain your composure in good time.

Your affectionate uncle

Twenty=four

Dear Simon,

From your tone I infer that my recent letters haven't convinced you. You complain about my habit of stating a strong position and then backing away from it. Let me point out that, while I intend the strong position as an ideal or standard, I do tend to stick quite close to it in my work. Only rarely do I show my patients what I'm feeling—I do generally play it cool. But I guess I'm hesitant to advocate that position too strongly to you, because it can be a mistake to take it too stringently when you're beginning to do therapy. It requires, you see, the kind of conviction that grows not out of theory, but out of the experience of how effective it can be in practice. And you'll need both the conviction from experience and the practice before you can do it well.

Anyway, I think I've written you enough about these general kinds of issues, and it's time to return to particulars. So let's proceed to the second stage of *Psychotherapy*, the Middle.

As in the middle game in chess, the Middle stage of therapy is where much of the exciting and creative action usually takes place. As in the middle section of a sonata, it is where the themes and motifs of the Beginning are subject to articulation, variation, and development. This is when the major reorganizations and transformations occur, the major revelations and insights, the major Transferences—and also the major impasses. By now your patient has had a substantial experience of the therapy and you have had a sub-

stantial experience of him. So this is when the chief work
consists in the formulation, the elaboration, and also the
repetition, of Interpretations. This is also when the main
struggle for and against change takes place.

The Beginning stage is often marked by an undercurrent
of optimism and enthusiasm. The Middle, by contrast, is
often marked by an undercurrent of despair and resistance,
because now the patient's basic unwillingness to change
becomes manifest and powerful, and it pits its strength
against the forces of change and development. (In psychoanalytic terms: this is when Ego—your big ally—struggles
against the combined forces of Superego, Id, and Reality.)
It is now that long-entrenched patterns of behavior must be
weakened and altered; it is now that the Transference Neurosis reaches its full intensity and exerts its full force.

It can be extremely useful to define the Middle for a patient. When the issues having to do with being in *Psychotherapy* (the common themes and concerns of the Beginning)
have been dealt with, and when he has recounted the main
events of his life, you can proclaim the advent of a new
stage in the therapy—no special ceremony, of course, but an
acknowledgment that a new stage has been reached. Usually, there are clear signs of it that can be articulated, and
the patient has a distinctive experience that the therapy has
matured.

Occasionally, this will take the form of a major impasse;
your patient may react to it by considering whether he
should continue in treatment. He may complain that he
despairs of benefiting from it, and that he is considering
either quitting outright or changing therapists. At such
times it can be very helpful to articulate his experience fully
and to offer at least a partial explanation of it that makes
reference to the new stage the therapy has reached. You
must convey an appreciation of the seriousness of his
conflicts. You must avoid explaining them away (more

about that, later), but you can reassure him by acknowledging their basis in the reality of the Middle: "I think that, in part anyway, your misgivings and doubts over whether to continue in therapy have something to do with the fact that we've reached a new stage in it." The same approach can often be taken with respect to the other common phenomena of the Middle that I will take up in this letter.

* * * * * * *

The shape that the reality of the Middle takes will naturally vary from patient to patient; each therapy can be expected to reach its own distinctive kind of Middle. So what I'll write you about in this letter are two of the most common expectable themes and issues. The first—and also the most basic—is resistance to change. In order to do justice to this subject I would have to write you a monograph on it. (While the same could be said for others I have touched on, this one is clearly most basic to the enterprise of psychotherapy as well as to human development.) I can hope to do little more than make some selected comments on it and indicate some of the ways it can be dealt with in *Psychotherapy*.

My first comment is one that can go without having to be said: the subject must be approached with especial sensitivity, Tact and patience. To simply level the charge, "You really don't want to change," is likely to be tactless, offensive, and self-defeating. But the resistance to change is something a patient must come to recognize in himself if meaningful change is to take place. For one thing, unless he becomes both intellectually and emotionally familiar with that fundamental fact, he'll be unable to recognize and analyze the variety of forms and shapes it can take—and it can take many.

The standard Interpretation for this theme can be formulated like this: "A part of you—and I believe you know it quite well—does not want to change. I think that part of you is now exerting a lot of pressure." What should follow is a specification of the "part" as well as an articulation of the current form and content of the "pressure." Often it's "the sick part" that's responsible; sometimes it's "the stubborn and angry child in you." Often it's based on a dread of certain consequences (secondary gain, so-called), or else because of some important adaptation that has been achieved on its account. In any case, it can be of critical importance to identify and explore the sources and functions of the unwillingness to change.

For a patient to acknowledge his resistance to change but to experience a substantial impotence against it—"I do want to change, but I just can't"—is very common. After all, it may have been just this sense of helplessness that brought him into therapy in the first place. So, to put the matter bluntly, it becomes the main task of therapy to transform this impotence by restoring to him his ability to act on himself and on his reality. That, of course, is no mean task. It requires, for one thing, that you yourself be fully convinced that the achievement is possible. You have to empathize with his sense of helplessness, but you mustn't lose sight of the fact that its basis is neurotic. This means that you will focus on the sense of helplessness as directly as you can and try to uncover its dynamic and genetic basis.

In my experience, a good tactic to follow at first is to try for a transformation of the experience of "I can't" into an experience of "I won't." Often this step can be achieved by introducing the experience of risk—"I can't" becomes "I can't risk it," which in turn becomes "I won't risk it." The same can be true for experiences of "must" and "ought." Basically, what we aim for is the transformation of what feels peremptory and automatic into feelings of volitional choice. This achievement takes time and patience—it's anything but quick or sudden, even when accompanied by a

sense of insightful revelation, and there are pitfalls along
the way. Sometimes a patient will accept the transformation
only at a semantic or cognitive level—"Alright, so it's not
that I can't, but that I won't; but it still feels just as impossible to do." The temptation will be to react with disappointment and resignation. The element of stubbornness may or
may not be implicated, but even if it is it may be recalcitrant to analysis for a period of time.

What's required of you, in my opinion and according to
my experience, is a dogged kind of determination, if not
faith. Your patient will often need for you to give up on
him, to declare him hopelessly helpless. That should not
only be interpreted to him, but you should resist actually
feeling it, for if you maintain the faith then that will count
for a great deal.

I can't put this too strongly, Simon, so let me repeat and
amplify. It can be of enormous value to your patient if you
proceed as if you were fully convinced that he can take
effective action and can change. For one thing, you will
then resist his attempts to enlist your support for his sense
of helplessness and resignation. It's neither difficult nor is it
hypocritical for you to have some private doubts and skepticism (especially when it is early in your career as a therapist), but do not allow them any significant influence on your
session-to-session work. You can simply accept the working hypothesis out of conviction that the hypothesis itself is
vital. Otherwise, not only will you be prone to self-fulfilling
expectations, but you won't be giving your patient's well-
being the full benefit of the doubt. The reason I am making this pitch here is because it's during the impasse of
the Middle—sometimes deep and protracted—that this matter becomes urgent. What I advocate as the best medicine
for it is a patient and determined and unswerving stick-to-
it-iveness on your part.

Familiarity with the variety of ways people maintain their

sense of helplessness, as well as the variety of reasons they need to maintain it, can be most useful. I believe that the former can often be more practically relevant than the latter. There's an inclination on our part to pay more attention to the dynamic bases of the phenomenon—for example, to ways in which it can be a resolution of conflicts over aggression, or the result of Superego pressures (matters of conscience or guilt), or interwoven with aspects of self-image. I in no way mean to minimize the value of a genetic approach to unraveling the skein of interrelated dynamic factors, but it's too easy to lose sight of the cognitive structures that support the sense of helplessness, of the fact that beliefs, attitudes, values (which do of course have a significant dynamic origin) can play a powerful part in maintaining the experience of "I just can't!"

One of the cognitive processes that tends to become involved is generalization (or overinclusion). It begins with those situations and circumstances which do in fact render people helpless. (There are, after all, events none of us can act against, and situations where our only recourse is acquiescence.) The next step is to associate or assimilate them with situations and circumstances which are not outside of control. By a process such as generalization we recruit the latter into the former. What was at first "I can, but I won't" becomes compounded with the "I can't, so I won't," and the crucial distinctions become submerged. The matter is not simple because there is a wide range of intermediary points along the continuum which represent circumstances in which helplessness is one of degree. The process then works by shifting from one relative position to another and by grouping events from further up the continuum with those at a lower position.

Whatever the process may be, it can be of enormous therapeutic value to pay attention to the purely cognitive aspects of the phenomenon, to work at unraveling the network of associations and groupings (I like to call them *schemas*) in order to help a patient restore the distinctions between circumstances that are indeed outside of his control and those that are not.

The therapy session itself provides an arena both for the playing out of the underlying dynamic conflict and for the kind of learning that will restore the cognitive dimension. Not only does a patient come to recognize the underpinnings of his sense of impotency, but he also learns about the range of real possibilities for action. For instance, you can (and should) often point out to him that he is structuring and controlling the sessions quite actively even while he experiences the event passively. Patients will often cling to a sense of helplessness in the sessions themselves. They will feel prey to whatever happens to come to their mind, as if they are nothing more than the passive object of their own thoughts and moods—"I don't know why, but I'm thinking about . . ." or, "For some reason the following thought comes to mind . . ." or, "A feeling of sadness is coming over me." And when you point out, as you often will, that it is no accident that such a thought or such a mood is upon them, you will be working with the fundamental phenomenon. By exposing the dynamic and cognitive causes you gradually chip away at the patient's sense of lack of control. As the therapy progresses, he will come to know that his thoughts and feelings do not simply impose themselves on him but rather are the products of relatively active processes. He doesn't "have to" feel what he is feeling or think the thoughts he is thinking; he's making and choosing and Willing. And out of such repeated experiences emerge both the sense and fact of control.

I don't want to give you the impression, Simon, that I believe people simply Will their thoughts and moods. That's not my point. It's far from simple—in fact the issue here is a terribly complex and profound one—but I believe that people can take active measures when they really want to and when they can free themselves from unrealistic (or irrational) constraints. *Psychotherapy* requires the assumption that a patient can exert, over a fairly wide range, a significant effect upon his actions, his thoughts, and his feelings. The way the sessions actuate this assumption is by providing him with a regular and extended exercise in it. The goal, you see, is to enlarge and strengthen his Ego control.

Simon, let me now imagine a major objection on your part. Let me put the following words in your mouth: "What about the fact that *Psychotherapy* entails a substantial powerlessness on the part of my patient to affect me? All of his efforts to control me—to provoke me to speech and to emotion, for instance—are generally frustrated. Surely the result can only be to reinforce his sense of helplessness with respect to his interpersonal relations. Or else he may learn how to exercise greater control over himself, but he learns nothing at all about how to control others. Is this not a basic flaw or contradiction between the goals and the methods of *Psychotherapy?*"

I think not, Simon. In my experience, it typically does not happen. I believe the reason it doesn't rests upon two separate aspects of the therapeutic interaction. First of all, there is a vital sense in which your patient is constantly exerting maximum control over you. Though he is powerless to move you to affect and to action, he nonetheless retains complete control over your attention and your train of thought. You take him seriously during each moment of each session, and your stream of thought (as revealed, for example, in your Interpretations) follows the same path that his takes. This represents a substantial—as well as unique—kind of interpersonal power.

Second, consider the fact that his power is limited to this. Here's another unique feature of your interpersonal relationship—in his everyday interpersonal relations he experiences nothing like it. Although he may feel in his everyday relationships as if he were in fact powerless, when he comes to see what a really powerless relationship is like— i.e., the one he has with you—he has the opportunity to discover the invalidity of that feeling. Your patient, after all, must come to recognize the diverse and subtle ways in which he manipulates people. When his efforts to move and manipulate you are so systematically frustrated, he can sense the real difference—and his recognition can be profound and meaningful.

Say, for example, he relates to people with a passive kind of helplessness that causes them either to nurture and protect him or else to reject him altogether. When (and if) you point it out to him, he will acquire an intellectual appreciation of the fact, but it may be little more than that. When, however, he experiences his interaction with you, in which his behavior has neither of those consequences, then his intellectual appreciation is supported by emotional recognition that can make it a deeper and more meaningful discovery. It's as if he comes to know what a really impotent relationship feels like, and as a result can feel what his everyday relationships really entail. This, after all, is the reason that Transferencelike experiences within the therapy can have such a profound effect on outside-of-the-therapy experiences—the intellectual recognition is accompanied by an emotional recognition, and both are vital ingredients in the process of Understanding.

Does that resolve the contradiction?

* * * * * * *

Now to a second big issue: dependency. The Middle is often characterized by conflicts over dependency. Since many patients experience a sense of dependency—if not upon their therapist, then upon the therapy itself—the vicissitudes of dependency are likely to play a prominant part in the Middle. First, let me indulge in some general remarks on the subject.

A conception of Ego Autonomy has to take account of the problem of dependency, and Relative Autonomy must formulate a kind of balance between dependency and independency. So we have to make distinctions between kinds and modes of dependencies—for example, the profound relationships between being dependent upon others and being depended upon by others must be carefully considered. It goes without saying that dependency is basic to the Human Condition, and so for many patients it will form the basis for their neurotic adaptation and their major personality problems. It's altogether prudent to assume, then, that when the matter emerges in force, the therapy is in a position to deal with a central aspect of their problems. And it needs to be said—though it's too facile to say it—that you must have a conception of it that is psychologically sound, that is balanced, judicious, and relatively free from cultural attitudes and values that attach premiums to dependency or to independency in ways that exaggerate or distort. Now to some particulars.

For some patients the growing sense of dependency in the therapy may become a source of anxiety. Missed sessions will evoke uneasiness if not a sense of dread, and that reaction can be unsettling and frightening. While forms of therapy which include support and direction are more likely to intensify a patient's dependency needs and conflicts, it also happens that *Psychotherapy* will do it as well. The reasons for this can be twofold: (1) dependency may accompany the regression and decompensation that often occur in therapy as a prelude to meaningful changes; (2) the Transference Neurosis may redintegrate a patient's underlying dependency needs and conflicts.

When you conduct *Psychotherapy* you do your best to avoid gratifying your patient's dependency needs. The special advantage of this is that you are then in a good position to Interpret their vicissitudes to him. Since there is little reality basis for his feeling dependent on you, he will be better able to recognize the degree to which it is an irrational—or an Internally determined—matter. But patients tend also to experience dependency upon the therapy situation itself. They feel that their well-being depends upon having regular sessions—and this can have a substantial reality basis. If your patient has plunged into an intensive Transference Neurosis, or if he has regressed significantly within the context of the therapy itself, then he does in fact need the sessions to preserve his well-being outside of them—his sense of dependency is then altogether reasonable and valid. It's easy to lose sight of that fact and to attempt too strenuously to "resolve" the dependency by means of active Interpretations. My point is this: you should both expect and accept a degree of dependency as natural to the process of therapy.

One reason I make this point is that dependency can be a problem for a therapist, particularly a beginner. It can be difficult to shake off feelings of guilt and uneasiness at having someone become so dependent upon us. Such feelings will lead us to over-emphasize the irrational and neurotic component in the patient's dependency at the expense of it's valid and realistic basis. The message may be, "Don't be so dependent," which can put him into a very difficult position. Some patients will be alarmed at the dependency, and the feeling will be unnecessarily intensified if they sense that we feel it too. Others will settle into it too comfortably.

Both reactions are important to watch for. The first is easier to see and easier to Interpret—"I believe that you are frightened by the fact that you seem to be needing these sessions so much, and so you react by wanting to withdraw in a way that is quite typical of you. . . ." The second may remain in the background only to emerge in force during the Ending stage. It can be very helpful to focus attention on the second reaction during the Middle—"While you occasionally complain about the fact that you've come to feel so dependent upon therapy, I believe that it gives you some pleasure and comfort. You seem to like the feelings of dependency, and in part it is your way of reassuring me that I am helping you." The thing to avoid, however, is too much emphasis on the dependency as if it were a symptom or a special problem. In general, it must be allowed to run its course naturally—and the Middle stage is its natural habitat.

* * * * * * *

The Middle is also the natural habitat of the impasse. Whatever its basis—and it probably stems from conflicts over dependency and over change more than any others—the impasse too must be expected and accepted. And because it's so likely to play a critical part in therapy, it merits most careful consideration. Therefore, Simon, I'll put it off until next time when I expect to feel fresher.

Your affectionate uncle

Twenty-five

Dear Simon,

I like to draw a distinction between the Therapeutic Process and a patient's psychological condition. It's a useful thing to do for several reasons. One is that it allows me to distinguish an *impasse* from a *crisis*. The former can be defined as an arrest or set-back of the Therapeutic Process; the latter is an arrest or setback of a patient's condition. By definition, then, an impasse denotes an occurrence whose source and function lie within the therapy itself, while a crisis may (and also may not) be based on events external to the therapy.

In any form of psychotherapy it's common for there to be periods during which things come to a protracted standstill. Furthermore, rather than remain on a plateau, things may take a turn for the worse. Such occurrences—whether they are conceptualized as periods of great Resistance tension or not—can be regarded as intrinsic to the Therapeutic Process, and the term *impasse* is best applied to them. It's equally common for a patient to suffer a serious relapse in his psychological condition, if not a new decompensation. There may be an intensification of a personality problem; he may fall into a severe depression or go into a manic flight; there may be an exacerbation of a neurotic feature, a phobia perhaps; he may experience an acute episode of anxiety. To many therapists the occurrence of such regressions is evidence that the therapy is "taking" (for if there is to be a significant restructuring of personality there may have to be

260

a significant destructuring). The term *crisis* denotes such occurrences.

Before I write about them separately, as I plan to do, let me point out that they often occur together. An impasse may be sparked by a crisis, and it may in turn be the source of a crisis. It's usually possible to discern the difference, nevertheless, and it's important to do so—for it is important whether my patient is suffering from the therapy, so to speak, or from events that lie external to it. In the first case, I can best serve him by maintaining my regular therapeutic posture, by sticking to *Psychotherapy;* in the second, I may have to modify that posture, because it may be that I can best serve him only by abandoning (temporarily at least) the business-as-usual position. What I mean is this, Simon: if, say, he falls into a depression, and if the precipitating event is largely unrelated to the therapy (a loved one, let us suppose, fell seriously ill or died), then my appropriate mode of behavior may no longer be the analytic one; but if the precipitating event was internal to the therapy (a major conflict, let's suppose, has surfaced) then it may still be the most efficacious one.

While the distinction is important insofar as it can have great practical implications, it is sometimes a subtle one that takes time to discern. This can pose particularly difficult decisions for us, because we may not be able to wait until the situation becomes clear enough for us to decide how to respond. You see, we may have no good way of judging at the outset whether it's an impasse we are confronting or whether it's a crisis. For one thing, it's not uncommon for a crisis to be pressed into the service of Resistance in a way that is functionally identical with an impasse. For another, it's not uncommon that a crisis has it source in the events of the therapy even though it occurs external to it. A patient may, for example, lose his job, or dissolve his marriage, or even fall ill, as a result of what he is experiencing in his therapy. In this way too what takes the form of a crisis may be functionally an impasse. (I'll enlarge on this subject soon.) From his—the patient's—viewpoint, however, the distinction is likely to be clear and sharp, and this fact has to play a major role in how we handle the situation.

A patient's paradigmatic experience of the impasse is this: "I don't see what good this therapy is doing me any more—it's not working, it's not getting anywhere." Usually it attaches itself to some feature of the therapy or to some aspect of the therapist that he had accepted during the Beginning but no longer can—for example, "This is too artificial," "too intellectual," "too infrequent," "too expensive"—or, "You are, as I thought at first, too young," "too middle-class," "too uptight," "too different from me." Neither is it uncommon for him to accept all the blame for the impasse—e.g., "I am, after all, too inhibited," "too rigid," "too neurotic," "too crazy."

Since it lies internal to the therapy, an impasse can readily be explained by what's going on in it. We can accept the working hypothesis that its occurrence is related to the current state of the treatment—a major defensive system may be undergoing change, an important conflict may be emerging into consciousness, a painful memory may be on the threshold of redintegration, or a Transference feeling may be burgeoning. The impasse can therefore be viewed by us as defense (Resistance, more strictly speaking). Sometimes it's quite new, but ordinarily it borrows its form from the patient's already familiar defenses. If we view it this way, we will eschew any serious modifications in Technique designed to overcome it.

Our business-as-usual posture in the face of our patient's anguish and distress is something that's very hard to feel right about. This, by the way, is perhaps the sorest spot in the public's view of the more traditional psychotherapies, and it's commonly encountered in movies and magazines.

The patient is pictured as suffering terrible anguish, and the smug and foolish therapist simply goes ahead doing his regular thing—which is depicted as cruelly incompetent. The one cries out desperately for the other to behave in a more human and reasonable way, and the other has nothing but deaf ears.

When a patient is in acute distress, the standard therapeutic methods tend to seem irrelevant, ill-suited to be helpful, and even ethically questionable. Now, first of all, let me acknowledge that they may be all of these. I've repeatedly written that *Psychotherapy* is not suitable for all patients, and soon I'll discuss the matter further when I write about the modifications required when your patient experiences a crisis. But my focus here is on the impasse, and my contention is that the regular methods of *Psychotherapy* are in fact the most efficacious ones to maintain in the face of an impasse—provided that you follow certain Technical considerations and precautions. My thesis is this: the advantages of the analytic (i.e., Interpretive) mode may be especially great during an impasse. My main Technical consideration is this: the manifest content of the impasse must be given extensive and intensive attention.

The rationale for my thesis is based on the assumption that the impasse can be a critical juncture in the development of the Therapeutic Process. The patient is not intellectualizing, he is feeling; he's experiencing the full impact of a basic impulse and a basic conflict; his defenses are in full force and in the forefront. Matters have surfaced to where they can be clearly experienced and observed, and therefore analyzed. It is, in short, a moment of great opportunity. But, like all such moments, it's also fraught with great hazards. Which brings me to the Technical consideration.

The biggest hazard—at least in my opinion—is to dismiss the manifest content of the impasse (or to minimize it) and to draw premature attention to its presumed underlying basis. To meet an impasse with the Interpretive mode is one thing; to use that mode inappropriately is quite another. And it can be a serious Technical mistake to regard an impasse as little more than a fortuitous reflection of an underlying conflict. That it does derive from a latent meaning, that it serves an unrecognized or unacknowledged function, is not at issue. All behaviors can be viewed as hierarchically layered and ordered, and all meanings are probably superimposed on deeper meanings, but this does not justify the conclusion that it's only the "other"—the "deeper" —meanings that really count. Like the manifest content of a dream, and like the form of a symptom, the actual impasse must be paid serious attention. To dismiss the overt in favor of the covert, the manifest in favor of the latent, the conscious in favor of the unconscious, is simply an error. Nothing can be so ineffective and even self-defeating as the claim, "Oh, it's just unconscious hostility," or, "It's nothing more than oedipal conflict in disguise." Moreover, it's not always we therapists who take this position; sometimes our patients do it with even greater haste and urgency.

So how do we go about paying due attention to the manifest content of an impasse? Let me use an example. Let's make the issue monetary, since it's far from uncommon or unreal. Your patient's financial condition hasn't changed, but a session ago he began by saying, "I was writing out cheques for my monthly bills last night, and it hit me how much this therapy is really costing me. A hundred bucks a week—almost a quarter of my earnings! It's insane, you know; I just can't see it any more. If I were getting much better that would be different, but things are going so slowly here, It just doesn't make sense to me anymore." Since then this topic has been so much in the forefront—he is so obsessed with the cost—that things have otherwise come to an effective standstill; little else comes to his mind during the sessions.

Suppose further, to make matters more simple than they usually are, that the main topic at the time the issue first arose was his rage at his father in respect to ungivingness. Your temptation will surely be to draw the connection between that theme and the nature of the impasse. It is that temptation you have to resist, Simon—for the time being anyway. For one thing, it's a connection you want him to draw for himself; for another, suggesting it to him now may be to deny that the issue is real enough, and that may only lead to argument and confrontation which would exacerbate the impasse.

The first step that has to be taken vis-à-vis an impasse is to make sure the patient understands that it is intrinsic to the therapy. In this example it's easy, because your patient has acknowledged that if things had been progressing better in the therapy the issue would not have come up with such force. Still, you must be careful not to minimize the reality consideration when you draw attention to its basis in the Therapeutic Process.

The next step is usually more difficult. It's to suggest that the reality issue is now serving the interests of Resistance— i.e., not only has it brought things to a standstill, but that may actually be its principal function. Because this one can be such a difficult step, it may work better if you delay it until after you have explored what it means to him that the therapy is so expensive. Is it, for instance, that he has recently grown worried about his future security?—Is that the main concern? Or is it his wish that you should show your love for him by lowering the fee? Or is it rather that he now feels more acutely a sense of deprivation? You see, it's possible that the underlying issue has to do with giving and getting—e.g., he is giving you so much and getting so little in return. While all of these themes may be at work, it's likely that one of them is most salient, and if that emerges with sufficient clarity then the underlying dynamic issue will have a better chance to emerge with it.

Next, your aim can be to show him that the theme is not specific to therapy alone but cuts across his personality and problems. If feeling cheated and deprived is the salient issue, then you might be able to point out, for example, that he has similar reactions when he takes girls out on dates.

[PATIENT:] That's true. Are you saying then that there's no basis for that feeling? It's unrealistic?

[YOU:] No, I don't mean to say that. This treatment is expensive; dates can be too. I'm suggesting that the problem is not altogether specific to here.

[PATIENT:] Okay; I do get caught up with whether I'm getting my money's worth in other situations too. But it seems to me I have every right to feel it here too. I've stopped getting much out of therapy, so maybe I'd be better off stopping and saving my money.

[YOU, focussing on the theme:] That's not so different from what you do with girls—you stop dating them. Then you feel lonely and unloved.

[PATIENT:] So what am I supposed to do? If I keep dating them, the feeling of being cheated just grows and grows, and that's no good. I get sore at them, and I start acting mean, and then they quit on me. . . .

The final step, for which groundwork has to be laid carefully, is to elucidate the meaning of the theme (and the impasse as well) by considering its relation to the topic that was interrupted by its advent. You can introduce it by saying, "I believe that part of the reason you've become obsessed with the idea that you're being cheated and deprived has to do with what you were talking about several sessions ago. Do you recall what that was?" What you aim for is the connection between the father's ungivingness and yours—i.e., the Transference implications. But what you hope for at first is merely the apposition of the two without necessarily drawing any causal connection. It's important that he find this apposition to be interesting and eye-opening, and that he not see it as an act of expediency on your part (to take the heat off you). If he recalls the topic, and if he reacts with some surprise, then much will have been gained.

[PATIENT:] That's right!—I was talking about how my old man was so stingy [grins with embarrassment]. I'm feeling foolish.

[YOU:] It must feel to you as if you've been caught doing something surreptitious. You're embarrassed, aren't you?

[PATIENT:] Yeah. You know something, when I was sitting there writing out cheques, I remembered how my father used to pay his bills. He would get himself into a big sweat; he'd criticize my mother for being a spendthrift; he'd complain about the high cost of everything. . . .

Now things are headed in a good direction. Whether he takes the route of identification with father or with the criticized mother matters little. Sooner or later he will remember the rage that he once experienced at his father, and the feelings of the impasse will have provided the emotional basis for this important redintegration. He may even come to recognize by himself that instead of having immersed himself in the memory of how cheated he felt by his father, he became obsessed with the fact that you are cheating him. But even if you have to formulate that for him, he'll be prepared to accept it, and the impasse will have been weathered while a significant advance in the Therapeutic Process will have been achieved.

Trust me, Simon; impasses frequently have that kind of salutary result—if you hew to good Interpretations and good Technique. Crises, however, are different. They pose new and often serious problems for the conduct of *Psychother-*

apy. If your patient suffers a serious relapse or decompensation, if his loved one falls seriously ill or dies, if he loses his job or something happens that seriously affects his psychological condition, he is experiencing a crisis that may be functionally unrelated to the therapy but can have a profound effect on it. At such times you can hardly maintain a business-as-usual position.

* * * * * * *

From the patient's viewpoint, a crisis, unlike an impasse, is most likely to be external to the therapy. That fact is of paramount importance even when you have reason to believe that the crisis was precipitated by therapy and designed to serve as a Resistance. By now it ought to be clear to you, Simon, that what counts is your patient's Mind. The crisis will remain extrinsic so long as he sees it that way, and you may have little choice but to regard it that way too.

The movie and magazine writers are quite right in their indictment of those traditional therapists who maintain business as usual when their patients are suffering a crisis. A patient in acute distress needs support and counsel, not explanations; he may not even benefit much from an articulation of how he feels. Of course, whether he needs counsel and support depends on the nature of the crisis as well as the patient; but the rule generally holds. That *Psychotherapy* is not appropriate for all patients, I have already written several times; one example I gave was the seriously depressed patient. Now, if your patient falls into such a serious depression during the course of *Psychotherapy*—no matter whether the precipitating event was internal or external to treatment—you are treating someone who, temporarily at least, is not suitable for the method. You must be fully prepared to change it to suit the new circumstances. You may abandon your attitude of neutrality and impassivity by

commiserating and sympathizing; you may offer reassur-
ances and support instead of Interpretations (which will
only serve to exacerbate the depression by providing nutriment for self-punishment); you may offer direction and
even certain kinds of real help. That much is quite clear.

Perhaps the only legitimate question is, "When he recov-
ers from the crisis will it be possible to resume *Psychotherapy?*" The answer, in my opinion, is a qualified
"Yes." (Some orthodox analysts would answer it with an
unqualified "No.") Before I defend this opinion it needs to
be mentioned that you cannot predicate your decision on
the answer, for even if it's a qualified or unqualified No, the
modifications may be unavoidable. Your answer may affect
you insofar as the speed and extent to which you act is concerned, but your patient's well-being is obviously paramount. A patient in crisis needs special clinical attention,
and this can mandate a radically modified position on your
part.

But once the crisis is past you will want to return to
your pre-crisis position. While that may be problematic, it
needn't be ruled out automatically. Generally, a patient
will have little difficulty understanding what it was that
prompted you to behave so differently and in ways that you
promised you wouldn't. He will likely balk at your efforts to
return to your pre-crisis behavior, for once having enjoyed
your direct gratification of his needs he will be loath to give
it up. But there should never have been any question in his
mind that, being a human being, you were always capable
of giving support, helpful direction, advice, and the rest. It
was clear that you didn't before because you chose not to;
so you can choose not to once more after the crisis is past.

Our neutrality, detachment, and impersonality are typically perceived by our patients as our therapeutic posture. If
that is not the case, then we must take appropriate steps to
guarantee that it is. If, for example, your patient perceives

your passivity as a personality trait, that merits attention. Of course you cannot say, "I am an active person in all but this particular situation." The most you can do is to point out that he is perceiving your passivity as if it were your every-day way of behaving; but you can elaborate on that with an Interpretation—e.g., "You need to see it that way because it makes that aspect of my behavior here more tolerable to you," and you might know enough about him to be able to suggest a reason why that perception is more tolerable. Still, it's one thing to point out that he is making an unverifiable generalization; it's another to give him proof that it's in fact untrue. Before the crisis he had no way to experience you as a giving, active, and resourceful person; he may have assumed that you were, but he could not have been certain. After the crisis he knows for certain; so in a sense he has learned something personal about you that he would not have learned otherwise. During the crisis you may well have revealed yourself as a person in a variety of ways—and it's no use pretending that you can go back into hiding, so to speak. Thus, there's little question that the crisis and the way you responded to it will continue to play an important part in the therapy. The important question is: "Will this alteration mitigate against the successful continuation of *Psychotherapy*?" My answer, again, is a qualified "No"—provided you remain sufficiently alert to a number of likely consequences.

One consequence revolves around the fact that your patient has learned a way to shake you away from your analytic position. The temptation will be strong—and it will take unwitting as well as witting forms—to engineer a new crisis in order to do that. This requires you to be alert to the slightest hint of such a temptation in order to meet it with appropriate Interpretations. Another consequence is one that is more difficult to articulate. Your response to a crisis will usually be taken as enduring proof that you Care, and sometimes this may take on some of the attributes of Love. In any event, this may free your patient from needing further proofs of it, and he may return to *Psychotherapy* with a new sense of security as well as a new Transference ingredient. While certain features of this may be quite comfortable for you as a therapist, it may represent a serious flaw in the therapy from then on. Despite the fact that you are again impersonal, impassive, and the rest, he *knows* now that you really are not. He may proceed as if nothing had changed—you must avoid that illusion.

Even when it is past, a crisis inevitably affects the nature of the therapy. For this reason you must be judicious, if not cautious, in your estimation of its magnitude and in your modifications. If you realize that the fate of *Psychotherapy* may be hanging in the balance, then you will be more reluctant to make modifications that may not be entirely necessary or to make them more radical than they need be. The big danger, however, is that you will react too slowly and too timidly, and fail to make all the necessary changes in time. It's yet another of our Scylla and Charybdis's.

Your affectionate uncle

Twenty-six

Dear Simon,

You're interested in my claim that it's an error to dismiss the overt in favor of the covert, the manifest in favor of the latent, and the conscious in favor of the unconscious. You're quite right to suggest that it's probably a legacy Freud left us. But I don't agree with your second point, that together with this has come the fact that traditional ("dynamic") psychotherapy is, as you put it, "a hassle." I can see how I've given you the impression that the Middle is typically a steady struggle against a series of impasses and Resistances, a continuous stream of problems and complaints, and an experience of unleavened anguish for the patient. That is my fault, and I'll try to correct it. First, the legacy.

Freud's topographic slogan, "To make conscious that which was unconscious," is perhaps too famous. Even though he later added the structural point of view to his metapsychology, we still encounter the slogan as if it were the best way to formulate the goal of psychotherapy. It does imply a kind of disrespect for the poor conscious mind in favor of its unconscious underpinnings, and it has undoubtedly had some unfortunate effects on the practice of therapy. The Client-centered, Existentialist-Humanist movements can be understood as attempts to correct for the bias, and I agree with them that the actual form of behavior and experience must occupy a central position in the considerations of *Psychotherapy*. The structure of experience, the texture of consciousness, must be studied and Understood. My advice to you is to avoid at all times a hasty plunge into the deeper layers of behavior and experience, and to take steps to keep your patient from doing it as well.

It's helpful to bear in mind that the too-hasty plunge is likely to be a defensive maneuver. It's not uncommon for both you and him to be more comfortable dealing with the more abstract—and therefore remote from actual experience—events such as "aggression," "sex," "conflict," and "pleasure." One's actual experiences of anger, disappointment, shame, lust, and pain can be more difficult to countenance. A patient who is experiencing a sense of disappointment in you can gain short-term relief from it through the intellectualization that he is in the sway of a Transference Conflict. Similarly, anger may be less tolerable than Unconscious Hostility. The intellectualization may sometimes be an altogether necessary short-term relief, but it should be regarded as a band-aid treatment and little more.

Your first—and I would add your principal—task is to articulate the experience itself, to make your patient aware of the full scope and texture of what it is he is feeling. This requires forebearance in explaining it (and explaining it away) and in tracing its less conscious sources. Both you and he must live with the experience for a time. An impasse, for instance, is not something to be broken and defeated—it is to be examined and resolved, not dissolved. Lest my rhetoric distort things, let me amplify. Recourse to dynamic and economic explanation or to genetic reconstruction is necessary and useful. In this respect I disagree with the Existentialists who seem to advocate nothing more than the articulation of actual experience. But my guiding consideration is this: the explanation serves the interests of enlarging, articulating, and re-ordering the conscious experience; it's not vice versa. The explanations are tools, not ends—means, and not goals. They should be used to enhance the realm of actual experience and behavior, to enhance its authenticity, its complexity, and also its immediacy.

Distortions and displacements need to be corrected, and explanations can achieve that. The mistake is to regard distortions and displacements as trivial in relation to deeper meanings and functions. (This is the medical model—its germ theory—that we must be on guard against.)

So—to return to the topic of last letter—an impasse, like a silence, is not something to be broken. It's an important opportunity, a valuable period of tension. Its resolution may be imperative, but resolution means something critically different from dissolution. In music, for analogy, a period of tension (dissonance, for instance) may call for an appropriate resolution but rarely for a dissolution. Don't lose sight of the fact that tensions, impasses, and Eriksonian crises form part of the developmental fabric. So, just as music without tension is apt to be lifeless and boring, a therapy without impasses is apt to be lifeless and directionless. This is not to say, of course, that therapy should proceed at a high level of tension—that one impasse should resolve directly into another, that there should be a constant high pitch of tension. There's a natural ebb and flow, warp and woof, dissonance-consonance; between the crises of human development are periods of relative calm consolidation.

This leads me nicely (and not accidentally) into the second point you raised. It may be unavoidable in letters like these to concentrate on the expectable problems and difficulties. That, after all, is when we therapists need all the counsel we can get and all the ideas we can use. But it would be unfortunate if I left you with the impression that the Middle, or *Psychotherapy* in general, is a steady "hassle." What about the good experiences—the moments of keen excitement at having Understood, the deep satisfactions that come from an authentic encounter with Self, the security that is based on achieved control, and the intrinsic rewards of enhanced Autonomy? These too can be expected to occur during the Middle, and we can play a big part in making them happen.

To leaven the stresses and strains that inhere in *Psychotherapy* should be one of your principal concerns too. Along with everything else you are concerned with, you must also strive to make your patient's experience of therapy a good one. This can mean a variety of things—from fostering a sense of excitement over self-discovery to occasionally offering an Interpretation whose main purpose is to alleviate dread and anxiety. *Psychotherapy* needn't be a constant ordeal. And when I say that it can be leavened from time to time with the exhilaration that springs from fresh Understanding, I don't mean by this the kind of gladness that comes with improvement or with success outside of therapy; that's another matter. I mean the old Gestalt experience of *Aha!*

A natural way to foster a sense of excitement is to convey it in your Interpretations, to include a note of *Aha!* in your formulations and articulations. Another is to show interest in your patient's fleeting thoughts at moments when something significant may be happening during the session. No matter what ways you choose, you should avoid combining your impassivity with deadness or flatness of affect. I have already advised some warmth; I would now add some sparkle. Your body, your eyes, your manner of speaking, should convey a sense of alertness and aliveness.

Some therapists deliberately behave dramatically in order to heighten their patient's involvement and to make the sessions lively and exciting. Drama, unfortunately, tends to melodrama; and even when it doesn't there can be little merit in encouraging histrionics. You can guard against a dry and spiritless atmosphere in other ways: you can convey a sense of intensity and excitement if and when you feel it; above all, you can take care not to discourage your patient's intensity and excitement by your interventions or by the model you present. If you notice, for example, that he tends to be impassive, you should suspect that he is emulating your behavior—and you can draw his attention to that fact. If you notice that he tends to speak in sober "interpretation," you should recognize that you are being imitated. Even more, since it's quite inevitable that he will take on some of your characteristics, you should make sure that your behavior during the sessions conveys a measure of sparkle, excitement, and intensity.

Many therapists occasionally use wit and humor in their interventions. Their rationale is not to lighten the spirit of the session by introducing some mirth into it, but rather to take advantage of the special properties of humor as a way of sharpening an observation, giving an Interpretation in a condensed and economical way, allowing for the discharge of tensions, and momentarily bypassing defense. Humor, however, because it too easily becomes tactless, has to be used with utmost discretion. A patient may react to your joke as if it were at his expense. If he perceives you as simply poking some fun, then the humor may sour. If he's in a sober mood, humorless and serious, then your joke can be jarring and distracting. In any event, you must be prepared for the challenge, "Why do you make a joke?"

In my opinion, Simon, we therapists should generally avoid the use of humor and levity, even in the face of a patient who has complained of how uniformly serious or sober we are. In the context of *Psychotherapy,* humor is too likely to serve the interests of defense. And while a patient who occasionally needs to entertain us with his wit or to provoke us to laughter with a joke needn't be slapped with an Interpretation, neither should we feel moved to compete with him. It's one thing to share a good joke, a funny incident, or a humorous development in his free associations; it's another to foster the mode. Therefore, the only occasions on which I regard the therapist's humor appropriate is when the patient is himself engaged in it, and when its defensive function is not paramount. That, at least, is my rule of thumb.

Let me try to construct an example that may or may not strike you as funny—and this, by the way, is one of the big problems with humor. Your patient is recounting an incident at the supper table where his wife and his mother were competing over who is the better cook. When the argument turned to the use of frozen ingredients, his wife was clearly on the defensive. She was momentarily speechless when his mother charged that freezing robbed the ingredients of their goodness, and at this point he experienced some anxiety along with the impulse to come to his wife's rescue. But all he could think to say was, "It tastes good enough for me," to which his mother triumphantly replied, "And you're the big gourmet in the family, eh?"—at which point his wife burst out with, "And who is to blame for that?" Now the patient tells you this: "When she said that I suddenly felt nauseated, and I had to burp, but I struggled to keep from burping because I knew it would make my mother furious. So I reached for my glass of water but instead I knocked it over, and the water spilled right into my mother's lap. She flew into a rage because she thought I did it on purpose."

Say, now, you believe that the burping and the spilling of water into his mother's lap both represent the same underlying act. It occurs to you that there's a humorous association between acting "on purpose" and "on burpose." Your impulse is to quip, "You actually did it on burpous." You give in to this impulse. If your patient gets the joke, it will mean that he has understood the association; if he laughs in recognition he will have apprehended your Interpretation (that the need to burp and to spill were indeed purposeful acts, and the latter was a substitute for the former). But suppose he does not get the joke—and you had laughed when you made it. Now the situation is quite different, for it he reacts with irritation and asks, "Why are you laughing at me?" that will necessarily become the focus of attention. You cannot simply apologize and then try to offer your Interpretation in a more straightforward way. You may instead have to deal with his reaction to your quip, to change the subject—impose a fresh topic. It may be quite true that, just as the act of spilling the water evoked an affect (rage) in his mother, so it now evokes an affect (amusement) in you, but it's hard to see what useful purpose will be served by pursuing that correspondence.

And—to make a weak joke—I'll pursue this correspondence next week.

Your affectionate uncle

Twenty-seven

My dear Simon,

Who among us can resist drawing a nice, clean distinction between facts and fictions, between actual events and hypothetical ones? It's really something of a human necessity to do that—that's what Reality Testing is about. Furthermore, distinguishing givens (data) from intellectual constructions (theory) is for many of us more than an Ego Function alone; it's a task in which our Superego takes a keen and sometimes overbearing interest. Blessed as we are with the power to symbolize our experience—with the ability to conjecture and to anticipate, to fantasize and to remember—we are also cursed with cognitive dissonance. And once we discover the dread power of the challenge, "How do you know?" our ignorance and uncertainties can take on a punitive aspect. It can be our conscience that nags us to make a sharp distinction between factual events and theoretical ones.

Why this rhetorical outburst? Because a discussion of theory is before us, and all men, not just psychologists, live in a world of mental events that brooks no easy distinction between fact and fiction. "I am feeling angry." Is that a fact? What kind? In what way can we be certain that it's true? How about, "You are right, doctor; I suppose I am feeling angry."? That sounds like an inference. Where does it belong in the realm of fact and fiction? How can we confirm it? And go on to consider this Interpretation: "When you were a small child you probably wanted to kill your father because you were angry with him."

Now, Simon, this correspondence is hardly the place for a disquisition on the nature of observation and theory in psychology. Unfortunately, however, the smallest step into the philosophy of natural and clinical observation would require an extensive excursion into the matter. There's no simply wetting our toes—the matter is too deep and complex to be dabbled in. At the same time, Simon, we cannot avoid these waters altogether because we deal so much in observations, inferences, and confirmations. And not only are many of our Interpretations theoretical in nature, but their substance and content are bound to reflect the kind of theory we profess. There's no justifiable way to sidestep a discussion of theory. All I can hope to do is keep it brief and to the point, and to focus on issues having maximum relevance for psychotherapy. After I'm done with it, Simon, I promise you I'll return to purely clinical matters and write you about the Ending stage of *Psychotherapy*.

Let's plunge into the murky waters by considering the fundamental fact-theory distinction. In one sense at least, this resolves into a separation of events that are observable from events that are not. Now, that seems—does it not?—like an altogether sensible and practical distinction to draw. But when the subject matter is psychology, unfortunately, it may be a trap for the unwary, for it turns out to be profoundly difficult to specify what is an observable psychological event. It's one thing to agree that when a person strikes another with force, that is a fact; it's quite another to agree that he intends harm or is experiencing anger. This is the basic reason why the orthodox Behaviorists concluded that only the former events are amenable to scientific study—conscious events, experience as experience, such things as intentions and affects, are not observable in principle. Better put: even though they are observable by the experiencing person, they cannot be confirmed or disconfirmed by him or anyone else. It's no simple sophistry to contend that he may actually be deluding himself (if not others), that he may be quite incapable of the experience. One can conclude that under certain circumstances that is improbable, but never that it's impossible. And Science, you know, is the search for certitude.

It's impossible to confirm with certainty that when a patient says, "Yes, I recall that such and such an event took place," or that he experienced such and such a feeling when he did, that he is recalling it and that he experienced it. If we define Science as that which deals with events that are confirmable according to certain agreed-upon rules, then we must confront the tough conclusion that until such time as conscious experience can be directly observed by another person, such events cannot be the raw data of a Science.

Now, Simon, it's no good to dismiss the matter by shrugging off the mantle of Science with, "So, who needs it!" The question, you see, is not semantic, it's material. It's the epistemological question, "How do you know?" that we're dealing with—how can we be sure? How can we confirm or disconfirm the validity of our observations? And insofar as Science rules out the role of good faith (but not, I should add, the role of good sense), we must ask ourselves whether the methods that are available to us to answer these questions are Scientific—or, better put, Scientific enough.

Let me simply assert that we psychotherapists have to accept with equanimity the unavoidable answer to the epistemological challenge, "We can never know for sure." Methodological considerations give us little choice but to countenance a fundamental limitation in our ability to confirm our observations, and we must settle for something like relative and conditional confirmation. Now, if that keeps us out of the kingdom of Science—if there's no place in it for those who traffic in data like ours—then so be it. But we will still place a high priority on the value of confirmation; we will continue to care that our observations are as valid as possible. And more than that, we will still draw distinctions between our formulations (and our patients') in respect to their relative factualness and theoreticalness. Why?—for two big reasons: (1) because we cannot escape the purely intellectual implications; and (2) because it can make a great practical difference in our work as therapists. Let me start with the first.

When I was a student, psychologists were arguing about whether this or that concept was animistic or not. To claim, as Tolman did, that a rat can have an expectation was regarded as dangerous because it let the psyche (i.e., the soul) back into psychology after it had been so painstakingly and painfully banished. But times changed. Hebb, for one, was able to dispel the taint of animism by the simple expediency of showing how events such as expectations and intentions could be translated, at least hypothetically, into neurophysiological ones. Does this mean that such psychological events can be regarded as factual *because* they bear a one-to-one relationship to C.N.S. events (which stands, according to Hebb, for Conceptual Nervous System) that can be directly observed in principle? Apparently Yes. Freud did it too in his often quoted statement about ultimately reducing all psychic events to neurochemistry. But notice, Simon, how this implies an anything-goes approach. It's quite possible, in principle, to contend that every and any psychological event you care to consider will one day be amenable to direct observation of its neural underpinnings. Does this free us of having to observe it directly? Obviously, to me anyway, the answer is No.

Consider the proposition that the earth is a roundish ball. Back in the fifteenth century it was a theoretical proposition because it could only be inferred and not yet directly observed. But it was only a matter of time and technology before it could, and then it simply lost its theoretical status. Are our propositions similar in kind? I'm afraid not. "You are (or I am) feeling angry" is not the same kind of fact as "the earth is round." The neural events that accompany it may be, but not the psychological event itself. We may some day discover that neural event, but we will still only be able to observe that event and not the "anger." We will still be left with the task of observing the psychological event—and with the philosophical problem of defining the observable and of formulating its rules of inference and confirmation.

But I'll leave the matter hanging right there. I may already have taken it further than I should have, Simon, and I'll leave it to you to ponder it, study it, and read about it. I'll only exhort you to avoid shirking the responsibility of articulating for yourself the rules of observation for psychological events. They may have to be different from those for physical events—perhaps very fundamentally different—but that won't necessarily make them any the less Scientific.

* * * * * * *

I turn now to the second reason we must care about the relative factualness and theoreticalness of our formulations: because of the practical difference it can make in our work. I'll try to give you the flavor of what I mean, Simon, though I won't go very deeply into the issues that I'll raise. (My aim in this letter is to provoke thought and not to settle matters.) So consider, please, these four Interpretations and assume with me that they are all equally true:

Interpretation 1. "You are feeling angry with me."

Interpretation 2. "You are feeling angry with me because that keeps you from feeling dependent on me."

Interpretation 3. "The reason you are feeling angry with me [in order to keep from feeling dependent] is because I remind you of your father."

Interpretation 4. "When you were five years old, and your

father went away from home, you were angry with him [because it threw your dependency into jeopardy]."

These four Interpretations differ in some fundamental ways that can make some fundamental differences. Your patient can respond "Yes" to all four, but he will mean different things thereby. The first and fourth are statements of fact, insofar as they say what he is feeling and had once felt; the second and third provide an explanation for that fact, insofar as they implicate another feeling (dependency) and also a defense mechanism (substitution).

When he responds to Interpretation 1, your patient means to say, "Yes I do feel angry with you—I recognize that I am experiencing that feeling now." But when he responds to Interpretation 2, he means something different: "Yes, I recognize that my feeling of anger is serving the function of preventing me from feeling dependent," and that is essentially an intellectual recognition. Even if it's more, even if he first acknowledges the dependent feeling too, he is left with the necessity of accepting the connection between the two feelings (i.e., the defense mechanism). Insofar as the connection between the two affective experiences is not itself directly experienced, it is an intellectual construction and therefore a theoretical proposition.

Interpretation 2 therefore entails the cognitive process of inference. Do you want to contend that the first Interpretation does it too—that "anger" is also based on an act of inference? That's altogether reasonable, but you must then acknowledge a difference between kinds and levels of inference. I do agree, strictly speaking, that when I say that I am behaving in anger I'm making an inference and a kind of theoretical assumption. But this sense of "theoretical" is built right into my phenomenological experience by cultural and linguistic usage. I'm applying a socially designated label ("anger") to my direct experience. And when I recall such an experience from the past—whether it happened yesterday, or when I was five, or even before I had learned the label for it—I am "theorizing" in a way that is intrinsic to all cognitive processes. Perception, both internal and external, operates on this kind of inferring, labeling, and "theorizing." Furthermore, there's no compelling reason to make any fundamental distinction between perceiving and remembering—except to bear in mind that the one is more subject to error and distortion than the other. It may make sense to consider a current feeling as less theoretical than one that is recalled from yesterday, and for both to be more factual than one recalled from age five. Here confirmability is relative, and therefore so is theoreticalness.

So the difference between the first two Interpretations comes down to a difference in kind and level of inference. In both cases there can be an experience of recognition, but it may be significantly more direct in one than in the other. The one can loosely be called an "emotional recognition," and the other an "intellectual recognition."

Before I continue, Simon, let me make it clear that in no way do I mean to minimize the efficacy of intellectual recognition—far from it. (It's not the defense mechanism of Intellectualization that I have in mind.) It may be truly insightful and revelatory and have substantial influence on the patient's behavior and experience. Still, it remains fundamentally different, I believe, from the propositions about his angry and dependent feelings. Moreover, the intellectual recognition may be accompanied by direct affect (excitement, relief, anxiety, etc.) without obviating my point here.

Interpretation 3 entails an intellectual recognition too, but here we have an added ingredient to consider. Can the patient experience directly that you "remind" him of his father? That he is behaving toward you in a way that is similar to the way he behaves (or behaved) towards his father is, again, something he may well recognize intellectually with utter conviction—but can he more directly experience it (like he can his anger)? That's a moot question.

Finally, consider Interpretation 4. It's not an explanation, not a description of a defense mechanism, but it is located in the patient's past. When he says, "Yes, I did feel angry with him then," he is accepting the validity of the remembrance. But two further questions may be raised: (1) Is he simply recalling the fact that he experienced anger then? (2) Is he also re-experiencing the feeling? In the case of the first, we are again dealing with a purely cognitive process. But if the second is answered in the affirmative, his experience has a significant affective component, and the interesting question arises: Is it the same feeling that he is now re-experiencing? You see, that he is now feeling some anger is one thing, that it's a feeling from the past is quite another. The old term Redintegration can be applied here to take account of the possibility—which I believe is far more than just a possibility—that we are capable of experiencing a feeling that seems old to us, that comes with a distinct sense of its pastness. Sometimes we can even date it with conviction. (The sense of conviction, by the way, is one that we must respect across a wide range of phenomenological experiences. It represents an important way that our propositions in therapy are confirmed—relatively, at least.)

Consider now these three Interpretations, each of which represents one of the classic Kantian trichotomy: affection, conation, and cognition.

Interpretation 1. "You are angry with me."

Interpretation 2. "You want to hurt me."

Interpretation 3. "You believe you'll hurt me if you get close to me."

Consider these three questions: (1) Is inference differently involved across the three types? (2) Can the three represent the same kind of fact? (3) Are the experiences they reflect experienced in the same way? These are difficult questions to answer. An impulse is probably experienced as an intention, and a belief as an expectation. They may be accompanied by an affect that is experienced directly, but the intention and expectation are probably based on inference. When we acknowledge the impulse to hurt someone we are inferring it from our actions and our feelings, not directly. The same is probably true for our attitudes and beliefs. Nevertheless, such intellectual recognitions can be readily articulated—and they matter a great deal.

I should perhaps have made the following point earlier in this correspondence because it has substantial bearing on our session-to-session work. Many student therapists make feelings their chief, if not exclusive, target; they give the biggest priority to their patients' feelings. It's as if they take too seriously the global diagnostic category of "emotional disorder" and view their patients' problems as chiefly emotional. How the patient thinks, how he perceives and remembers, what he knows and believes in, what he aspires to and what he dreams about, are given a back seat in the single-minded pursuit of feelings. "But what do you feel?" is the ruling question. This simplifies matters nicely (and maybe that's what makes the thing so popular). But trust me, Simon, cognition counts too—and often very much.

Bear in mind too that feelings are generally less effable than thoughts. We can articulate our thoughts into words—we can say what we want, what we like, what we fear, what we believe—far better than we can articulate many of our feelings. English, you know, is quite poor in words that describe inner states of experiencing and feeling, particularly the finer shadings and nuances. It's therefore inevitable that English-speaking people will use the same words to denote different shades of meanings. That can be quite a problem in psychotherapy, for it's our job both to understand and to articulate the patient's experience. More than that, because Understanding must be communicated—

and both ways—we must learn our patient's language—
what his words mean, what their referents in behavior
and experience are—and he must learn ours.

One final consideration for this letter, Simon. Suppose
that instead of saying to your patient, "You are feeling angry," you chose to say "You are under the sway of the
Death Instinct." I know you don't plan to say such things to
your patients, but let's suppose it anyway. It sounds—does it
not?—like a blatant theoretical conception, and so you
probably dismiss it as a flagrantly intellectual construction
with no possible place in the phenomenology of your patient's direct experience. No person can be expected to directly experience his death instinct, so the matter of confirmability by observation is altogether different from the
first Interpretation.

But it's a most intriguing question—and one that has
some major implications—whether a dyed-in-the-wool Freudian who has grown up in that tradition experiences his
"death instinct" in a way that is no different from the way
the rest of us experience our "anger." After all, if "anger"
too is a matter of culture and language and learning, then
why not "death instinct"?

A patient's culture—broadly defined—must play a vital
role in our work, and I should be alluding to it more in
these letters. When we estimate the extent of inference and
judge the kind of confirmation we naturally take into consideration the particular experiences of the particular patient.
And this brings me back to the basic question of whether a
Science of conscious experience—of inside-the-person events
as seen from inside him —is sensible to conceive of. It raises
the grim possibility that there can be no fundamental distinction between the facts of phenomenology and the theories, between the raw data that a Science requires and its
abstract concepts. However, short of doing all that, it deep-
ens the urgency of our need to pay close attention to the

role inference plays across the entire range of events that we observe in therapy.

Simon, I'll spare you a discussion of the often encountered claim that the analytic couch is our test tube. I'll simply tell you how it's usually worded. To wit: not only is our treatment method therapeutic, it's also scientific insofar as it provides the optimal setting for the confirmation of our theoretical propositions. There's an important sense in which this claim is true, and also an important sense in which it's quite false. But to try and explain would be over-reaching myself. If you're interested in having me do it, then please say so by return mail.

Your affectionate uncle

Twenty=eight

Dear Simon,

I appreciate your bluntness. Not only are you not interested in having my views on how therapy can provide for the confirmation of our theoretical concepts, you're impatient with my disquisitions on the philosophy of clinical observation. Let's leave it to the philosophers, you imply. Alright—though, as they say about war, it's too serious a matter to leave to them. You're more interested in having my opinion on two "theoretical" questions: (1) "How much theory is actually necessary for the conduct of *Psychotherapy?*" and (2) "Does *Psychotherapy* require a particular kind of psychological theory?"

I'll turn my attention to these two questions (but I warn you that I may sneak back to some considerations from my last letter). Let me begin by claiming that some theoretical framework is necessary in order to Understand a patient's experiences and actions. To remain atheoretical is probably impossible; and even if it weren't it would probably weaken if not impair our effectiveness. It is a fair question, however, whether it's better to work out of one particular theory or to draw from a variety of theories the way the Eclectic does. The Eclectic is willing to sacrifice the consistency (he calls it the rigidity) of one point of view in favor of the advantages of drawing the best and most fitting concepts and formulations from a variety of different points of view.

Given the relatively primitive state of our theories and their limited basis in critical empirical evidence, the eclectic's position is attractive. But how does the Eclectic decide which concepts and formulations to choose from which theories? How does he integrate the diverse kinds of explanations that different theories offer? Answers to these questions are likely to lead to the conclusion that he generally does have a single theory at the back of his mind which guides his choices and shapes his integrations. It's a broadly based one perhaps, it may remain relatively unarticulated, but it's a theory nonetheless.

The Eclectics have a good lesson to teach us. It is to recognize that all of the theories available to us are in various states of incompleteness, unevenness, and disrepair. We should certainly work away at them, but in the meantime it might be better to eschew a wholehearted reliance on any single one. We should, at the very least, pay serious attention to what other theories may have to offer. Ours, you see, may be strong for certain kinds of phenomena but weak for others. We should therefore be aware of another theory's potential strength in that area of weakness.

The eclectic versatility and flexibility can be of enormous value to a psychotherapist. It broadens the range of options he has with respect to how to Understand his patients. If he can draw from Freudian thought, from Interpersonal theory, from Existentialism, and even also from Behavior Theory, then he will be rich with ideas during his day-to-day work. And—within limits, of course—that wealth of ideas can result in more effective Understanding. It can also be useful from the patient's point of view, for it may be that the concepts and formulations of one theory are more comprehensible to him than those from another.

Every human being has—whether he knows it or not—a theory of psychology. It is his way of making sense out of the behavior of others as well as his own. Some are more articulated than others, more unified and coherent, but every one has a real theory at the cognitive level of functioning. This means, then, that our patient has one too—and it can play a significant part in his psychotherapy. Consequently, one of our big tasks as therapists is to discover, to elucidate, and to otherwise deal with our patients' theories of behavior. This is clear enough when they exhibit paranoid features. But it pertains equally to our narcissistic patients, our obsessional ones, our hysterical ones, and all the rest. Patients can suffer not only from their reminiscences but also from their theories.

But I'm writing you about our theory, and I can't resist pointing out that we too can suffer from it. The relationship between observation and theory—most particularly in psychology—is complicated and treacherous. It can be argued that the function of theory is little more than to improve observation, that theory is necessary only because our powers of observation are limited and selective. This is certainly the case for descriptive theory, and it's easy to accept the contention that the principal function of our clinical theory is to aid and abet our clinical observation. But if you accept this contention then you must also accept its corollary: that if the theory happens to be bad it will undermine and arrest clinical observation. This is the major peril. Clinical theory can mislead and distort clinical observation—and it does. That's why Criticalness must be valued and nurtured, and the domain of observation be protected from undue encroachment from theory. There are a number of ways that such protection can be ensured. One is to keep the level of inference as low as possible. Another is to keep polishing our lenses.

What I believe, Simon, is this: as a therapist you need, not a variety of theories and points of view, but a single coherent one which is not bounded by rigid and impermeable boundaries. You should be committed to a theory that makes sense to you, that satisfies your intellectual demands, and that meets with your philosophical requirements (which means also that it conforms with your view of the fundamental character of Human Nature). But your commitment should not take on ideological properties which can transform your theory into a dogma. Flexibility and balance are prime virtues; so is openness to new ideas. But, as I wrote you some time ago, flexibility easily becomes fickleness, openness easily becomes intellectual anarchy, and it's tempting to hide our confusion and unclarity behind the banner of Eclecticism.

The hoary idiographic-nomothetic antinomy sometimes gets combined with eclecticism in the following way. The argument against involving theory in psychotherapy is based on the truism—practically a cliche, really—that every person, and therefore every patient, is unique. The major implication of this truism is that Understanding must be particular rather than general, and therefore theory is irrelevant if not detrimental to the efficacy of psychotherapy. Now, the major implication is not only true, in my opinion, but it's very important. The conclusion, however, is misleading. It is truly very useful to keep in mind that we are not striving in our work to understand people in general (for example, the "average hysteric" of whom our particular patient is a representative). We are indeed striving to Understand a particular person, and it serves that purpose to emphasize that he's a unique and particular person. For one thing, this helps us resist the temptation to ever say to him, "Well, people like you tend to behave in such and such ways for such and such reasons." Neither should we justify our Interpretations on the grounds that they are based either on our theory or our experience (e.g., "The reason I think you are fearful of expressing hostility is that people who suffer from symptoms or character structures such as yours generally are."). And can you picture a therapist saying, not to a colleague but to a patient of his, "I once had a patient who. . . ."? It's abundantly clear that such formulations are without effective merit, can serve only as reassurance, and can be generally proscribed.

But does that mean that such thoughts should never occur to us—that we must even avoid thinking it and allowing it to guide our listening and further our Understanding? Even if it were possible (and I believe it simply isn't) for us to avoid thinking in terms of theory or of our experience with other patients (or indeed the experience of others that we've assimilated from the clinical tradition, which is embodied in clinical theory and in the teaching of our supervisors), it does not follow that we will Understand the patient better. My guess is that we would Understand him less well. Our ability to Understand a particular and unique patient can only improve if we can bring to bear the experience we've gleaned from other particular and unique patients. As long as we can avoid thinking of our patient as an average this or an average that, and if we can avoid applying normative standards, we can only benefit from the life experiences of other people.

The following lecture may also be relevant to this issue, though I would want to give it to you even if it weren't. We commonly hear the criticism of orthodox psychoanalysis that it simply teaches the patient the theory—that it is little more than an indoctrination into the varieties of psychoanalytic explanation. The analyzed person is often caricatured as the one who speaks smugly of his "oedipus complex" or his "castration anxiety." Now, there's no use denying that this happens, but it does not happen in the hands of a good analyst. The good analyst, who fully subscribes to every part of the orthodox theory, conducts an analysis that makes little if any reference to the theoretical hypotheses or concepts. The way he does it and the way he formulates his Interpretations is very instructive.

The good analyst uses his theory as a guide, the way a navigator uses a map. For him a concept such as Castration Anxiety serves to organize his Understanding of a patient's actual life experiences and self-image. Suppose his patient is recounting an incident in which he was injured and then experienced recurring episodes of anxiety about it. The analyst may think Castration Anxiety (if not consciously then preconsciously) but not say it in that form. Instead he will make Interpretations that speak of the dread of mutilation and loss of body parts. More than that, he will encourage the patient to reminisce about earlier accidents and related fears and fantasies, for his theory tells him that all such experiences form a unified structure, each related both backwards and forwards.

Moreover, very few analysts nowadays believe in total anamnesis or anything approaching it. The fear of actual castration is available as a memory to very few people, and it's not necessary that an analysis uncover it. Instead, it is regarded as important that the patient recognize a connected chain of experiences, affects, and fantasies having to do with the fear of loss of a vital body part—that he recognize the many forms that such a fear takes in his current life and how they are historically linked up for him.

You know, Simon, it is often supposed that the orthodox analyst Understands his patient according to the concepts and formulations of his metapsychology. Certainly, when he writes his formal case presentations he tends to translate behavior and experience into the theory's abstract terms. So it can come as a big surprise to listen to a good analyst speak informally about his patients and tell about how he understands their session-to-session behavior. Instead of "oral impulses" and "death wishes" he speaks of concrete and often mundane kinds of everyday experiences—like the yearning to be cuddled and comforted and the wish to hurt someone. Instead of "castration anxiety" he talks of the patient's fear of being incomplete, being different from others, and perhaps of being crazy. The "primal scene" becomes little more than a fear of witnessing something that is forbidden and unbearably exciting. And all of these behaviors are concretely tied to current realities, not to some remote past. That they stem from early history is, of course, never denied; but that fact can be quite irrelevant to the session-to-session work with such experiences. Sometimes the early or "primal" experiences are merely added, like so much intellectual icing to an already baked cake.

* * * * * * *

I just remembered something that I wanted to write you about when I was writing you about the Middle stage of *Psychotherapy.* It has to do with a question that's often asked: "At what distance from the patient does a therapist work? How close to the manifest content, to the concrete details, does he stay?" I think my favorite answer is relevant to the considerations of this letter. It goes like this.

It's commonly supposed that by the time the Middle is reached we therapists have a well-formed conception of our patients' problems and personalities, that we have a dynamic formulation all worked out. By analogy, then, we are like a geographer who has, during the Beginning stage, charted the entire terrain. Now, during the Middle, our function is to lead the patient on an exploration (a guided tour) of the terrain, showing him the highlights, pointing out landmarks, and generally acquainting him with the lay of the land. We are like the local guide who already knows the lay of the land, and even if we choose to encourage our client to discover it for himself, we know where the danger points are as well as the important highlights. So if our client misses them, we can subtly guide and steer. We still conduct the excursion, you see—we may choose to follow but we steer from behind.

This picture, in my opinion, is misleading (no pun) and inapt. The therapist is more like an experienced guide or geographer who knows about different kinds of terrain in a general way but is unfamiliar with the particular land that he and his patient are exploring together. The venture should be regarded as a mutual one. Moreover, since it's the patient's terrain that is being explored, he alone knows it to begin with. The therapist is essentially a stranger to it, and it is the patient who is guide. What the therapist provides is an expertise of exploring, of charting the terrain of personality and behavior. Therefore, he must stick very close to his patient during the entire excursion. He may be expert at recognizing certain meanings and functions, but he remains unfamiliar with the lay of the land until his patient reveals it to him.

To pursue the analogy a bit further, your patient knows the trees while you can see the forest. You can remove yourself sufficiently from the details in order to appreciate their larger design, and you can occasionally be helpful by showing him how the details form a larger pattern, but you must allow the pattern to emerge from the details and not commit yourself to it too soon. Neither should you regard it as your function alone to deal in the larger patterns. Your patient may be one of those who is more comfortable with forests than with trees, and then you have to be the one to draw attention to the details.

* * * * * * *

So much for analogies and for your first question. Let me now turn to your second one: "Does *Psychotherapy* require a particular kind of psychological theory?" I seem to have been saying (in this letter and also in many of my earlier ones) that Psychoanalytic theory, in one or another of its modern forms, is the theory we must use when we conduct *Psychotherapy*. Do I mean to say that? No, because I'm not convinced that I mean it. I'm tempted to write, "It happens to be my theory," but the implications of "it happens" worry me. I would like to suppose that there is a variety of different and nonpsychoanalytic theories that are compatible with the structure and principles of *Psychotherapy*. I guess what I'm saying is that I would like to think so but I'm not sure.

For one thing, I'm not prepared at this point to test the proposition out—that is, to consider in detail some form of nonpsychoanalytic theory and see whether it is compatible with *Psychotherapy*. Moreover, the principles of it have, after all, emerged from the psychoanalytic tradition. Still, insofar as the therapist's chief function is concerned—namely, the formulation and communication of Interpretations—it is conceivable that he can at least avoid the sort of causal and functional explanations that a dynamic theory entails—certain of them, at least. It's possible, for instance, to do without the so-called instinctual terms and concepts; I find it less easy, however, to consider dispensing with the concepts of Defense, Resistance, and Transference, but I suppose it could be done. At the very least, I'd guess, one can do with a minimum of Psychoanalytic theory and rely instead on some form of Cognitive theory or Existential theory or Interpersonal theory—not that I'm recommending it, but I see no compelling reason to rule it out.

Let me now amplify. That behavior is goal-directed and purposeful—that it's motivated—is a theoretical point of view that I regard as essential for our purposes. It means that we assume every psychological act is either instrumental or consummatory with respect to a goal. We traditional therapists subsume this basic assumption under the heading of "dynamic." The term itself is rather unfortunate because it derives from physics and connotes an energy concept that is not only unnecessary, but unnecessarily fraught with implications. True, the term has a good feel for many of us—so much better than its antonym, "static." But then we get ourselves enmeshed in metaphysical conceptions of energy—

and that, I believe, is really quite irrelevant. To presume that behavior serves needs and drives and purposes—that it's motivated—really suffices. And if that's all we'll mean by "dynamic," we can be perfectly content with the term.

But the Dynamic point of view is more than simply a motivational conception; it construes behavior to be the resultant of forces acting in concert and in conflict. It makes the crucial assumption that no behavior (with the exception perhaps of the simple reflexes and responses) is simply the result of a single motive, drive, purpose. Rather, there are always two or more at work. When these forces act together, we describe the behavior as Overdetermined or Multiply Functioned; when they act in dissonance, we describe it as Conflict. The point of view enjoins me to make two kinds of assumptions: (1) when my patient says, "I hate my father," I make the assumption that he is giving expression to an ambivalent feeling (i.e., to Conflict) and that he is also saying, "I love my father too"; (2) when he says, "I hate my father because I dread the prospect of becoming like him," I make the assumption that there are other reasons too (i.e., it's Overdetermined), for example, ". . . because I dread the prospect of not becoming like him." Now these, for the most part, are assumptions or working hypotheses; but they are especially powerful ones. If you apply them in your work, you will find—as so many of us have found—that they are extremely efficacious. They work—and sometimes wonders.

Now, how about those two key psychoanalytic concepts: Resistance and Transference? Are they dispensible? I strongly doubt it, though I wouldn't go so far as to claim—as many analysts do—that they are the sine qua non of analytic therapy. I do, however, regard them to be among the most powerful processes at work in *Psychotherapy,* and I hope I haven't seemed to give them short shrift in my letters. These, after all, are the main ways that our patients can bring their fundamental problems into the treatment itself, and not merely by recounting them verbally but by recreating them *in vivo*.

Many nonanalytic therapists, particularly of the Existentialist-Humanist persuasion, regard both Resistance and Transference to be overplayed and even tangential. About Transference, they claim that not only is it artificial to deliberately induce it, but it is without much effect to resolve it. Their emphasis, you see, is ever on the Real Relationship—that's what really counts. Insofar as the so-called Transference is unreal, it can be unreal to work with it. Well, I of course disagree—provided that Transference is not elevated to the ruling process and made into the central therapeutic issue. Let me hasten to say that with some patients, at certain stages in their treatment, it may well be the ruling and central process. But that's different from asserting that it has to be in all cases and throughout most of the treatment. Many orthodox analysts, by the way, share my opinion; "Keep the Transference in the background," is a piece of advice I've often heard from them. (At the same time, equally orthodox analysts will disagree and insist that it's our obligation to be ever alert to Tranference phenomena and to interpret them assiduously—which only supports a point I made in an early letter to you about the substantial heterodoxy within the analytic orthodoxy.) In any case, I would put it this way: *When the Transference is in the background, keep it there!* And the same applies to Resistance.

In closing, there's a sense in which this slogan can be applied to theory in general—keep it in the background! But, Simon—like Transference and Resistance—keep it in the picture nonetheless. Don't let any of these vital considerations slip out of view entirely.

Your affectionate uncle

Twenty=nine

Dear Simon,

This seems like a good time to keep the promise I made in my first letters and give you a reading list. If I recall correctly, I had in mind to show you thereby some of the main sources of my principles and methods. Another purpose will be to recommend some readings that you might find instructive and interesting. So this is going to be a personal, and therefore selective, list. I'm bound to omit important items, and not all of them deliberately—some omissions will be sheer oversight. I won't let that worry me because I'm sure you have access to good bibliographies on psychotherapy-in-the-large, and I know from my own experience that lengthy reading lists can be something of an aversive stimulus to reading. I'll keep this letter as brief as I can, and then I'll return to *Psychotherapy* proper and write you about the Ending.

For straight, rigorous, and systematic Psychoanalytic theory you can do little better than to read the essays of my teacher, David Rapaport. Not only does his work have depth, but his constant attention to the empirical bases of the theory is a model of its kind. Get yourself a copy of his collected papers (*The Collected Papers of David Rapaport*, edited by M. M. Gill, New York: Basic Books, 1967) and you'll have all of his important works. I'd begin with his valiant effort to formalize Psychoanalytic theory, and then read his papers on the models of Affect and of Thinking and his paper on Ego Autonomy. All of his theoretical writings are terse, pithy, and very much to the point.

Next, for sheer lucidity and relevancy, I'd recommend you read Erik Erikson—anything and everything of his that you can get hold of. His attention to social and cultural factors (his so-called psychosocial approach) is a refreshing tonic to the dominant approach of most analyst-theoreticians. His classic, *Childhood and Society* (New York: Norton, 1951) is still a marvelously fresh and instructive book. And I'd especially recommend you read his monograph titled *Identity and the Life Cycle: Selected Papers (Psychological Issues,* Monograph 1, New York: International Universities Press, 1959).

If you can get hold of a copy of a book called *Psychoanalytic Psychiatry and Psychology: Clinical and Theoretical Papers* (edited by R. P. Knight and C. R. Friedman, New York: International Universities Press, 1954) you will be able to read some of the writings of teachers who have greatly influenced me. Along with important papers by Rapaport and Erikson, there are papers by Robert Knight and Merton Gill, both of whom have not published their views very extensively. Knight's papers are of great clinical relevancy, and I recommend them to you highly. Merton Gill has been especially influential in shaping many of the methods and principles of what I've been calling *Psychotherapy.* Unfortunately, he has published only his theoretical views (see, for example, his superb essay, *Topography and Systems in Psychoanalytic Theory, Psychological Issues,* Monograph 10, New York: International Universities Press, 1963), and they don't reflect his often radical and always incisive views on psychotherapy upon which I have leaned heavily.

I was also much influenced by George Klein, and I recommend you try to read as much of his writings as you can. His interests and expertise ranged across a wide field, covering much of academic psychology as well as Psychoanalytic theory. The way he combined his clinical experience with research and theory is a superb example for all of us. Some of his later papers are now available in a book of his called *Perception, Motives, and Personality* (New York: Knopf, 1970). Especially important to me was his effort to draw a distinction between psychoanalysis's metapsychology and its clinical theory. He was coming to the opinion that the former was quite dispensable, and only the latter remained of vital relevancy. His deliberations on the subject and his attempt to formalize the clinical theory are well worth studying.

In *Motives and Thought: Essays in Memory of David Rapaport* (edited by R. R. Holt, New York: International Universities Press, 1967) you will find—along with a paper of mine that I'm proud of—excellent pieces by Klein, Gill, Schafer, Wolff, and Holt, whose views reflect the same tradition as mine. There's a report of a research effort, by Lester Luborsky, using the psychotherapy situation as its laboratory, that you should find interesting and thought-provoking. Finally, there is a superb essay by Benjamin Rubinstein that addresses the kinds of philosophical issues that I wrote you about several letters ago. So this is a book I highly recommend.

Psychoanalytic theory and practice has a really voluminous journal literature, and I don't know where to start recommending any of it to you. Because it's a genuine classic and has had so much impact on both theory and practice, I'd single out Robert Waelder's paper called "The Principle of Multiple Function: Observations on Overdetermination" *(Psychoanalytic Quarterly,* 5, 1936). Also in that journal (20, 1951) you'll find a valuable group of papers on technical issues by the likes of Merton Gill, Heinz Hartmann, Rudolph Loewenstein, and Leo Stone. And I can also recommend a group of papers in the 1954 volume of the *Journal of the American Psychoanalytic Association,* under the title of "Psychoanalysis and Psychotherapy: Similarities and Differences."

The essays of Hartmann, Kris, and Loewenstein are acknowledged classics. You must read them not only for their elaboration of the Ego-Psychological point of view, but for their careful integrations and articulations of Psychoanalytic theory as a whole. Their papers, by the way, have a steady relevancy for our clinical work, and they both complement and supplement Rapaport's contributions. Fortunately, these important essays have been assembled in a single monograph called *Papers on Psychoanalytic Psychology* (*Psychological Issues,* Monograph 14, New York: International Universities Press, 1964).

If you want to read a remarkably sound and lucid account of orthodox clinical theory and technique, try to get a copy of Otto Fenichel's slim book called *Problems of Psychoanalytic Technique* (New York: Psychoanalytic Quarterly, 1941). It was written mainly as a polemic against what he encountered among third-generation analysts during the 1930's. He was trying to correct the distortions, the extremes, and the misapprehensions, so it's a down-to-earth book that's filled with the balance, the good sense, and the humaneness of what I've been calling the good analyst.

You'll find a number of good papers in *Psychoanalytic Techniques: A Handbook for the Practicing Psychoanalyst* (edited by B. B. Wolman, New York: Basic Books, 1967). And Karl Menninger is always worth reading for his close attention to matters practical and technical as well as for his theoretical sweep (for instance, his *Theory of Psychoanalytic Technique,* New York: Basic Books, 1958). I know that Rudolph Loewenstein is at work on a comprehensive presentation of psychoanalytic methods and techniques, and I'm sure that when it emerges it will be the definitive work of its kind.

I want especially to single out for you the contributions of Helmuth Kaiser, not only for his methods and principles, but also for his style. If you read his papers (in *Effective*

Psychotherapy: The Contribution of Helmuth Kaiser, edited by L. B. Fierman, New York: Free Press, 1965)—and I strongly recommend that you do—you will recognize the great influence he had on me. While I deeply admire his self-searching attitude, his criticalness, and his acuity, I can't follow him into the extreme reaches of his metapsychology. But judge for yourself.

Kaiser follows the tradition of Wilhelm Reich, whose classic *Character Analysis* (New York: Noonday Press, 1949) is still a must. In that tradition too was another teacher of mine, David Shapiro. If you haven't already read his superb book *Neurotic Styles* (New York: Basic Books, 1965) then you've been missing a lucid and sensitive portrayal of character types and styles which has, I believe, major relevancy for *Psychotherapy.*

(By the way, Simon, get yourself a copy of a book called *Use of Interpretation in Treatment: Technique and Art,* [edited by E. F. Hammer, New York: Grune & Stratton, 1968]. It is a collection of rather brief pieces by a great variety of therapists, and it focuses on Interpretation. It's a dazzling book, in several senses of the word, and it's a consistently interesting one.)

Now, you may have noticed with amazement that I've so far left out Freud—both of them. Well, Anna Freud's monograph on the Defenses (*The Ego and the Mechanisms of Defense,* New York: International Universities Press, 1966) is still the classic in the field, and I recommend you study it. But what can I recommend about her father? Reading the master can be a lifetime vocation, so one has to pick and choose. (I have the impulse to cite for you the *Standard Edition* of his collected works, but obviously that won't do.)

Robert Holt's sensitive analysis of the several modes and voices that Freud wrote in can help greatly in our picking and choosing (it's called *Freud's Cognitive Style,* and has appeared in *American Imago,* 22, 1965). Holt alerts us to the different functions that the various oeuvres had for Freud and to the different voices that he wrote in. Another of Holt's essays, titled "A Review of Some of Freud's Biological Assumptions and Their Influence on His Theories," is also a valuable guide insofar as it analyses the historico-scientific context of Freud's metapsychology (it has appeared in a book that contains a number of excellent papers: *Psychoanalysis and Current Biological Thought* [Edited by N. S. Greenfield and W. C. Lewis, Madison: University of Wisconsin Press, 1965, pp. 93-124]).

As you probably already know, Freud has to be read largely in historical perspective. There's no gainsaying that his work is rooted in nineteenth-century biology, physiology, sociology, and philosophy. It can be quite misleading—and it has been—to read him as we would a contemporary. That's not to deny that much of his thinking remains timeless—not at all!—but many of his patterns of thought, his conceptual formulations, and his biases can only be properly understood against the backdrop of his contemporaries. This is likely to be especially true for his papers on Technique. They are rich with marvelous insights and suggestions, but as a model for psychotherapy they are uneven and incomplete (partly because he never wrote a comprehensive work on psychoanalysis as a therapeutic enterprise). Anyway, I'll avoid listing his individual works for you; I assume you'll want to read as many of them as you can.

So much for the more or less orthodox psychoanalytic tradition and literature. How about the neo- and the non-psychoanalytic? My generation of psychologists was much influenced by the teachings of Harry Stack Sullivan and Carl Rogers. Among the neo-Freudians, Sullivan is perhaps the most comprehensive and profound, but also the most difficult to read. His contributions (e.g., *Interpersonal Theory of Psychiatry* and *Clinical Studies in Psychiatry,* New York: Norton, 1953 and 1956 respectively), whether read first-hand or passed along by others, have had much impact. The same is true for Rogers, whose influence on psychologists has perhaps been greater than any other. I'd recommend you read both of his major books, *Client-Centered Therapy* and *On Becoming a Person* (New York: Houghton Mifflin, 1951 and 1961 respectively). An excellent book in the Rogerian tradition is *The Psychotherapy Relationship* (W. U. Snyder, New York: Macmillan, 1961).

Out of the Gestalt and Holistic tradition of Kurt Goldstein, there's an excellent book of Andras Angyal's *(Neurosis and Treatment: A Holistic Theory,* edited by E. Hanfmann and R. M. Jones, New York: Wiley, 1965). It's a comprehensive, dynamic, and insightful work, and you may find it altogether persuasive. I did, as you'll be able to tell if you read it. Moreover, it's a good antidote to what is currently going under the name of Gestalt Therapy.

I'm not sure what to recommend from the Existential-Humanist point of view. Perhaps a good place to begin is *The Search for Authenticity* (J. F. T. Bugental, New York: Holt, Rinehart, & Winston, 1965). More turgid, but equally instructive, is *Psychoanalysis and Daseinsanalysis* (M. Boss, New York: Basic Books, 1963). And Rollo May's writings are well worth studying, particularly his ambitious treatise *Love and Will* (New York: Norton, 1969).

Now I must take account of the rapidly burgeoning area that goes under the rubric of Behavior Modification. The innovations that are being made in this area ought to be familiar to every practicing therapist. For one thing, one or another of these methods may be more efficacious and economical for certain patients or for certain of their problems; for another, some traditional therapists are already experimenting with an adjunctive use of some of the Modification methods. But I needn't be so apologetic—even though my methods and principles are antithetical to those of Behavior Modification, they may well have been influenced by them in a negative kind of way.

You should certainly read John Wolpe's classic, *Psycho-*

therapy by Reciprocal Inhibition (Stanford: Stanford University Press, 1958); and read also a book he wrote with Arnold Lazarus called *Behavior Therapy Techniques* (New York: Pergamon Press, 1966). Then there are a number of good books that summarize much of the theory and research: Bandura's lucid *Principles of Behavior Modification* (New York: Holt, Rinehart & Winston, 1969), a collection of papers in *Behavior Therapy: Appraisal and Status* (edited by C. M. Franks, New York: McGraw Hill, 1969); and a rich volume of papers including good pieces by Rogers, Fromm-Reichman, and others, called *Sources of Gain in Counseling and Psychotherapy* (edited by B. G. Berenson and R. R. Carkhoff, New York: Holt, Rinehart & Winston, 1967). I know of a book that presents a detailed account of methods and techniques (J. Marquis and W. Morgan, *A Guidebook for Systematic Desensitization,* Palo Alto: Veterans Workshop, 1968), but it may be hard to get hold of.

This leads me into the last area we must consider, the research literature. The past twenty years have witnessed an impressive burgeoning of research into both the outcome and efficacy of psychotherapy and the processes of therapies. No therapist, I believe, should allow himself to remain unaware of the various researches and their findings. There are at least three volumes of reports (*The Investigation of Psychotherapy: Commentaries and Readings,* edited by A. P. Goldstein and S. J. Dean, New York: Wiley, 1966; *Psychotherapy Research: Selected Readings,* edited by G. E. Stollak, B. G. Guerney, and M. Rothberg, Chicago: Rand McNally, 1966; *Research in Psychotherapy,* edited by H. H. Strupp and L. Luborsky, Washington: American Psychological Association, 1962) and two comprehensive attempts to integrate them (*Psychotherapy and the Psychology of Behavior Change,* A. P. Goldstein, K. Heller, and L. B. Sechrest, New York: Wiley, 1966; Meltzoff, J. and Kornreich, M., *Research in Psychotherapy,* New York: Atherton Press,

1970). Let me recommend especially the book by Meltzoff and Kornreich, since it comes to the reassuring conclusion that the traditional psychotherapies do seem to work.

I can't resist a small lecture on the relevancy of research. It's controversial, this, and I have some views. Briefly, then: Aside from what we learn directly from our patients, we therapists have two main sources of knowledge. On the one side are the observations that have emerged from the clinical experience of others; on the other side are the findings that have emerged from objective and controlled researches. They range from the Scientific to the Anectodal. As I once wrote you, I regard the Anectodal method to be a valid source of knowledge—but so do I regard the Scientific, provided that we apply the same kind of critical attitude to it that we apply to the other.

The body of empirical knowledge about human behavior is, at best, modest. Psychology, you see, is a difficult science, and it produces reliable knowledge at a slow pace. It is hampered by many complex and subtle constraints that limit the reliability of its findings. Moreover, there's a significant and substantial correlation between the size of the unit of observation and the reliability of its data. At the microscopic level (or call it part functions—e.g., the reflex, the perception of form, the acquisition of syllables) it can generate objective data more fully than it can at the macroscopic level (e.g., the aggressive act, the perception of events, the acquisition of language, the function of fantasy). So if we turn to the sources of empirical knowledge we are more likely to find knowledge about behavior that is less reliable and less applicable to our clinical work. Bear in mind that the two principal requirements of empirical research—objectivity and control—become more difficult to achieve as we approach the macroscopic level. Researches into matters such as aggressive behavior, fantasy and imagery, and the function of symptoms are necessarily the product of investigations that have made crucial and limiting decisions concerning objectivity and control. Such research is inevitably open to a variety of interpretations as well as to serious limitations of generality. Their relevancy or applicability to our clinical work is therefore subject to greater ambiguity—and this limits their utility. Still, Simon, the situation is not nearly so bad as to merit their out-of-hand dismissal (as some of my colleagues would argue). The empirical research must be assimilated judiciously and critically, and its relevancy must always be judged carefully. Skepticism and criticalness, yes; disregard, no. After all, the same tempered and judicious attitude must be applied when we read the Anectodal literature.

And read we must!—not only the works of our professional colleagues and forebears, but also of those whose powers of observation and insights into human affairs are expressed in novels and essays, in plays and poetry. Our novelists and sociologists, our critics, commentators, and philosophers, our dramatists and poets, have a great deal to teach us that is relevant to our day-to-day work.

Your affectionate uncle

Thirty

Dear Simon,

The most problemful and most ambiguous of the three stages is unquestionably the Ending. Not only does it call into play some of the most basic of human problems but it raises some of the biggest questions about *Psychotherapy*. Separation is the most basic of the problems, and the biggest of the questions are probably: (1) Does *Psychotherapy* have a natural kind of conclusion and, if so, what are its characteristics? (2) What marks the 'cure' "?

Most traditional psychotherapists believe that therapy has a natural conclusion, though they find it hard to agree about its nature and characteristics. But about the nature of the "cure" there is major disagreement—indeed, the concept itself is wholly rejected by many. Perhaps the only point of general concurrence is that separation—that fundamental problem every one of us must learn to resolve—is likely to be the main theme of the Ending. Otherwise the stage is marked by substantial disagreements, and not only among therapists but also between them and their patients. It's not uncommon, you see, for a patient to believe that his treatment is in its final stage at a time when his therapist judges that it's still in the Middle, or for him to resist acknowledging the Ending when the therapist deems he is there.

Because it can evoke such profound and mixed feelings, a patient is often strongly motivated to avoid the experience of the Ending altogether. Sometimes he will arrange for circumstances to conspire against it (for example, by taking a job in another city); sometimes he will decide to terminate precipitously (for such excellent reasons as that he feels all cured); and sometimes his therapist will conspire with him to avoid the full experience of termination—for it can evoke profound and mixed feelings in a therapist too. One way of evading the reality of the stage is to set an arbitrary date for termination, or one that is based on circumstances extrinsic to the therapy. What I have in mind is actually a very common practice—to make it coincide with the beginning of a major vacation interruption (typically, the summer). The rationale for that seems altogether sensible: take advantage of an already scheduled termination and simply transform it from temporary to permanent. Now, I don't mean to contend that this practice is always and necessarily an evasion of the Ending, only that it sometimes is. And it is likely to be when the therapist's professional and economic needs play a major part. Optimally, you see, any extrinsic consideration (such as a therapist's need to replace his patient) should play no part whatsoever in the crucial and delicate matter of termination—but, realistically, such considerations simply do. I believe that's always unfortunate and sometimes borders on the unethical, for when such factors play the major part, any natural Ending may not have a chance to occur and run its full course—a most valuable opportunity for promoting a patient's well-being will have been lost.

So much for a general Introduction to the Ending. Before I consider in greater detail the matter of its evasion, I want to consider what are the principal criteria for judging termination when extraneous factors play little if any part. From your patient's vantage point they are most commonly related to his reasons for having entered psychotherapy in the first place and his expectations about what it would achieve for him. The question I'll now raise is: Must we share these criteria?

* * * * * * *

Whether they had been discussed earlier in the therapy or not, whether they had been the subject of analytic work or not, it is only the rare patient who comes to feel that all of the expectations he entered therapy with are fulfilled. What complicates the matter is that his expectations typically undergo a change during the course of extended treatment. Therapy may uncover problems that weren't salient at the beginning, or else bring about an alteration in the hierarchy of problems, making certain of the initial ones less pressing and raising the urgency of others. It also happens frequently that the symptom which motivated him into therapy persists, but its role in his life changes in such a way that he can continue to live with it, so to speak. To further complicate the matter, it also commonly happens that as the Ending approaches new problems and issues become ascendant. Sometimes this happens out of a need to forestall termination, sometimes not.

In any case, the critical questions are these: When has he been "cured"? or, more accurately put, "cured enough"? When has he gained the strength to live well enough without therapy? When has he gained or regained sufficient involvement with, and control over, his Inner and Outer Realities? When is he optimally Relatively Autonomous? Questions such as these are always difficult to answer with much assurance, and some degree of ambiguity and uncertainty is bound to remain. But there is a radically different way to formulate the matter, Simon, and I will argue its merits to you. It does not involve judgments about cure, achievements, or expectations; instead, it revolves around my conception that psychotherapy in general, and *Psychotherapy* in particular, has a natural developmental course.

I have already written you about my conviction that the

Therapeutic Process, like an organic process, is characterized by naturally occurring stages of maturation. Just as there's a Beginning and a Middle with distinct defining characteristics, so there's an Ending. I'll devote the bulk of this letter to those defining characteristics; but first I must make a most difficult point.

The development of *Psychotherapy* itself can be substantially unrelated to—can stand independent from—the patient's condition (his problems, difficulties, and symptoms). This means nothing less than that the therapy can run its full natural course without there being substantial alteration in a patient's behavior and experience outside of it. And that, you may well believe, is an outrageous kind of principle to accept.

I seem to be contending that *Psychotherapy* can be divorced from reality—that a patient can enjoy a full and meaningful therapeutic experience without at the same time changing his real behavior (and, if so, what then is the point of the thing?). Okay, I'll face that contention. Why? Because the thing happens. It happens only rarely, but when it does it needn't follow that the therapy was without efficacy, because—and this is the crucial point—the effects may reveal themselves only after it has been completed. The majority of our patients do change during therapy, some very dramatically, but some only do it afterward. I am aware of how question-begging, if not defensive, this point may seem, insofar as I may be defending the efficacy of *Psychotherapy* in all cases, even when there is no objective basis for it. It may seem glib to contend that if the benefits of the therapy are not apparent by the time it's finished that is not conclusive evidence that it was without efficacy (which brings to mind the cognitive dissonance phenomenon, exemplified in the greater faith that some members of a Millenial movement show after the predicted holocaust fails to occur—they too move the date ahead!). But my contention is based upon clinical experience, and it can be readily explained.

There are several different explanations for this phenomenon. The one I believe is most often relevant centers on the Transference Neurosis and its resolution. Some patients form an intense Transference and cannot experience a sufficient resolution of it during the therapy itself. This may or may not be a function of the fact that Transference generally has a reality basis (or a real component) which is therefore recalcitrant to analysis. In any event, if it's intense and not substantially enough resolved, there may be little change in the patient's condition while the therapy is in progress. But afterward, in the absence of the sessions, the processes and forces that were latent can exert their influence. In the absence of real stimulation, you see, the intensity will subside and the Transference will loosen its grip; and then changes can occur that are the delayed result of the therapy.

Another explanation puts the onus on the patient's use of the therapy as a kind of large-scale defense against change. Instead of putting his energies into change he has put them into the therapy, and so it serves as a form of diversion. Only when it is no longer available to serve that function—when it's finished with—does he actually face the necessity of real change; up until that point, being in therapy exhausted his motivation for change. The trouble with this explanation is that it seems to minimize our responsibility to have dealt with the phenomenon during the course of the therapy. After all, whenever we discern it—and it's far from an uncommon phenomenon, so we should be alert to it—we must take energetic steps to expose and analyze it. Therefore, unlike the incomplete resolution of the Transference, if the therapy continues to be used as a defense against change (and against living too) there is a serious flaw. Still, for a variety of reasons, most therapies do remain flawed—some more seriously than others. (More about this soon.) And so I recognize the possibility that this one can persist despite our concerted efforts.

Whatever the reasons for it, then, changes in your patient's psychological condition may sometimes occur only after therapy is concluded. Not only is it important for you to be aware of this, but it can be very useful to tell your patient about it too. When, during the Ending, he says (or complains) that he hasn't changed—or, more typically, hasn't changed enough—you can discuss with him the possibility that he can expect to experience changes afterward. If you have an explanation that you feel confident about, there can be some benefit in sharing it with him too.

The only alternative—and it's the reason that I regard this point to be such an urgent one—is to forestall termination and continue the therapy. (Bear in mind that referring him to another therapist is tantamount to continuing the therapy.) That, in general, can be a serious mistake. Some patients remain in treatment for too long when the criterion of change is the ruling one. And when psychotherapy continues for too many years, it can change its characteristic and central function—it can become a way of living for the patient, if not a crutch. I don't mean to take a harsh or sanctimonious attitude toward protracted and even interminable psychotherapy. There are patients who continue to need therapy, for whom being in treatment once or several times a week serves a vital function. You have to be prepared to make the appropriate clinical judgment for such cases, but you also have to be prepared to make the clinical judgment that your patient has had a sufficient therapeutic experience and that continuation may not only be without benefit to him, but even detrimental to his well-being. It goes without saying that this is a most difficult judgment to make.

But I have oversimplified. There's a third alternative which amounts to regarding termination as a kind of trial.

Just as the beginning of the Beginning can be viewed as a period of trial, so the ending of the Ending can be viewed as not irrevocable. There remains, after all, the possibility that your patient can return to psychotherapy at some later date. I'll soon want to consider the question: Is it prudent to proceed on the assumption that your patient is going to be finished with psychotherapy? Since my answer is going to be No, it has direct bearing on the issue before us now. Yet I want to drop the matter for now and continue with a consideration of the defining characteristics of the Ending.

* * * * * * *

The Ending is often as distinctive as the Beginning. This is particularly true when it is substantially taken up with the issue of termination. But it can be distinctive in other ways as well—as, for example, when a patient turns his efforts to consolidating the gains he has experienced from therapy, when he turns his attention to his future. I'll take up the distinctive features of the Ending in the context of considering the transition between the Middle and the Ending.

The transition is sometimes so gradual and so subtle that it's difficult for us to discern it. In most cases, however, there are likely to be signs that it had occurred even when the transition itself went by unnoticed. It can be useful for you to mark the transition and to articulate it for your patient even when it is after the fact. "I believe we have moved into a new stage of the therapy, the Ending stage of it" can be an important kind of Interpretation to offer. You may want to point out that this stage is not to be regarded as a brief one; it can take a good deal of time (up to a full year). Because the issues raised are generally painful and it is common for patients to want to elude and short-circuit them, they will want to keep the stage short and get through it quickly.

The transition between the Middle and the Ending can take many forms. Sometimes it's marked by a major impasse based on a sense of an impending change of direction— "I've come this far; so far so good—but where do I go from here?" The Therapeutic Process may seem to have come to a grinding stop, and your patient experiences a sense of perplexity that can be understood as an unwillingness to face termination. This can provoke a major struggle, both within him and between him and you, that is based on the underlying question, "Where do we go from here?" When you answer the question with a reference to termination, you must do it judiciously and tactfully—and then you must steel yourself for a struggle.

Sometimes the transition is marked by a burst of intense analytic work—the very opposite of an impasse. Then it can be quite difficult to discern. You can be guided here by a sense of something paradoxical happening. The Middle has apparently run its course, and just when the time for the beginning of the Ending has come, your patient renews the work of the Middle with surprising intensity. Sometimes the intensity will have a strain to it that will be the clue, but sometimes not, and then all you can go on is your sense of surprise and paradox.

The Ending may be heralded by the appearance of a fresh theme—something your patient has not talked about at all or else mentioned at the outset but not again. Usually this theme will have a clear enough reference to termination (as, for a good example, a fantasy concerning death), but sometimes the reference may be obscure or absent. Its distinctive feature may be little more than its novelty, and the question it can provoke in your mind is, "Why now?—why, after such a long period of opportunities, does this important theme make its first appearance at this time?" If the theme refers to termination or to some aspect of the Ending stage, it can readily be interpreted as such. Otherwise, it will be difficult for you to press it into the service of articulating the transition.

It's not uncommon for the transition to be marked by a "regression" of some sort. Most typically this takes the form of the return of an old symptom. Sometimes it's even the symptom that originally motivated your patient to seek therapy, but which subsided soon after the treatment began. When this happens after the Middle has seemed to run its natural course, it can be taken as a likely sign that the Ending is at hand, for Its function is typically to prevent that stage from occurring. It's vital that the patient be made to recognize that fact—for example, "Just as it was this phobia that led you to start therapy, so it is now this phobia that keeps you in it." It sometimes happens that the symptom never subsided in reality but was kept out of the therapy itself; then it is invited in, so to speak, to serve its big function. Again, you may experience a sense of "Why now?—Why did this symptom wait so long?" These questions can be the clue, for it's a fair assumption that the transition between the major stages (including also the one between the Beginning and the Middle) will be marked by Resistance and struggle. Few people, particularly average patients in *Psychotherapy*, like changes.

Occasionally it will be a dramatic mental experience that ushers in the Ending—a dream, the emergence of a powerful fantasy, or the recovery of a significant early memory. The content of that experience often bears a direct relationship to the new and final stage of the treatment. If it revolves around the theme of separation, or mortality, or of everlasting union, then it can be unmistakable. If the theme is more obscure than that, you may have to listen hard for it; if you are alert to the function of such an event, you will more likely hear it.

Let's see if I can give you some illustrative examples. I'll make them up in pairs: one that clearly reflects the advent of the Ending, and one that is obscure.

[CLEAR] In the past few days I have become obsessed with the memory of my grandfather's death. I don't know why it's haunting me so much. He was old at the time; he had had a full life; but everyone took it hard anyway. He was such a cheerful and active person right up to the end, and I loved him very much. He died peacefully in his sleep [pause]. I don't believe I have ever told you about it. I wonder why I didn't. Anyway, we were sitting at breakfast, and my mother sent me up to fetch him. . . .

[OBSCURE] Recently I have been obsessed with the memory of my first day at school. I have no idea how come, because there was nothing traumatic about it like there is for so many kids. I had looked forward to going to school, and I was very excited when the time finally came, and. . . .

[CLEAR] I just now remembered something—something I had forgotten till now. The memory comes back in a rush, and it's so vivid [flushes and seems excited]. I guess I was four or five at the time. My father had to go on a business trip, or something, and it must have been a big trip because he packed a big suitcase. And I remember not wanting him to go away, so I hid his shaving kit, and. . . .

[OBSCURE] Last night, while I was going to sleep, I remembered something I never recalled before. I'm not even sure it really happened. Anyway, it was when I was very little. I was with my mother and my brother somewhere in the country. We were walking in the woods, I think, and my brother must have gotten lost. Anyway, my mother was very upset because I can remember that she yelled at him and slapped his face when he came back [pause]. Maybe he didn't get lost; maybe he just did something bad—I don't know. I remember crying, so I must have felt very bad about it. . . .

[CLEAR] I haven't told you this. I don't know why, really. I guess I've been hoping it would just go away. But [pause] I had the fantasy that I had cancer. I had the fantasy last Sunday morning, and it stayed with me pretty much all day long [pause]. It was an incurable cancer, and I was going to die within the year. . . .

[OBSCURE] I had the fantasy that you needed a heart transplant, and mine was the only heart that would be suitable for you. So. . . .

[CLEAR] Over the week end, I had a ball with a new fantasy that I developed for myself. I found myself imagining how it would be to take a trip to Europe. I pictured myself going all alone, and staying for a full year. . . .

[OBSCURE] In the middle of my studying, I had this funny fantasy, and it really grabbed me. I was, of all things, an astronaut. And I was in training. The thing I pictured myself practicing was moving around in the weightless condition. . . .

[CLEAR] I had a vivid dream last night, and I still feel under its spell. I dreamt I was at a funeral, but everyone was smiling and laughing, and I felt puzzled. Whose funeral was it? At first I thought it was someone I didn't know, even though my family and friends were there. But when they opened the coffin for the last look at the body I saw that it was me lying there. . . .

[OBSCURE] I dreamt I was at a party of some kind. My wife was there, and some of my friends, and I think you were there too. We were all sitting around a large living room, and I was lying down on what could have

been a couch. It might have been the couch here
[pause]. Anyway, the thing I remember most vividly
was that my wife was crying. I don't know why, because no one else was. . . .

[CLEAR] In my dream I was in a small boat, and it was drift-
ing slowly away from the shore. There were people on
the shore, but they didn't seem to be paying any attention. I tried to call for help, but I couldn't. . . .

[OBSCURE] One part of my dream was very strange. I was
riding on an escalator, going down, and when the escalator came to an end, I just kept on going down anyway. It was weird. . . .

* * * * * * *

So much for the earmarks of the Ending; now for some
of the problems. It's one thing for you to discern and articulate the transition, Simon, it's another for your patient to
acknowledge and accept it. So you should not be surprised
when he tries his hardest to resist the advent of the Ending.
And you should prepare yourself for something of a struggle. How? First, by resolving your own misgivings about
termination.

You too can expect to experience a variety of feelings
about the Ending. Some will constitute resistances against it,
but others will amount to pressures toward it. Some will be
based on Countertransference feelings specific to the patient, others on aspects of your professional work (e.g., the
need to fill the open time with a new patient, and some on
the process of separation itself. I think you will find that pressures to speed termination can be more difficult to face and
also more pernicious in effect than pressures to forestall it.
You may find, at certain times and with certain patients,
that you prefer to finish for reasons of pessimism, or even
boredom, or because you generally find the Beginning stage

more interesting and more congenial to work in. In any event, it's important to realize how your feelings can work both ways. Without dwelling on the problem, let me simply assert that they need to be resolved—and adequately. So you prepare yourself for the Ending by examining your mind and heart, for there are bound to be forces there that will influence and shape the kind of Ending your patient experiences.

Having resolved your feelings, you now face a series of hurdles and pitfalls. The major one, according to my experience, is imposing the Ending on your patient. It is vital that he acknowledge his own part in the advent of the stage—that he see it as the product of his own activity, in significant part at least. Ideally, just as he played the active part in starting therapy, so he should play the active part in ending it. This, again, is an ideal, and so it is usually only approximated; for it's quite typical of patients to experience termination as the therapist's decision. "You want to be rid of me," "You are tired of me," "You're giving up on me," are some of the complaints you can expect to hear. And they are likely to be made because he refuses to accept the fact that it was his own actions and experiences that led you to judge that the Ending stage had been reached. You must be in a position to say in good conscience, "It was my Interpretation, yes, but it was based directly on your experience of the therapy."

Your patient can, of course, reject the validity of that Interpretation—"I see what you based it on, but I disagree that it means what you say it means"—and he may contend that he cannot be in the Ending because he does not feel prepared to terminate the therapy. The basis of this feeling, the nature of the "I am not ready," will then become the main subject for consideration. The key question is, "Not ready for what?" For some patients it may be growing up and all it entails; for some it may independence—being cut off and alone; for some it may be facing mortality. The meanings may coalesce around the basic theme of auton-omy-and-separation.

Before you turn your attention to this large question, you should take the precaution of determining how he conceives of the stage. Many patients believe that the Ending is a brief period—little more than an extended goodbye. If so, then feeling unprepared for it can be based on that simple misconception—after all, one doesn't begin to say goodbye until one is ready to depart. Despite the fact that such a misconception is likely to be based on the dynamics of sep-aration, it can be useful to clear it up by notifying him that the Ending of *Psychotherapy* is not to be regarded as a brief farewell; rather, it is a stage of equivalent proportions to the others and can last as long. It is prudent, in my opin-ion, to allow up to a full year for it, and to tell a patient that. Our aim here is not to mollify and reassure him (though that will usually be the short-term effect), but to lend weight to the issues of termination—to give them a sufficient significance. It's as if you were to say, "The prob-lems that are going to be brought to the fore by the pending termination are of utmost seriousness and relevance to your psychological well-being. We must give them a thorough and careful working over." You yourself must be convinced that termination is an integral part of the treatment, that no course of *Psychotherapy* can be considered complete before it has amply dealt with the conflicts and fantasies associated with it—most notably, separation. Moreover, since it is cen-tral to Relative Ego Autonomy, separation is central to the fundamental dynamics of *Psychotherapy*. To be Autonomous and Free is to have come to terms with separation, and so it is one of the most important lessons patients can learn in *Psychotherapy*.

I'll write you about separation in another letter.

Your affectionate uncle

Thirty-one

Dear Simon,

You put two questions to me about the Ending: (1) "Do you think it's a good idea to do like the Rankians do, and establish the date of termination right at the outset of therapy?" (2) "What, if any, modifications in attitude and Technique can a therapist make in deference to the Ending?" My answer to both is going to fall on the negative side.

It's apparently familiar and intriguing to you how the Rankians elevate separation anxiety into the paramount psychological problem, how for them the whole of psychotherapy is concerned with it. A Rankian therapist therefore sets the termination date right at the start and actively keeps it in the forefront. There are, in my opinion, several big disadvantages to this procedure. The biggest is that it artificially imposes the issue of separation on all patients in a way that is likely to be premature for many. Dread of separation can serve to prevent full involvement in therapy. I'm sure you know people who cannot commit themselves to any relationship (or to an involving activity) because they can't shake off their anxiety about terminability. When they are our patients, then psychotherapy must of course deal with that problem—it has to be regarded as a central one. But I question whether the best way is to set it up at the very outset so that it casts its shadow over every aspect of the Therapeutic Process. Why not allow the thing to emerge spontaneously as the therapy proceeds, all the while maintaining a sensitive alertness to its implications not only for the therapy itself, but for the patient's personality?

325

Some patients will show an overweening preoccupation with the time-limitedness of the therapy; others will show an absence of any such concerns; both positions merit careful exploration and analysis. Often the temporary interruptions of therapy (vacations, for example) will provide the setting for such exploration. There is the patient for whom every interruption is a trauma because, among other things, it signals mortality; then there is the one who protects himself from such separations by means of the fantasy that they are only temporary. Your patient's reaction to temporary interruption of treatment will provide your first glimpse into the dynamics of separation. You must be alert to their relevance for your patient's personality as well as to their implications for termination. I strongly advise you to use such opportunities to make him aware of these implications.

The summer vacation most typically provides an opportunity to deal with separation, and in a sense it can be regarded as a trial separation. The value of so regarding it is twofold: (1) separation issues will not be novel during the Ending; (2) the Ending will not be entirely taken up with termination. I agree with the Rankians that separation is such a basic issue it can't wait until the Ending. Furthermore, if it comes up for consideration only when final termination is pending, then the issue may not be adequately dealt with. A prudent working hypothesis is: *it's insufficient to deal with separation matters only during the Ending.* In fact, when the final stage is entirely taken up with termination, then you are open to the criticism that you weren't active enough in listening for termination themes during the earlier stages of the therapy. In the majority of cases such themes will have been discussed and analyzed before the Ending is reached, and this means that you will offer no new major Interpretations about separation; you will merely repeat, amplify, and articulate Interpretations that you had occasion to make before and after summer vacations, interruptions due to illness, and the like.

But again I have oversimplified, and I must beat a retreat. To say of the Ending that no new major Interpretations occur during it is an overstatement. This is not to deny
that one of its earmarks is that process we Freudians call
"working through," which entails the repetition, elaboration,
and specification of Interpretations that were formulated
during the Middle; but it seems to minimize the uniqueness
of the Ending. While terminations occur throughout the
course of treatment, when it terminates for good there can
be no easy recourse to the expectation that it will resume.
The rhythm of the weekly schedule, of the holiday and
summer vacation schedule, quickly establish themselves for
a patient, and that rhythm serves to structure the separations and to organize defenses against separation anxiety.
But termination proper takes on the properties of irrevocability and finality, and it is these properties which are
unique to it.

The Ending can therefore provide a patient with an experience of separation that's especially profound, even when
it's made up of already familiar ingredients. Paradoxically,
it's this very profundity that can limit its analysis and resolution. What I mean is this: only death is irrevocable and
final; psychotherapy can resume (if not with the same therapist, then with another)—and just as the Transference can
never be fully resolved, so separation too is ever relative.

* * * * * * *

Let me continue on this subject from another vantage
point by answering your second question, as to whether
modifications can be made during the Ending. There are
therapists who believe that it's useful, if not necessary, to
modify their basic posture during the final stage. So instead
of remaining neutral and impersonal they gradually move
into a more personal and partial position; they ease themselves out of the standard therapeutic mode into one that

has the characteristics of a friendship. Where they would have remained silent and impassive earlier in the therapy, they now engage in more conversation, and they show their feelings and share their thoughts in a freer, looser, and more "human" way. I strongly disagree with this move.

Consider the various rationales for it. For some therapists it may be a way to speed and maximize the resolution of the Transference; for others it's the best way to actualize a patient's problems over separation (he learns to separate from a real and meaningful relationship instead of an artificial and unreal one); and for some it's based on the more general conviction that the patient has had a sufficient experience of the standard therapeutic mode and now needs something different. While one or another of these rationales may be cogent for certain patients under certain conditions, I find none of them persuasive as a general principle—i.e., for the average expectable patient in *Psychotherapy*. The main reason I disagree with the idea of introducing modifications is quite simply that I'm convinced the standard position is the most efficacious one to maintain right up to the very end.

Modifications in the interest of resolving Transference can be seriously misplaced—they can also boomerang. As I've already written, insofar as Transference is the product of your patient's Inner Reality, it has to be subjected to analysis because it remains the chief instrumentality by which he gains Understanding of his Inner Reality. Any real changes in your behavior can obscure that process. And if this was deemed to hold for the Middle, why should it cease to hold for the Ending? The same is true for that component of Transference which I've been calling "real." Your patient must come to recognize its reality, and it is of little help that you try to change it. Moreover, as I wrote before, if you are really a warm and comforting person, can you take steps to change that during the Ending? Are you

to play-act a different role? And are you prepared to act coldly and uncomfortingly to a patient whose Transference has
included perceiving you as the good father figure? The distinction between the so-called Neurotic and Real Transference is a useful one throughout the entire course of *Psychotherapy*. The former is best resolved by the standard
analytic methods, and the latter remains so embedded in
reality that it's likely to be futile to try and resolve it even
when circumstances suggest that it might be useful.

An interesting and important thing sometimes happens
during the Ending: your patient perceives changes in your
behavior and attitude where none has actually taken place.
"You seem more friendly to me than you used to be," he
may say; or, "You seem more relaxed lately, less inhibited
and less removed from me." He may also claim that you
speak to him more than you used to. The Interpretation you
can offer him will draw attention to the fact that the perception is based upon changes in him and not in you. If you
have in fact maintained your regular position, it is he who
is more relaxed, less inhibited, less defensive.

Such changes in perception and feeling, however, are likely to be complicated and overdetermined. For one thing,
there may be a significant ingredient of gratitude in his new
appraisal of you—it may be his way of saying "thank you."
For another, there may also be some relief that the conclusion to the ordeal of therapy is in sight—he may be saying,
"Thank God!" You should be sensitive to the workings of
such feelings, and at the same time be convinced that
changes in perception are likely to be more meaningful for
a patient if they truly reflect changes in his Inner Reality.
Then, you see, he will have learned a meaningful lesson for
himself.

Which leads me to a point that you may regard as unnecessarily harsh and uncompromising. I know how uncongenial it may seem for you to offer the following kind of In-

terpretation to your patient during the Ending, but it can be most valuable for his continuing well-being. To wit: "You say I am more friendly toward you now than I used to be. But I don't think I've changed in how I behave here; or if I have, then it hasn't been as great a change as the one you perceive. So I wonder whether the fact that you perceive such a change means that your feelings toward me and toward the therapy have undergone a change." This theme can be pursued in a number of different ways. For some patients it may be appropriate to suggest, "It may be your way of expressing gratitude;" for others, "It may be that it is easier for you to separate from me if I am friendlier and warmer toward you;" for some, "If I am partial to you, if I approve of you, then it makes our parting less frightening— less of a rejection, perhaps." In other words: *everything remains grist for the analytic mill during the Ending no less than during the other stages.*

Your uncompromising uncle

Thirty-two

My dear nephew,

I'm glad you've been sharing these letters with some fellow-students and flattered that you think they should be published. You have my permission.

Now, back to the Ending. You have anticipated correctly, and you've brought my attention to a crucial consideration. First, the anticipation.

Yes—it is my conviction that even the final session should be approached by you in no different a way than any of the preceding ones. The fact that there's no tomorrow may influence you to some extent, but it should not do it unduly. If you believe (as you should) that the analytic work can (and should) continue without you—that your patient will not suddenly cease reflecting and examining his Mind—then there is no reason to withhold Interpretations because there is no time left in the therapy to pursue them. Naturally, a major new Interpretation during the final session will be a rarity, but that's not because there are going to be no more sessions afterwards; ideally, it's because so many sessions have gone before. Still, the principle holds: if you learn something about him during the final session, and if you deem that he can benefit from that knowledge, you can offer it without feeling constrained by its being the final session. The treatment may be coming to a close, but the Therapeutic Process (not to mention your patient himself) extends beyond it. I mean nothing mystical or fanciful; I mean that he has learned a way to experience himself and to work with his behavior that is not bound to the reality of the psychotherapy but has become part of his mode of living his Inner and Outer Realities.

So my position on the question of modifications in Technique during the Ending is clearly "No." And I base it not only on the conviction that the standard Technical principles remain efficacious right up to the very end, but also on the fact that they serve a number of critical functions for a patient's future potential benefit from the therapeutic mode. This raises a question that I have postponed: Is it prudent to proceed on the assumption that your patient is going to be finished with psychotherapy? This question can be construed in two ways. One has to do with the possibility of resuming at a later date, either with you or with another therapist. The second has to do with the continuation of the therapeutic mode in the absence of formal therapy sessions. Both of these possibilities must, in my opinion, be allowed for—and adequately.

As I discussed it some time ago, every therapy is flawed—and some more seriously than others. The formulations I've presented throughout this correspondence are all of them ideals, and therefore never fully realizable in practice. Every therapy, and every patient, will arrive at a position that is more or less short of this ideal in one way or another. Therefore, further attempts are always possible. Advisable? It depends. In some cases the shortcomings will not merit the cost of further therapy; in some cases they will. In some cases the disadvantages of prolonging therapy will outweigh the advantages; in other they won't. Still, the fact that your patient might potentially benefit from a further course of therapy has to remain as a real consideration. If it does, then two consequences necessarily follow (and both of them I've already written you about): (1) the termination of *Psychotherapy* needn't wait until perfection has been achieved; (2) the Ending should not be conducted in such a way as to "spoil" the patient for further *Psychotherapy*.

If you choose to notify a patient of the fact that resumed

therapy is an open possibility, he may accept termination with greater equanimity. The matter must of course be analyzed as much as possible and worked through as thoroughly as possible, for it generally has to do with the finality and irrevocability of separation; and it is too easy to bypass this vital matter with a promise of resumption at a later date. Still, only death is irrevocable as a separation, and there's little reason to elevate therapy to that status. If a patient takes some comfort in the knowledge that you and therapy will remain available to him, and if that knowledge makes termination more tolerable for him, then it needn't be viewed as such a serious flaw in the therapy. Which leads me to the crucial consideration that you wrote about in your last letter.

You pointed out to me, Simon, that the experience of separation actually takes place after termination, not before. That's a most relevant point. In a vital sense, then, the patient must confront the experience—must learn to deal with it—after the final session is over, and therefore in the absence of a therapist and the therapy. Separation is something each of us must achieve alone.

That consideration lends further weight to the second way of construing the question (Is it prudent to proceed on the assumption that the patient is going to be finished with psychotherapy?). The therapeutic mode—particularly that of *Psychotherapy*—can and should continue past formal termination. Not only is it important for us to bear that in mind, but it can be equally important to share it with the patient. He has learned a way of experiencing that can continue to serve his well-being—he knows how to reflect, to examine his Mind and Heart, to confront his experience with directness and honesty, to be authentic—and there is no reason he cannot expect to continue doing it without our presence and help. He should have been doing so between the regular sessions too.

It can be helpful if you bear this point in mind through-

out the entire course of the therapy. You may often find an
opportunity to draw your patient's attention to the fact that
analytic work is possible outside of the sessions too. It isn't
uncommon that he will report during a session having done
some analytic work outside of it, and you should take pains
to support that move. At the very least you should be wary
of ever seeming to criticize him for it—for instance, by interpreting the action as a defense against the therapy or you
(something like, "So you worked it through this morning in
order that you wouldn't have to do it here."). Not that this
doesn't often happen for that very reason, but it has to be
carefully handled insofar as it can be a tacit reproach
against continuing the analytic mode on the outside.

It's perhaps more common that a patient avoids any outside analytic work; that, in my opinion, always merits attention. Sometimes, you see, it's based on the expectation (or
fantasy) that you will disapprove, or that you will regard it
as a rejection of a sort. Whatever its basis, it can be vital to
pay particular attention to it—for example, "I believe you
avoided dwelling on the experience you had, avoided working on it the way you do here, because that would have
meant you can do without me, that you don't need therapy
and me." Sometimes the issue revolves around the discussion with others of his problems and experiences; he may
even have been informed that such behavior is prohibited
(i.e., it is "acting out"). This matter is complicated and
many-faceted, particularly when it occurs during the Beginning and Middle stages. I'm not suggesting that you minimize its complexity or that you fail to acknowledge the variety of Acting Out defenses that tend to become implicated.
What I am suggesting is that you bear in mind throughout
what are the implications for termination. It should be your
goal to be in a position to say to your patient, when the end
of the Ending approaches, "You have, after all, been doing
a substantial amount of therapeutic work on your own,"

and to mean thereby not only that he had been doing it during the sessions but also outside of them. On balance, that's an aspect of Autonomy to be valued and nurtured.

To foster this goal during the Ending, many therapists make it a practice to reduce the frequency of the sessions. Some do it for other reasons as well—to reduce the intensity of their patient's dependency and Transference, to gradually shift the balance from therapy to living. Now, this is one major modification that I do not disagree with. Why not? Because it does not necessarily entail a modification of Technique per se, and neither does it "spoil" a patient for further therapy. Nevertheless, Simon, I don't recommend it as a routine step; neither do I believe it's a good idea for you to initiate this step or even to suggest it to a patient. If, however, it arises as his idea, and if you judge that it is likely to serve a useful practical purpose without—and this is the critical judgment—diluting the vital work of the Ending, you can support it. Otherwise, I continue to advocate a business-as-usual approach throughout the course of the Ending.

* * * * * * *

The final session, then, can be expected to be no different than the preceding ones, with the exception of the parting exchange—the goodbye and farewell. Here no ceremony is called for, no grand summing up or resume of the therapy, obviously also no final words of advice or commiseration. In my opinion, Simon, little more than a wish for good fortune is appropriate. Which reminds me that I never told you how to end each of the regular sessions. So let me do it now.

It's worth paying attention to the way you will end each session. Some signal from you that the session is over is obviously called for (though I've heard of therapists who expect their patient to end it himself by referring to a clearly visible clock). I recommend that your way of signalling the end of the hour be an invariant one—a kind of automatic habit. "Our time is up," is the one I routinely use; it seems to me the simplest and least freighted with overtones. "We'll have to stop now," is okay too. But "I'm afraid we'll have to stop," or "I'm afraid our time is up," is obviously to be avoided insofar as it conveys a sense of regret (it seems to say, "I'm sorry that we cannot continue with this vital subject; I wish we could because it's a good and important subject").

To interrupt a patient in midsentence in order to close the session is potentially tactless. You won't have to do that ordinarily because you don't need to clock the session to the second—or even to the minute. To allow a range of up to five minutes is good practice, and within that period it's usually easy to decide when the session is appropriately terminated. Still, most patients will at least occasionally have to be interrupted in order to bring the session to a close. So you will simply say, "I have to interrupt you now, because our time is up," or even, "Excuse me for interrupting, but our time is up." To add anything to this is likely to be gratuitous—to say, for example, that he can continue with the topic next time is both gratuitous and directive.

There are, however, patients for whom the ending of each session is a minor separation trauma, and they manifest it in a variety of ways. Some will stop talking altogether when they sense that the ending is approaching; others will try to forestall it and prolong the session by plunging into a fresh topic or engaging you in some pressing matter. Such tactics are obviously well worth paying analytic attention to, and you will naturally find ample opportunities to formulate Interpretations that revolve around them. Sometimes this can pose a Technical problem insofar as the appropriate time to do it falls right at the end of the session when there's no time left for it. Your temptation at the time will be to draw his attention to the tactic (i.e., confront him with it) in order that he may try to control it—namely, to stop it. But I think you'll agree that it can be a pointless and tactless thing to do, insofar as you're imposing the topic without allowing the opportunity to work on it. Take, for example, "I have to interrupt you now because our time is up, But let me point out to you how you regularly make it necessary for me to interrupt you right in the middle of something." Where does that leave him? Do you mean for him to consider the matter after he leaves? "Why do you point it out to me now when there's no time left to discuss it?" is an altogether fair rejoinder.

But when else can you do it without imposing the topic? At the outset of the next session? Well, you may have no other choice. The preferable thing, of course, is to find an opportunity during the course of an hour when your patient is into a subject that may be relevant to the matter. But sometimes you'll have little choice but to impose the topic, and then the time to do it is at the outset of a session.

I see no compelling reason not to interrupt a patient in order to raise an issue that I judge needs to be raised. But it's best, in my opinion, to do this always right at the beginning, before he has gotten far into the topic of the session. It seems somehow less of an interruption and imposition if it comes early—right after he's begun to speak, for instance. Before he begins? Perhaps—but why not wait to hear what he intends to begin with?

Incidentally, Simon, this applies to all occasions on which I have something to bring to my patient's attention. Most typically this will be some "business"—i.e., if I have to cancel a forthcoming session, arrange a change in the schedule, or discuss the fee, I do it at the beginning of a session rather than during the course of it or at the end. I also think that the beginning of a session is the time to hand him the monthly bill, not the end of it. However, in the case of a nonbusiness matter—such as how he ends the session—I may want to wait a moment or two to see what he begins with. For one thing, there's the possibility that he'll begin with exactly the topic I intend to broach; for another, it may well be that he happens to have a topic of some urgency, and then I may want to change my mind and not introduce "my" topic during this session. But if he begins with a nonrelated topic which doesn't strike me as especially urgent, I'll then proceed with my interruption-imposition—"Let me interrupt you and raise another issue. I think this may be a good occasion for us to consider the matter of. . . ."

* * * * * * *

But all of that was a digression. Let's return to the main topic of this letter: the final session. Obviously a little something more than your routine "Our time is up" is called for this time. But as I've written, aside from a warm expression of farewell and good luck, I see little merit in any kind of closing ceremony. For you to ask your departing patient to keep in touch with you is inadvisable for a variety of reasons that should be amply clear to you by now. If he, however, offers to keep in touch, then that can be accepted graciously; it remains, after all, up to him.

Let me construct for you some examples of the final moments that may convey the flavor and spirit I regard to be optimal. I'll try to show how your posture can remain Analytic and Tactful, but at the same time responsive to the special moment.

Example 1

[PATIENT:] You know, I've been talking away this hour as if it were no different from any other hour. I seem to have forgotten that it's the last one.
[YOU:] It's not hard to surmise why you would want to forget it.

[PATIENT:] It sure isn't. It still scares the hell out of me [big sigh]. And I can see that I haven't given you the chance to say much today.

[YOU:] You've been worried about what I might say to you today?

[PATIENT:] I guess so. I dread goodbyes, as you know, and I guess I dread this one more than anything [falls silent].

[YOU:] I think you dread it also because you're worried that I might express to you how I feel about this goodbye.

[PATIENT:] Well, I guess I knew that you wouldn't do anything different today. But I suppose I must have been worried that you would show me your feelings—for once, at least [pause]. I feel relieved that you haven't, but I don't know whether that's because I didn't give you any chance to.

[YOU:] I can tell you that I didn't intend to do that.

[PATIENT:] I guess that's a relief [smiles].

[YOU:] But I do want to wish you the best of luck. Our time is up.

[PATIENT:] So it's really goodbye [big sigh]. I want to thank you so much for everything [warm smiles are exchanged, and the routine walk to the door is executed perhaps a bit more slowly than usual].

You will notice, Simon, that you didn't choose really to explore or Interpret your patient's dread that you would show him your feelings. This was hardly the appropriate occasion to do that—let him do it himself, if he wants to.

Example 2

[PATIENT:] Well, I guess this is it [falls silent].

[YOU:] I take it you're having mixed feelings.

[PATIENT:] Yes. I feel kind of glad and maybe even relieved. You know, this final session wasn't as bad as I imagined it would be. I thought I'd feel very nervous today, and that I'd be sort of embarrassed. Actually, I feel quite good. But I'm not really sure what else I feel [pause]. I guess I feel a bit scared too.

[YOU:] Maybe also some of the anger with me you've been feeling over the past few weeks.

[PATIENT:] Maybe. But most of the anger is gone. Now I'm just scared.

[YOU:] Scared over the prospect of being alone—without me and without therapy.

[PATIENT:] Yes [pause]. I'd like to keep in touch with you, if that's alright.

[YOU:] Sure; I'll be glad to hear from you.

[PATIENT:] I guess I feel I'm going to need it [falls silent].

[YOU:] I understand. Our time is up [as both of you rise, patient offers hand; you take it in handshake].

Example 3

[PATIENT:] I just remembered a fragment of a dream I had last night. I'd completely forgotten it till now, and suddenly it came back to me. That's great! Let's see now, how much time do we have left? [glances at wristwatch] A cool ten minutes. Oh well, I guess we're going to have to have another session to work on it [laugh]. Should I tell it to you or not? That's the question.

[YOU:] Sounds like it's a going away present.

[PATIENT:] Marvelous! That's what it was about. It was about a party of some sort—maybe a birthday party. You were there; so maybe it was yours. Anyway, the fragment I recall was about a present that I brought. It was one of those oversized trick boxes; you know, the kind that contains boxes within boxes. And I was unwrapping it. And each time there was another, a smaller, box. That's all I remember [pause]. I never did get to find out whether there was anything in the last box.

[YOU:] The boxes, perhaps, were all empty.

[PATIENT:] Perhaps. Nothing left—nothing left to give you.

[YOU:] I wonder, then, whether the idea of a birthday reflects how you feel about this final session.

[PATIENT:] I guess so. This is my day of birth, eh?

[YOU:] I suppose I should wish you a happy birthday.

[PATIENT, laughing:] Thank you, doctor. But not, if you please, many happy returns [falls silent].

[YOU:] I think you're wondering whether this is really going to be your final session with me, or whether you will want to return at some future date.

[PATIENT:] Yes, that's true. I was thinking yesterday about what you said awhile ago that there was always the possibility that I could come back for more therapy later on, if I felt I needed to. I guess that makes it easier for me to accept this termination. But I feel a bit guilty about it too.

[YOU:] As if it lends a false note to this ending. Maybe the trick boxes in the dream have that meaning.

[PATIENT, big sigh]: I do hope I'm really finished with therapy, but I guess I'm still conflicted about it [falls silent].

[YOU:] Our time is up now.

[PATIENT:] Thanks for everything; thank you very much. It's been a rough ride, but a good one. I really appreciate everything you've done for me.

[YOU:] The best of luck to you.

And the best of luck to you too, Simon.

Your affectionate uncle